THE
ORIGINAL
SIX

THE ORIGINAL SIX

HOW THE CANADIENS, BRUINS, RANGERS, BLACKHAWKS, MAPLE LEAFS, AND RED WINGS LAID THE GROUNDWORK FOR TODAY'S NHL

LEW FREEDMAN

SPORTS
PUBLISHING

Copyright © 2016 by Lew Freedman

Sports Publishing books may be purchased in bulk at special discounts for sales promotion, corporate gifts, fund-raising, or educational purposes. Special editions can also be created to specifications. For details, contact the Special Sales Department, Sports Publishing, 307 West 36th Street, 11th Floor, New York, NY 10018 or sportspubbooks@skyhorsepublishing.com.

Sports Publishing® is a registered trademark of Skyhorse Publishing, Inc.®, a Delaware corporation.

Visit our website at www.sportspubbooks.com.

10 9 8 7 6 5 4 3 2 1

Library of Congress Cataloging-in-Publication Data is available on file.

Cover design by Brian Peterson
Cover images: iStock

Print ISBN: 978-1-61321-949-2
Ebook ISBN: 978-1-61321-952-2

Printed in the United States of America

Lew Freedman is a longtime journalist and sports book author. He has written more than ninety books, including *Clouds Over the Goalpost, A Summer to Remember, The Rise of the Seminoles,* and *Knuckleball,* among others. He has also worked as a newspaperman for numerous papers, including the *Philadelphia Enquirer, Chicago Tribune,* and *Anchorage Daily News.*

Currently a writer for the *Cody Enterprise* in Wyoming, Freedman and his wife Debra split their time between Wyoming and Indiana.

CONTENTS

INTRODUCTION

THE FANS STREAMED through downtown Toronto on their way to an early-season hockey game at the Air Canada Centre. It was a long time before first-puck drop between the Maple Leafs and the visiting Colorado Avalanche.

Still, you could tell where everyone was headed after stopping for dinner, for a brew, or a snack in the restaurants, bars, or shops nearby. They call the weekly television viewing of National Hockey League games across the country "*Hockey Night in Canada.*" But really, every night a home game is scheduled it is Hockey Night in Toronto.

The same is true in Boston, Detroit, Chicago, New York, and Montreal. In those cities, hockey is in the DNA of the citizenry. Maybe a little more rooted here, maybe a little less there. Those are the teams that constitute what is termed "The Original Six." They are the cornerstone franchises of the NHL, the ones that go way back, well before the establishment of many of the league's other teams.

For decades in the twentieth century those clubs were the whole league, a six-team league small in size, but intense in passion.

There never was an easy night when the Leafs, Bruins, Red Wings, Blackhawks, Rangers, and Canadiens played. There was so much familiarity respect was bred more than contempt.

Being a hockey player at the top level in North America was as much fraternity as profession. It may also have been considered a brotherhood, but the type where brothers battle one another in the living room and overturn the coffee table and occasionally break a lamp with their bodychecking.

In 2016, there were thirty teams in the NHL, twenty-three in the United States and seven in Canada. That represents expansion of twenty-four teams, a 500 percent larger league. Hockey even thrives in the Sun Belt, in American cities such as Dallas and Los Angeles. Yet despite the thousands of skaters who benefited from the expansion opportunities and the millions of fresh followers the sport created, a somewhat indefinable hold on the spirit of the game is retained by the Original Six, especially among older fans.

Mention names such as Maurice "Rocket" Richard, Frank Mahovlich, Bobby Hull, Gordie Howe, Andy Bathgate, or Phil Esposito and old-timers get misty-eyed and nostalgic. Oh, the memories.

Yes, they play serious NHL hockey in St. Louis, Pittsburgh, and Nashville, but there is a little bit louder buzz in those teams' arenas when an Original Six team comes to town. There is more excitement yet at the Joe Louis Arena when the Blackhawks visit the Red Wings. They have been playing against one another so long, since 1926, and so often, going on 900 meetings. Just another game? Not quite. It is history speaking out loud at the face-off, tradition in the flesh.

High in the arenas there are banners signifying championships won and names of Hall of Famers who played long before the other twenty-four teams were born. Heck, long-gone grandparents in the same family watched the Original Six in their colorful, memorable sweaters. Later generations still cheer Grandpa's team.

"There's a long tradition of great hockey between the two," said Blackhawks general manager Stan Bowman of Chicago-Detroit. "It's an intense rivalry."

That's one rivalry. Toronto-Montreal is another. Boston-New York (in any sport), still another.

I was a child of an Original Six team. I grew up in the Boston area and the Bruins were Our Team. Later, they came to be known as the Big Bad Bruins. But in the 1960s they were just bad. For eight straight seasons, beginning with 1959–60 and ending with the 1966–67 season, the Bruins did not make the playoffs. That was in a six-team league with four teams qualifying.

In some ways, Boston didn't seem to even care, because losers or not, the fans still came to the Boston Garden and filled it to the rafters. Those rafters were enveloped in a sort of cloud because arena smoking was still allowed. The smoke rose and those in the $2 upper balcony seats sometimes had foggy views. But that year Bobby Orr came to town and after that things were all right.

I lived in Chicago when the Blackhawks hit bottom, drawing an announced 10,000 fans to the 20,000-seat United Center. Then the Blackhawks got Patrick Kane and Jonathan Toews and after that things were all right there, too.

There were so many Maple Leafs jerseys, jackets, and caps in view as the 19,800 fans filed into the Air Canada Centre for that game against the Avalanche that I wondered why apparel was still for sale in the gift shops. It appeared fans had it all already. But I suppose there was always Christmas for relatives.

Maple Leafs games are always sold out. I came by a ticket for $100 US on the secondary market. Looking at a map I thought my seat was in a balcony halfway up from the ice, but when I began climbing it was as if I was scaling Mount Everest—the summit was always just over the next ridge. No one nearby, despite not wearing ropes, keeled over, however, from altitude sickness.

When I reached my seat I was in the next-to-last row of the building. Silly me, my binoculars were at home.

A few pre-game vacant seats to my left sat Paul Ayres, forty-one, an elementary school teacher, and his son Ben, eleven. This was the youngster's first live game after only following the Leafs on TV. Soaking in the scene, his eyes were as wide around as the tires on my car.

Like so many Ontario residents, Paul Ayres was a lifelong Leafs fan even though the Leafs hadn't won a Stanley Cup since 1967, since seven years before he was born. When Ben was born Dad put the family on Toronto's season-ticket waiting list. The Ayreses were number 7,796. Before the 2015–16 season started, after eleven years of patience, the team contacted Ayres to tell him his turn had come to buy two tickets.

The only problem was that Ayres really couldn't afford the indulgence on his salary. He asked the Maple Leafs what happened if he passed. They told him he would go to the bottom of the list, then 15,000 names long.

There was a bit of anguish in the household.

"I figured if I didn't do it I would probably never see a Leafs game again," Ayres said. "I told my wife we had to look at it like a rental property, an investment."

So Ayres bought the tickets, is selling enough of them to break even, and then going to the rest of the games.

It turned out that a number of people in the section were like me. They bought their tickets from a broker. I assumed that meant there were a lot of people like Ayres, selling seats to get back some of their costs. The guy next to me was thirty-four and it was the first Maple Leafs game he saw in person after a lifetime of fandom. He only lived an hour away, but had no idea when he would have another chance to come to the Air Canada Centre.

The Maple Leafs, still looking to draft their Orr, Kane or Toews, were playing better than they had in years. They beat Colorado, 5–1, in Ben Ayres's first game.

The boy discovered real life can be more vivid than television. "It was awesome," Ben said.

The Blackhawks last won the Stanley Cup in 2015, the Bruins in 2011, the Red Wings in 2008, the Rangers in 1994, the Canadiens in 1993, and the Maple Leafs forty-nine years ago.

More irritating to the fans who view hockey, the NHL, and the Maple Leafs as a birthright, not an acquired taste, is that since the Stanley Cup's home address is in Toronto they can pretty much reach out and touch it without winning it whenever it is not traveling. Even then, a duplicate of the most famous trophy in sports is perpetually on display at the Hockey Hall of Fame, also in Toronto.

Pretending is not ideal, though. Toronto residents want to possess the Cup, not pay to see it in a museum. Being home to an Original Six team should come with some privileges, they believe.

When Toronto wins the Cup again, the city will go mad, singing, dancing, high-fiving hands so often and hard they will bruise. In Toronto they will just figure the Cup has come home to stay at last.

Lew Freedman
May 2016

1

MONTREAL CANADIENS

Founded: 1909
Home Arenas: Jubilee Arena 1909–10 and 1918–19; Mount Royal
Arena, 1920–26; Montreal Forum, 1926–96; Bell Centre, 1996–
present (know at Molson Centre from 1996–2002)
Stanley Cups: 1916, 1924, 1930, 1931, 1944, 1946, 1953, 1956,
1957, 1958, 1959, 1960, 1965, 1966, 1968, 1969, 1971, 1973,
1976, 1977, 1978, 1979, 1986, 1993

Beginnings

FOUNDED IN 1909, the Montreal Canadiens, the standard-
bearer of French-speaking Quebec and the greatest dynasty in
National Hockey League history, is the only team that was created
before the league itself started in 1917.

The official team name was le Club de hockey Canadien. The
Canadiens have also been fondly referred to as Les Habitants, and
from there the diminutive of the Habs has been applied. The early
French settlers of the region were called Les Habitants. There was some
minor tweaking of the name in French, but the CH logo has remained
a constant since the 1917–18 season with only minimal variations.

Montreal has been the New York Yankees of the NHL. The
Canadiens own 24 Stanley Cup titles, one won before the NHL

opened for business, and 23 since. One Montreal player, Henri Richard, alias "The Pocket Rocket" because he was the younger brother of superstar Maurice "Rocket" Richard, played for 11 Stanley Cup winners, more than any other NHL player.

Although the Canadiens have not won a Stanley Cup since 1993, they are regarded as much civic institution as sports team in Montreal and throughout Quebec. Every boy aspires to grow up and wear the *bleu, blanc, rouge* of the Canadiens. Founders wanted the club to be emblematic of the French-Canadian community, and in the late 1910s and early 1920s especially, owners sought to suit up only French Canadians.

That point of emphasis has fallen by the wayside in a more cosmopolitan National Hockey League with stars from all over the world, but for decades it was important to the franchise to feature a French-Canadian star. Fans did not really even want players whose first language was English. This was certainly true through the end of the Original Six era. However, for years the Canadiens have broadcast their games in French and English.

The Canadiens go back so far they have a theme that dates from World War I and relates to a poem written in 1915 called "In Flanders Fields" by John McCrae. One line of the poem was etched on the wall at the old Montreal Forum and read, "To you from failing hands we throw the torch. Be yours to hold it high." The inspirational slogan followed the Canadiens to their new rink.

The name Georges Vezina has been kept alive much longer than the man. The name is attached to one of the most coveted awards in professional hockey. The Vezina Trophy goes to the most outstanding goalie of the year at the end of the NHL regular season.

Vezina was born in 1887 in Chicoutimi, Quebec, and his nickname was "The Chicoutimi Cucumber" because he was so cool in goal. Vezina moved in as protector of the Montreal net in 1910 and played every single game for the Canadiens in that spot through the 1924–25 season. That included 328 regular-season games and 39 playoff games. Vezina was the goaltender when the Canadiens won their first Cup in 1916 and he was in goal when they won it in 1924.

He was the first goalie in NHL history to record a shutout. So popular at one time, Vezina wrote a column for a newspaper translated from French to English. In one piece, appearing during World War I, he quoted from the English novelist John Galsworthy, who later won a Nobel Prize for literature. The phrase revolved around the comment that at that time of war "only one flag that is still flying high and true, and that is the one of Sport."

Montreal found Vezina in his hometown when the Canadiens made a barnstorming trip to play against the locals. Vezina pitched a shutout on a frozen pond and the pros demanded his signature on a contract. Not that Vezina grew up dreaming of being an ice hockey star. He actually did not learn how to skate until he was eighteen, previously manning the net in leather footwear.

On the night of November 28, 1925, Vezina occupied his familiar post. But he felt dizzy, and when reeling from chest pains he pulled himself from the lineup. After the first period Vezina threw up blood, and was rushed to the hospital where he was diagnosed with tuberculosis.

Vezina passed away on March 27, 1926, at age thirty-nine. Crushed by the loss of their star, the Canadiens, working with the NHL, established the Vezina Trophy, awarded each season to the goalie surrendering the fewest goals. Later, the award was given to the goalie voted the best during the season.

More than 1,500 people attended Vezina's funeral in his hometown, where the local rink was later named for him. Vezina was also one of the first inductees of the Hockey Hall of Fame when it opened in 1945.

Decades later, the only pads Vezina wore during his career were sold by a private collector of memorabilia to a producer of hockey cards. That company cut up the pads into small pieces less than two inches by two inches and inserted 320 pad cards into packs of cards for collectors. There was an outcry about the destruction of history because the pads were one of a kind.

The early Canadiens featured some other players who live on in team lore. Jack Laviolette was the first captain, coach, and general manager of the Canadiens. He was born in Ontario in 1879 and shifted between wing and defense on the ice. Laviolette was an early standout from the 1916 Cup team and was part of a group that earned the nickname "The Flying Frenchmen." That nickname stuck with the Canadiens of French heritage.

Laviolette, also a star lacrosse player, saw his on-rink career end in 1919 because of injuries suffered while automobile racing. The crash cost him his right foot.

Although he was not the owner, the 5-foot-11, 170-pound Laviolette was the man who pieced together the Canadiens' first success stories. Laviolette died at eighty in 1960 and was inducted into the Hall of Fame in 1962.

Newsy Lalonde

Practically no one knows the real name of the star hockey player called Newsy Lalonde because he had jobs for a newspaper. Lalonde, who was as adept at lacrosse as he was at hockey during a Hall of Fame career, was given the name Edouard when born in 1887.

Lalonde, like Laviolette, was an original Flying Frenchman, perhaps the original for whom the nickname was coined. Not only did Newsy score a goal in the first official NHL game played on December 19, 1917, in a Canadiens' win over the Ottawa Senators, he scored in his first six games. During the 1919–20 season Lalonde scored 37 goals in 23 games for Montreal.

While Lalonde only played in 99 NHL games (in addition to others in different pro leagues), he scored 124 goals. Overall, Lalonde scored 413 goals in 20 seasons of some kind of pro play. He led four leagues in scoring in some very short seasons, but once scored nine goals in a game. He later coached for 11 seasons, mostly with Montreal.

When Lalonde was player-coach during the 1918–19 season, the NHL called off the Cup Finals because of the international Spanish flu epidemic that was killing people around the world. The Canadiens were matched with Seattle of the National Hockey Association, but so many players on both teams became ill that play ceased. Future Hall of Famer Joe Hall of the Canadiens died from that flu strain.

Lalonde turned pro with Sault Ste. Marie of the International Hockey League in 1907 for $35 a week and was expected to watch his first game, so he didn't bring gear to the arena. However, when a player was injured, the team needed him, and Newsy stepped in on a pair of borrowed skates. He quickly absorbed a crushing hit, but he couldn't leave the game because the team had no substitute and would have to play shorthanded.

"It hurt and I didn't feel good," Lalonde said.

A boxer in the house named Jack Hammond tried to help him during a break. He presented Lalonde with what he said was a bottle of whiskey.

"I took a big swig," Lalonde said. "It burned my mouth and my gums and my throat. I thought I was a goner. But I came around. I couldn't eat anything but poached eggs for a week."

It was later learned that in the confusion of the moment Hammond had handed Lalonde a bottle of ammonia, not whiskey.

Much later, in 1920, while on the ice for the Canadiens, Lalonde committed a serious faux pas. Montreal led the Quebec Bulldogs by a goal and goalie Georges Vezina made a spectacular save. The rebound bounced to Newsy, who thought he heard a whistle for offsides. Thrilled because of the stoppage in play while his team was under pressure, Lalonde kiddingly tossed the puck into his own net. Only there had been no whistle and the goal counted for the other side. Mortified, Lalonde later scored the winning goal to make up for the big mistake.

Long after he retired from hockey and lacrosse, Lalonde was honored with a special day in his hometown of Cornwall, Ontario, taking note of accomplishments. The event included a city hall reception, a civic luncheon, a dinner, a lacrosse game, and other activities.

Newsy Lalonde admitted getting more enjoyment out of lacrosse than hockey "because it's played out of doors where you get lots of fresh air."

Howie Morenz

Howie Morenz was most closely identified with the Montreal Canadiens, the team he started his NHL career with, ended it with, and spent the most time with (12 years) as he amassed 271 goals in 550 games.

A 5-foot-9, 165-pound center from Ontario, Morenz was the star of the playoffs in 1924 when the Canadiens won their second Stanley Cup and first after the National Hockey League was formed. During 1927–28, Morenz became the first player to score 50 points in one season with 51 when he netted 33 goals in 43 games. In the 1929–30 season, Morenz scored 40 goals in 44 games.

Morenz won the Hart Trophy three times as the league's Most Valuable Player and played on three Stanley Cup championship teams as a member of the Canadiens. He became a beloved local player because of his speed and passion on the ice. Explosive and dashing, in 1950 Morenz was voted the best hockey player of the first half of the twentieth century.

Fun-loving off the ice, Morenz sang songs and played the ukulele. The 1920s has been called the decade when sports figures first became bigger than life with Babe Ruth in baseball leading the way, Jack Dempsey in boxing, and followed by Red Grange in football, Bobby Jones in golf, and Bill Tilden in tennis. Morenz was that guy for hockey.

"Howie was in a class by himself," said Toronto's King Clancy, "the greatest player I ever saw. He was the best in his day, the best I played against, and the best I watched. He could get to top speed in one stride. He was a threat to go end-to-end through an entire team at any time."

It was said Tex Rickard, the boxing impresario who built Madison Square Garden, had not thought of installing a hockey rink in the building until watching the Canadiens led by Morenz.

In a brilliant characterization of Morenz long after his career, a Canadian sportswriter said of him, "They say that Howie

Morenz could skate so fast that he finished thirty years ahead of television."

"When he came down the ice, he was like the wind," said Earl Seibert, a Morenz contemporary and fellow Hall of Famer in 1987. "If he were around today there wouldn't be a player who could touch him."

However, Seibert did. He delivered what he thought was a routine check on Morenz in a game between Montreal and the Blackhawks. Morenz fell, rammed the boards, and caught his left skate on the wood, twisting his leg. The impact was violent and snapping bones could be heard around the arena. Morenz's leg was fractured in four places.

"People say I killed him, but that really isn't true," Seibert said. "I hit him with a check and he broke his leg and I take the full blame for that. He wound up in the hospital. But it was all his friends coming in to visit him, bringing him drinks and things. They were the ones who killed him."

Technically, Morenz died of a broken leg, but things went awry in the hospital that contributed. It was later stated there was whiskey on the dresser and beer under the bed in Morenz's room as visitors violated rules. The Canadiens took a nosedive in the standings and Morenz was stuck in the hospital fretting about his recovery. When the team doctor came he stated Morenz had suffered a nervous breakdown.

Soon after, Morenz complained of chest pains. He had a heart attack and died on March 8, 1937, trying to climb out of bed. He was only thirty-four.

"I think Howie died of a broken heart," said Montreal teammate Aurele Joliat. "He loved to play hockey more than anyone ever loved anything and when he realized he would not ever play hockey again he couldn't live with it."

A funeral service for Morenz was conducted at the Montreal Forum and an estimated 50,000 people filed past the casket placed in the center of the arena. Some 15,000 people stayed for the service and it was estimated 250,000 people lined the road to the cemetery.

"At the rink, it was so quiet," Howie Morenz Jr. said of the event. "For the first time in my life I realized just how much my father meant to everyone."

Canadiens part-owner Leo Dandurand spoke for the organization, saying, "Howie Morenz was the athlete in whom modesty, loyalty, and honesty were truly personified. His heart bubbled for his friends and the game he loved and played so well. His sense of responsibility to his club and his teammates endeared him forever to all those who knew him."

In an era long before cell phones, texting, and email, Howie Morenz wrote letters from the hospital. At least one sent to his father and family went public.

In part it read, "Dear Dad and All, just a note to let you know I am still very much alive. Mary [his wife] and the children are all well. . . . Hoping you will be able to make this writing out as I am in quite an awkward position. Had intended to write you at an earlier date, but had been suffering from a lot of pain from my leg.

"My leg is pretty badly fractured, but I have got a lot of confidence in the Drs. With love to all, Howie."

Morenz died about five weeks later.

The following November the Canadiens retired Morenz's Number 7 sweater, the first retired number in team history. A benefit All-Star game was also played with the proceeds going to

Morenz's family. Later, Morenz's daughter Marlene married future Canadiens' legend Bernie "Boom Boom" Geoffrion.

Aurele Joliat

At 5-foot-7 and 135 pounds, Aurele Joliat was called "The Mighty Atom" or "The Little Giant" when he skated 16 years for the Montreal Canadiens.

A member of three Canadiens' Stanley Cup championship teams, Joliat led the NHL in goals once with 28, his career high. He accumulated 460 points in 655 games before retiring after the 1937–38 season. Joliat and Howie Morenz played on the same line for 13 seasons. Joliat put up with a lot of injuries, including six shoulder separations, five broken noses, and three broken ribs.

While later celebrated enough to become a Hall of Famer, Joliat's arrival in Montreal was at first met with dismay by local fans. He was an unknown, but owner Leo Dandurand traded the famed Newsy Lalonde for Joliat.

Joliat definitely did not get rich from hockey.

"I remember I made $1,100 my first year in the National League," he said. "I think the most I ever made was $5,500. You didn't dicker, you know. We didn't know how much we were getting half the time. I went in once to sign a contract and they just stuck it out and said, 'Sign here.' I started to read it and he said, 'I didn't say read it. I said sign it.' So I signed."

The money wasn't like it would become, so after hockey Joliat, besides spending time being viewed as an elder statesman, became a ticket agent for the Canadian National Railway. Actually, Joliat wasn't so sure he was going to have a long life and especially not a long life after hockey. He underwent a spinal fusion operation in 1942 that frightened him.

"I thought I was finished," Joliat said. "I still can't understand how I'm still alive in this funny world."

After retiring from the railroad, Joliat stayed in Ottawa and closed his favorite pub many nights while drinking beer. That particular pub was located six miles from his home, and at closing time he took the long stroll for the exercise at age seventy-eight.

"The walking is good for me," Joliat said. "How the hell do you think I keep young?"

That was after he drank beer, smoked cigarettes, entertained the bar crowd with tales of the old days with the Canadiens and signed autographs. Sometimes, after all of that, in the early morning when the sun was rising, Joliat strapped on his skates to cruise around a pond before heading to his bed.

Back when he was playing, long before the days when players wore helmets as they competed, Joliat wore a weird appendage. He played wearing a black cap. Nobody wanted to emulate him and officials didn't seem to care.

"I've had about six of these," Joliat said decades later. "Most of them rotted away with all of the sweat. I used to wear them because it was cold in the rinks in those days. But the peaks were too big, like a baseball cap. So I trimmed them down and got them good and tight so they couldn't knock it off."

When he was seventy-nine, Joliat decided to suit up for an old-timers hockey game, wearing the gear for the first time in forty-three years. Joliat played for a team called the Old Pros, fundraising to fight Parkinson's disease. Joliat did not merely dress out and wave. He skated about a half hour's worth.

"Aw, that's nothing," he said. "Skating is easy."

Years into retirement, when Joliat agreed to meet with a sportswriter for five minutes and instead talked for about five hours, he critiqued his listed height as really being 5-foot-6, not 5-foot-7, but he had shrunk by then anyway, so who really knew?

Joliat was a small guy despite having a father who stood over six feet tall and weighed 240 pounds. Emile Joliat was so muscular he made his career as a butcher, mine worker, and as a police officer.

For all the contact, Joliat believed in self-preservation and had the quickness to avoid many trying situations when players gunned for him. Boston Bruin Bill Cowley did so once as a rookie.

"One shift my first year I remember I tried to run him through the boards," Cowley said. "He put a deke on me and I almost went through the boards myself. I was trying to knock that black cap off his head and he skated by me and told me, 'Don't try that again, young fella.' He was small, but nobody hit him—they couldn't. And if they did, he could handle himself."

Joliat was feisty as an active player and as an old-timer. In 1960 while at a charity dinner in Boston, Joliat, who long before tangled with Harry "Punch" Broadbent, was seated near his nemesis. In the middle of the meal Joliat leapt over the table to attack Broadbent and they fought again. Other players locked them in their rooms for a cooling off period.

He was not afraid to fight during his active skating days, but Joliat admitted his size mitigated against going after many players.

"I lost most of the fights, of course," Joliat said. "But I won one in Montreal. It was against the chief of police. He jumped on the ice during a brawl against the [Montreal] Maroons and I belted him. He was wearing a big, raccoon coat. I got the better of that one, all right."

At eighty, Joliat bowled a 195 game and with his pub mates joked about making an NHL comeback for one exhibition game.

Joliat was looked at for a long time as perhaps the greatest stick-handler in the game. He provided thrills to Montreal fans, and a poet named Wilson MacDonald focused some verse on the exploits of the swift skater. In part, it read,

> When Joliat skate out I yell
> Unteel I have a pain.
> I trow my 'at up in de hair
> And shout, 'Hurrah,' again. . . .
> Dat was a ver' exciting game
> De score eet was a tie;
> An' den dat leetle Joliat
> Get hanger een hees eyes.

And, naturally, scored the winning goal.

Elmer Lach

When Elmer Lach retired in 1954 his name had been engraved on the Stanley Cup three times. He had won the Hart Trophy as the Most Valuable Player, won the Art Ross Trophy twice as single-season scoring leader, and was the all-time leading National Hockey League scorer.

Those distinctions helped secure his spot in the Hall of Fame. Lach spent his entire 14-year NHL career with the Montreal Canadiens and served on a line with Maurice "Rocket" Richard and Toe Blake. Blake attained greater fame later by coaching the Canadiens. The trio was called "The Punch Line." Lach, who suffered numerous broken bones during his career, caused the end of the partnership by breaking an ankle.

Lach, who lived to be ninety-seven before passing away in 2015, had his Number 16 jersey retired by the Canadiens after collecting 623 points in 664 games. At the time of his death Lach was the oldest surviving member of the Canadiens and the oldest living member of the Hall of Fame.

Before Lach began playing junior hockey in the mid-1930s he worked in a pool hall and was paid 25 cents daily for racking the balls. The Maple Leafs rejected Lach as being too small. Lach grew to 5-foot-9 and 165 pounds and proved he belonged with the Canadiens after the team gave him $100 to show up for a tryout.

When Lach was promoted to the Canadiens in 1940 he took a train into town and the only luggage he carried was a toothbrush and a handkerchief.

Some called Lach "Elegant Elmer" for his stylish passing, although the things that happened to his body on the ice could not come under that heading. Among other woes, Lach suffered a broken nose seven times, a fractured skull, and a thrice-broken jaw, although he admitted to only two breaks so he could stay in the lineup. When he was a younger man Lach's mother always told him "Don't get hurt" when he went out to skate. Apparently that advice didn't take.

Supposedly, Lach's insurance company offered him $17,000 if he would give up hockey. He ignored the offer. Also, some felt Lach got what he deserved in the contact sport. Detroit Red Wings general manager Jack Adams called him "the meanest, shrewdest, nastiest so-and-so in the league." But Adams said he would love to have him on his team.

When Lach's wife gave birth to a son in 1945 Lach was on the road with the Canadiens and sent her a telegram reading, "Nice going, honey."

Lach later said of some opponents classified him as "a son of a gun who used his stick like a saber. But I never minded a swordfight."

He also recognized what he signed up for in the rugged days of Original Six hockey.

"It's no game for little gentlemen," Lach said. "Those guys take the bread and butter out of my mouth when they beat me. Injuries are a part of hockey, and I guess if you don't want to get hurt, I figure you better not play."

When Lach scored the Cup-winning goal in 1953, Rocket Richard leapt into his arms for a hug. Only he hit him so hard he caused one of Lach's broken noses. Near the end of his life someone asked Lach his best memory of teammate Richard. Going fishing together, Lach said.

Born in Nokomis, Saskatchewan, in 1918, Lach grew up not far from a famous provincial psychiatric hospital. Once, teasingly, Lach asked, "Do you think I should have checked in?"

During Lach's Hart-winning year he scored 26 goals and contributed 54 assists. When Richard scored his 50th goal for a new one-season record, Lach had the only assist on the play.

In his nineties, Lach not only still played golf, he also shot scores in the 90s, matching his age.

Overall, retirement from hockey was good for Lach's health. He went decades without breaking any bones, until late in life he broke both ankles falling off his porch while shoveling snow, and then his hip.

"I was still breathing, which was good," Lach said of his last big injury.

Maurice "Rocket" Richard

No one exemplified the hockey player as hero the way Maurice Richard did. The fastest flying of all the Frenchmen, the Rocket carried the hopes and dreams of the Montreal Canadiens, the city of Montreal, the province of Quebec, and most Canadians during his 18-year career.

Richard played hockey with great flair and great success. He was the first player to score 50 goals in one season and he did it in 50 games. He was the first player to score 500 goals and he did so with incredible passion.

When the Montreal Canadiens were the best team in hockey, Richard was the face of the franchise. He remains one of the all-time greats, one of the finest players in the history of the sport, probably a top-five figure. It didn't hurt that he had a colorful nickname—and with his 544 goals, the Rocket was worthy of it.

Born in Montreal in 1921, Richard stood 5-foot-10 and played at 180-plus pounds. He was the homegrown star and a symbol of the French influence of the province for Canadiens fans who worshipped him.

Where Richard skated success followed. He played on eight Montreal Stanley Cup winners and was honored by selection to 14 NHL postseason All-Star teams. Richard's Number 9 jersey was retired when he did.

One of eight children of a poverty-stricken family during the Great Depression, Richard was initially looked at as a player with limited strength and staying power. He proved he was tough enough on the ice, but one infamous incident the Rocket is remembered for is hitting a linesman on March 13, 1955. That is one of the major no-nos in professional sport.

A few days later, NHL president Clarence Campbell suspended Richard for the remainder of the regular season and the playoffs, an action which precipitated a riot in the streets of Montreal. Although he had been warned away by police and Mayor Jean

Drapeau, Campbell boldly attended the next Montreal home game, even after receiving death threats. A crowd of 6,000 people gathered outside the Forum as 16,000 attended inside.

Campbell was relentlessly booed; fans threw everything from vegetables, bottles, and game programs at him. The crowd grew more restless as the Canadiens fell behind Detroit 4–1 and a man evaded security to attack Campbell, landing several punches. Then a tear gas bomb was thrown into the mix, landing perhaps 25 feet away. Eyes tearing, in a panic, the crowd fled the Forum. Campbell forfeited the game to the Red Wings.

The retreating game crowd mixed with the thousands outside. The riot on St. Patrick's Day and the angry crowd believed the length of Richard's suspension represented prejudice against French Canadians.

The disruption caused $100,000 in property damage and resulted in 37 injuries and 100 arrests.

In later years the protest took on larger political overtones as residents of Quebec sought to maintain their identity and heritage in a country that is mostly English-speaking.

Richard never forgave Campbell for attending the game that night or his playoff suspension.

"I expected to be suspended," Richard said on the fortieth anniversary of the riot, "maybe for the rest of the regular schedule and even some games the following season. But the playoffs? Never."

This was one of the most unfortunate events in NHL history, forever linked to Richard, who wasn't even able to dress for the game. It was an illustration of how much his fans loved him and his importance as a symbol.

Richard was by far the best goal scorer who had come along. During his early years with the Canadiens the record for most goals in NHL history was 323 by Nels Stewart. Richard surpassed that total by more than 200.

"Richard is the standout player in the game today," said New York Rangers' general manager Frank Boucher. "He's the Babe Ruth of Montreal."

That was during the 1949–50 season, and Richard played another decade. He retired at thirty-eight, and many believed he could have played on. Richard was reluctant because he set such high standards.

"Pride," Richard said. "That's what made me quit. When my gifts were gone I didn't want to hang on and end up being pitied. I wouldn't let that happen."

What gifts they were. Richard had a hard shot, was a swift skater, had a nose for the net, and an instinct for how to skate through defenses. Scoring turned him on, no doubt. Even later, when he played in old-timers games, Richard demonstrated the same hunger for the net.

"I just couldn't go out and have a nice little skate," Richard said. "I wasn't built that way. I liked to put the puck in the net, even when I got older. But after a while there's no way for you to beat young legs."

Toe Blake, who played on the Punch Line with Richard and then coached him, said Richard always displayed that burning fire to score. Even when Richard was going to quit he still went all out in practice drills.

"He still couldn't let up," Blake said. "Even in practice, even if the goal was wide open, he would ram the puck in as if he wanted to put it into the street outside."

When Richard retired, the Canadiens were on a run of winning five straight Stanley Cups. Without him, the Chicago Blackhawks won the next year.

"With the Rocket there—for heart and courage there was none like him—I'm sure we would have won at least the sixth," Blake said.

Richard could score, but didn't think he was better than everyone else at various aspects of the game.

"Lots of guys were better players than me," Richard said, "for sure, better skaters, better stick-handlers, better passers. But if your shot doesn't hit the net, there's no way it goes in. If a guy isn't scoring it's usually because he makes the same play all the time. The goaltender, he knows the player makes the same move nine times in ten. Every time, I would try something different. Hell, I didn't know what I would do next, so how could they?"

Richard was like a dog going after raw meat when he went to the goal. Blake, who might have been Richard's biggest cheerleader, did have a favorite Richard goal. It occurred during the 1945–46 season against the Detroit Red Wings. Blake started the play with a pass to Richard, who rushed up ice. At the blue line he encountered defenseman Earl Seibert.

"The Rocket, he must have been forty feet from the net and he didn't even break stride," Blake said. "Here's this 200-pound guy riding him and all you could do is watch him get closer, closer to Harry Lumley in the nets."

Richard faked Lumley out of his skates and deposited the puck in the net at the same time he shrugged off Seibert, sending him into the corner.

"Greatest goal I ever saw," Blake said.

Howe and Richard were tremendous rivals, but when Richard died in 2000 Howe said it was Richard who made the NHL.

His popularity went beyond the league and helped hockey players make a living.

Doug Harvey, the Hall of Fame defenseman who was a teammate of Richard's, said the Rocket was "the hungriest hockey player I ever saw. Intense? He even fished intensely. I don't know how you can fish and be intense, but he was."

Once, when Blake was coaching and gave the players a spicy pep talk, Harvey had his eyes on Richard until he exploded.

"Well, he decides he's had enough," Harvey said. "He goes to the door and crunch, he puts his skate through it. Now he can't get it out. It's kinda funny, now that I think about it, but nobody was laughing that night."

Goalies weren't Richard's friends, but they respected him.

"When I think about Richard," said Hall of Famer Glenn Hall, "the thing I see most are his eyes. When he was coming down on you, the puck glued to the end of his stick, his eyes were flashing and gleaming like the lights of a pinball machine. He was frightening."

One accomplishment that provided Richard with early fame was scoring 50 goals in 50 games during the 1944–45 season. It was previously thought to be impossible. Richard notched his 50th on March 18 in Boston against a rookie goalie named Harvey Bennett.

Bennett claimed the puck was kicked into the net. He told that story many times, though not to sportswriters until decades passed. Bennett didn't want to tarnish the goal even a half century later.

"He's too good an athlete," Bennett said. "He deserved everything he got. He's better than any hockey player that ever lived."

Teammate Jean Beliveau noted Richard did not say much, but was still the Canadiens' leader.

"He was an inspiration and an idol to my generation," said Beliveau, one of the greatest of Canadiens players. "He was not the greatest talker, but he was a leader. He inspired us to win by his desire to win."

When Richard died at seventy-eight in 2000, he was treated like a prime minister. The family rejected holding the funeral at the Molson Center in front of 21,000 people in favor of the Notre Dame Basilica in Montreal. But Richard's body lay in state for 14 hours and it was estimated somehow that 115,000 people filed passed his coffin.

The 90-minute high Mass conducted in French was broadcast across Canada.

"Maurice Richard is part of all of us, whether you're rich or poor, educated or uneducated," said Montreal's Mayor Pierre Bourque. "He made Montreal known worldwide as the city of hockey."

Richard understood he was a hero to many, but he was somewhat uncomfortable with the designation. Once, he said, "I'm afraid to let the French people down."

He never did that.

"Yes, I realize I was important to a lot of people as a symbol," Richard once said, "but I could not look at the politics of it. How would you feel to be discussed by historians like this? I was a hockey player. I have always been a hockey player. It was my métier. A hockey player, just a hockey player."

Henri Richard

The oldest sibling was the famed Maurice Richard. Henri Richard was fifteen years younger and was nicknamed "The Pocket Rocket" as an homage to the Rocket. It was impossible to live up to the achievements of Maurice, but Henri gave it a good run and in one respect exceeded his brother's achievements.

Henri Richard's contributions to 11 Stanley Cup winners make him the most decorated player in National Hockey League history. His name is engraved all over the Stanley Cup. Teammate Jean Beliveau was part of ten Cup winners as a player and another seven as an executive, however.

The younger Richard differed from Maurice in more ways than age. They shot from different sides, and Henri was smaller at 5-foot-7 and 160 pounds. As fierce a goal scorer as the Rocket was, Henri was more of a passer, leading the NHL in assists twice. Not that Henri was a slouch going to the goal. He scored 358 goals while collecting 1,046 points in 1,256 games between 1955 and 1975. Richard played his entire career with Montreal and over-lapped with his brother's final five seasons.

As a youngster, Henri attended games in the Forum to watch Maurice play. A decade later when he was breaking in with the Habs he understood the magnitude of trying to follow Maurice. He said if he led the NHL in scoring perhaps "someone will point to one of my sons and say, 'That's Henri Richard's boy.' Now they are certain to say, 'That's Rocket Richard's nephew.'"

Henri had plenty to be proud of, also playing in nine All-Star games. Given the age gap between the brothers, almost being of different generations, and Henri's achievements, it was silly to sug-gest that he wouldn't have made it in the NHL without Maurice's assistance.

"Maurice never taught me anything about hockey," Henri said. "But it doesn't mean that I never learned anything from him or that he never helped me. I learned so much just by watching him and playing on the same line with him. There were times I tried to copy his style, but I realized that no one could do that—that there was only one Maurice Richard."

Likewise, the Rocket told inquisitors that Henri was in charge of his own destiny.

"Henri did it on his own," Maurice said. "Maybe there was even more pressure on him because he was my brother. But he showed everybody what he could do and he's still doing it. I get a big kick out of watching him now that my playing days are over. Henri is a tough little fellow who needs no help from anyone."

Henri's career was a little bit longer, and since he was so much younger he was still playing with the Canadiens fifteen years after the Rocket retired.

"Henri is a better all-around player than I ever was," the Rocket said. "He stick-handles better, controls the puck more, and skates faster. He's better in every way except in goal scoring. He has his pride, and more, he has great natural ability."

As anyone who grew up in a large family knows when there is great age disparity, the oldest may well be out of the household when the youngest siblings are born. They may not even live under the same roof for more than a few years.

"Remember, Maurice left home when I was only six years old," Henri said. "When I went up to the Canadiens he was more like a father to me. We never roomed together. I never thought I would wear the uniform of the Canadiens at the same time as my brother Maurice. Imagine, I was six years old when Maurice made his debut with the Canadiens and I played five years with him."

In some ways Henri was like every other boy growing up with hockey in his blood in Quebec.

"I was only nineteen when I went to the Canadiens' training camp," he said. "That was in 1955. During the second week of practice they put me on the same line with Maurice. What a thrill that was! I never thought that some day I would play with my idol."

For his part, with his own schedule and travels, Maurice only saw Henri play hockey three or four times while the youngster was growing up.

One way in which the brothers were similar was being taciturn. Once, a sportswriter asked Toe Blake if Henri spoke English. The coach replied, "I don't think he even speaks French. He just doesn't speak."

The bold-faced statistic on Henri Richard's résumé is the 11 Stanley Cups. The only other player in any North American sport to match that figure is the Boston Celtics' Bill Russell in the NBA. He also won 11 world titles.

"I admit that I was lucky to play on talented teams that won 11 Stanley Cups," Henri Richard said. "To win the Cup five years in a row in your first five seasons is enough for a player in twenty years."

In 1971, as his career neared its end, Henri almost single-handedly won the seventh game of the Stanley Cup Finals, gathering the game-winning goal and two assists in a 3–2 victory over Chicago.

"I'll remember it all my life," he said.

Henri's secret, or most obvious characteristic, was his skating speed and the manner in which he could maintain it while also moving the puck.

"Lots of fellows will win skating races," said Montreal general manager Frank Selke. "But what makes this boy different is that he carries the puck with him and still leaves everybody behind. He's got to try to show the French Canadians in the balcony that he's as tough and brave as his brother."

When Henri Richard retired in 1975 he was coming off a season in which a broken ankle limited him. He operated a bar and played about 40 games a winter for a Canadiens' old-timers team.

In retirement the Richard brothers led separate lives with their own families, but a savvy businessman put them together on a tourist cruise to Greece with the assignment of entertaining passengers with hockey tales. Someone asked Henri what he would say to Maurice at the start of the journey.

"I'll say to him that he looks familiar," Henri said. "Something like a guy I used to play hockey with fifteen years ago."

The Defense

Doug Harvey

If Bobby Orr wins the title of best defenseman ever, then his partner on the ice would probably be Doug Harvey, a seven-time Norris Trophy winner and the bruiser on the blue line who helped protect the Canadiens' goalies during many of their glory years.

Harvey made 11 straight All-Star teams, beginning with the 1951–52 season. He was a 5-foot-11, 190-pound strong man who took the first steps toward making defensemen more offensive during a 19-year career that began with 14 seasons affiliated with Montreal.

A member of six Stanley Cup championship teams and the Hall of Fame, Harvey was appreciated for the tough style he brought to the game more than any commitment to offense. However, he was a good playmaker. Harvey scored just 88 goals in 1,113 games, but his passing often got things going.

"The thing I remember most about him is he was the best defenseman of our day," said rival George Armstrong of the Toronto

Maple Leafs when Harvey died at sixty-five in 1989. "It's like playing against [Wayne] Gretzky and Orr. It didn't matter what they did, they always beat you."

Harvey stayed on the ice any way he could, going back to the minors, coaching part-time, as long as he could into his forties. When someone asked why, he replied, "Aw, don't you know? I love it."

He was also very good at what he did and sometimes that frustrated his favorite opponents.

"All I know is the son of a gun came out of nowhere to be the biggest thorn in the side of the Leafs in our glory days," said Toronto's Howie Meeker. "He was an early Bobby Orr, except he did it in semi-slow motion. You always knew what was coming—you could see it happening—but you couldn't do anything about it. He was so good that he played mind games with the opposition."

To the surprise of many, the Hall of Fame did not choose Harvey in his first year of eligibility—he wasn't even nominated. That irritated him.

"I know what I did myself," he said. "And it's all written down in the record books. I don't care what the world thinks. It's my life."

It did not take long for the oversight to be rectified. Harvey drank heavily as a player—and did not hide it. He believed that's why he was not voted into the club in his first year of eligibility. Alcohol eventually contributed to his death—he died from cirrhosis of the liver.

"What they're telling me," Harvey said, "is that they won't put me in because I'm not averse to sampling the nectar of the gods now and then. The difference is that I'll hoist a few in full view of everyone where some other guys will sneak around the corner to do theirs."

Someone suggested Harvey was right up there with the best Canadian athletes of all time, not merely in hockey, because of his football and baseball talents. He practically blushed at that description, though.

"Ah, I don't think I was even the best in our house," he said, citing his older brother Alfie, whose sporting career was derailed by World War II navy service.

Harvey, who also was in the navy during the war, said he did not experience significant combat activity with the Germans.

"The biggest action we had was in Liverpool," he said.

Alfie and Doug played football for the Montreal Hornets, predecessor of the Alouettes of the Canadian Football League. Harvey was drafted by the National League Boston Braves for baseball and when someone teasingly asked if he could hit the curveball, he said, "I guess so, if I hit .351."

Harvey also won boxing championships and played lacrosse and said the only reason he didn't play more tennis was "I didn't have enough time."

In the NHL, Harvey was a co-founder of the Players' Association. Although he said he was blackballed because of his union activities, right up until the end of his skating days Harvey could find a job. It was Scotty Bowman, the greatest coach of all time, who suited Harvey up in his forties with the St. Louis Blues right after the Original Six era concluded.

When Harvey died, many Canadiens teammates were in attendance at the service. Dickie Moore, another Montreal star, said of Harvey, "He lived his own life, in his own way, but he was always there when you needed a friend, a true friend."

Harvey was most at home on the ice.

"As far as I'm concerned," said Montreal coach Toe Blake, "he's far and away the best defenseman ever."

Tom Johnson

One of the grand achievements of Tom Johnson's playing career was claiming the Norris Trophy as best defenseman in 1959. That's because teammate Doug Harvey had a stranglehold on the award at the time. Harvey won it seven times, including the year before Johnson and the year after. Johnson said he was lucky to gain the honor even once.

"That was the year Doug was hurt," he said.

Johnson was named to play in eight All-Star games. Johnson's name was also written on the Stanley Cup six times as a player with the Canadiens. Then, he won it twice more, as a coach and as assistant general manager for the Boston Bruins as part of his thirty-four-year off-ice affiliation with that franchise.

A low-key man who wore bow ties, Johnson was six feet tall, weighed 180 pounds, and came to the Canadiens from Manitoba in 1947. Not only did Johnson thrive in the outdoor brand of hockey in the town of 400 people, he never played inside a building until he was eighteen.

He played 14 seasons for Montreal and his final two NHL years for Boston. As a defensive specialist, Johnson scored just 51 goals in 979 games. When chosen for the Hall of Fame in 1970 he was the most surprised person in the neighborhood.

"Surprised? I'm amazed," said Johnson, who was just assuming his Bruins coaching job at the time. "Do you think my players will be impressed?"

Johnson was smoking a cigar when he got the news and it fell out of his mouth.

Johnson was caught off guard by his selection because he was the quiet man in the corner of a locker room that included Maurice Richard, "Boom Boom" Geoffrion, and Jacques Plante.

"Johnson's trouble was playing on the most colorful team in hockey history," said New York executive Emile Francis. "But he was the real worker on the team."

Johnson got into his share of fights, and one of his most memorable was with Toronto's Teeder Kennedy. Even as the men were being led to the penalty box, Johnson, who was bleeding slightly from the nose, took another crack at Kennedy. He gauged the angle over a policeman's shoulder and connected one extra time. That got him ejected from the game and fined $75. But what bothered Johnson was the doctoring of a picture in a Toronto newspaper. One photo showed the real deal. The other showed him with blood all over his face and not merely the little trickle from the nose.

"Some guy had painted blood all over my chin," an indignant Johnson said.

Johnson pretty much had hockey on the brain his entire life. He was a third grader when a teacher asked pupils to write down what they wanted to be when they grew up. Johnson wrote "professional hockey player." He was much older when a friend invited him to his first basketball game. When asked what he thought of the action, Johnson said, "I'd just as soon watch a guy fishing."

Jean Beliveau

As great a hockey player as Jean Beliveau was, he gained legions of admirers for his demeanor, gentlemanly behavior and off-ice post-retirement activities.

Remarkably, Beliveau, who played for the Montreal Canadiens for 20 years, scored nearly as many goals as Maurice "Rocket" Richard, 507 to 544, and received virtually the same level of adulation.

He was the fourth player to score 500 goals and the second to score 1,000 points.

A native of Trois-Rivieres, Quebec, the 6-foot-3, 205-pound Beliveau was a hard-to-stop center who was somehow both superstar and complementary player, making those around him better. He scored 1,219 points in 1,125 regular-season games, was a member of ten Stanley Cup championship teams as a player and seven more as an administrator. That makes Beliveau the most decorated all-around figure in National Hockey League history.

Beliveau, who played in 13 All-Star games, also won the Hart Trophy twice and the first Conn Smythe Award as Most Valuable Player in the playoffs.

"Who better than him to make history?" said Dick Duff, then with the Maple Leafs, but also a Beliveau Montreal teammate during his career.

The words "elegance," "class," and "grace" were often attached to Beliveau's name, although it took a trivia buff to realize his well-known first name of Jean was in reality his middle name and he had been christened Joseph.

Although the Canadiens were great for most of Beliveau's time on skates, they did reach a point late in his career of passing through a rebuilding phase with younger players.

"I figured my experience would help until some of the younger players got going," he said. "Now I guess I'm trying to show that an old man of thirty-nine can still keep up with the kids."

As testimony to Beliveau's stature in Quebec and across Canada he was awarded honorary degrees from some universities, including Ryerson University. At the time, Sheldon Levy, the school president, said of Beliveau, "In a country known for hockey heroes, Jean Beliveau stands out as one of the greatest legends of the game.

His leadership with children's charities, his dedication to making a difference, and his enthusiasm for the lessons of experience all embody the values we seek to instill in our students at Ryerson."

Beliveau was made a Knight of the National Order of Quebec, and also a Companion of the Order of Canada, the nation's highest civilian award. Beliveau was also honored on Canada's Walk of Fame and on a postage stamp. Beliveau was once offered the position of governor general of Canada, the federal representative of the English monarchy, but turned it down for family reasons.

For all of his impact with the Canadiens, Beliveau was slow to respond to overtures from the Montreal team, although it held his NHL rights for a few years before he dressed out. Beliveau played a couple of games for the Canadiens during the 1950–51 season and a few more two years later, but mostly stuck with a Quebec senior league team as he turned from teenager to twenty-one-year-old. There was a good reason. Although he was playing amateur hockey he did promotional work for companies and made $20,000 a year, more than any player in the NHL. Finally, the impatient Canadiens actually bought the senior league team.

For a player renowned as a gentleman, an attitude that was in his blood, Beliveau never won the Lady Byng Trophy for being a gentlemanly player. He could not because he ended up using his size in a physical way. When he came into the league Beliveau had no intention of fighting, but was repeatedly challenged, pushed around, and gained a reputation as an easy mark. So in his third season he resolved to fight back. He was smacked with 143 penalty minutes, but also led the league in scoring.

Beliveau had to maintain his reputation as someone who could take care of himself. It was not until the latter stages of his career that the challenges dropped off. Over his last six seasons Beliveau's penalty minutes declined until during the 1969–70 season when he was thirty-eight, his season total was 10 minutes in 63 games.

"Jean Beliveau played on instinct, incredible instinct," Dick Duff said. "He would control the center of the ice and knew how to create space for himself. If you cut and were open he'd get you the puck. He had size, strength, reach. It was a treat to play with him, a treat to watch him play."

Beliveau, whose greatest achievement might have been answering every fan letter personally, like Maurice Richard, was one symbol of the team, the city, and province.

"The two greatest figures of the Canadiens in the past sixty years are the Rocket and Jean Beliveau," said goaltender Ken Dryden, another famous Canadien. "One of them evokes love and the other evokes admiration."

Beliveau understood the special bond linking Quebec residents with the Canadiens.

"There are a lot of people who still see the Canadiens as a representation of themselves," he said, "and the fans invest their emotions and identities, especially when it's going well."

Beliveau began skating when he was three. He listened to Montreal games on the radio in the 1940s dreaming of how he might someday wear the blue, white, and red with the big "CH" in front. He did spend 20 years skating for the Canadiens and remained involved with and close to the franchise the rest of his life, attending home games regularly until his death at eighty-three in December 2014.

Beliveau was present in the arena when the Canadiens celebrated the hundredth anniversary of their founding in 2009.

"I guess you could say I've spent my life with this team," he said on that occasion, when he was seventy-eight.

When Beliveau died his funeral produced a massive turnout of the hockey elite. Several former Canadiens teammates served as pallbearers. Another handful of former Canadiens gave eulogies. One of the best-remembered comments was uttered by Yvan Cournoyer, who quoted a Walt Whitman poem in saying, "O captain, my captain, bon voyage."

Bernie "Boom Boom" Geoffrion

Was there ever a greater nickname to describe a hard-shooting hockey player than Boom Boom? Bernie Geoffrion, par excellence proponent of the slap shot, once scored 50 goals in a season when it was still a rarity.

Geoffrion shot so hard it made goalies cringe despite their padding. Of course, not all of them were wearing masks while Geoffrion was still patrolling the ice during his 16-year National Hockey League career.

Rookie of the year, twice NHL leader in points and twice in goals, Geoffrion played 14 seasons with the Canadiens (plus his last two with the New York Rangers).

Geoffrion claimed invention of the slap shot when he was a youngster and in many quarters is credited with the innovation. He certainly was an early practitioner of the art and one of its best-known as he accumulated 393 NHL goals, including those 50 during the 1960–61 season.

Geoffrion's wife Marlene was the daughter of Howie Morenz, another Canadiens legend, and his son Danny played in the NHL, as did his grandson Blake. Danny played in both the NHL and the World Hockey Association, suiting up for the Canadiens and Quebec Nordiques. He has remained in the sport as a scout with the Toronto Maple Leafs. Blake also made it to the NHL for three years, played briefly for the Canadiens, and won the Hobey Baker Award as the best player in American college hockey at the University of Wisconsin. It is difficult to beat the Morenz-Geoffrion family tree in the hockey world.

An 11-time All-Star, and a member of six Stanley Cup winners, Geoffrion was both a fortunate and unfortunate beneficiary of the suspension of Maurice Richard in 1955 when the Richard Riot ensued and Canadiens fans were incensed. When Richard was suspended for the rest of the season and the playoffs, he was leading the NHL in scoring. After president Clarence Campbell sat him down, Geoffrion won the scoring championship. However, his home fans booed him.

"I couldn't deliberately not score," a dismayed Geoffrion said. He felt awful about the circumstances, especially since he so admired Richard. "Ever since I was a kid, there was only one hockey player for me. Always, he was my idol."

Eventually, the Canadiens retired Geoffrion's Number 5 jersey. The banner hangs near the Number 7 banner honoring his father-in-law Morenz. Geoffrion actually predicted to his wife that one day that would happen. However, on the day Geoffrion's sweater was to be retired, he passed away from stomach cancer, turning a joyous evening into a sad one. It was one of Geoffrion's last wishes that the ceremony go on as planned. A Hall of Famer, Boom Boom passed away at seventy-five.

"This is the realization of dad's dream and brings closure to his career," said Danny Geoffrion that night. "I know dad wanted to celebrate it all with you."

In turn, just as Geoffrion followed Richard, Rod Gilbert, the New York Rangers great, said Geoffrion was his idol when he was growing up. Gilbert is from Montreal and said Geoffrion's uncle was a friend of the family and that he styled his own slap shot after Geoffrion's.

Geoffrion was the first coach of the Atlanta Flames, now in Calgary, coached the New York Rangers for a year, and also coached the Canadiens. Boom Boom took over Montreal when the team was coming off four Stanley Cup victories in a row, but was replaced after half a season.

He had long dreamed of being the man behind the bench and when appointed called himself a "sincere fellow" ready for the responsibility of running the esteemed franchise.

"You change, eh?" Geoffrion said. "When you reach forty-nine years old it is time to take stock. I wanted to prove for the people I am a more reserved person than before. I have done almost everything possible in my life, except maybe be humble. Now what matters to me is the Montreal Canadiens."

Geoffrion's tenure did not last long. The Canadiens were 15–9–6 and in first place in 1979–80 when it was announced Boom Boom was resigning due to health problems. There might have been more to his departure.

"I wasn't tough enough," he said.

Geoffrion was known for his fun-loving personality as a player. Sometimes he celebrated big moments on the ice by climbing on tables or benches and breaking into song. Like Richard he was a tiger around the net, thriving on notching the big goal. When Bernie didn't score he didn't celebrate.

"When goals don't come, there is no song," he said. "That is a mistake, I know, but how can I sing when I am not happy?"

It is unlikely he broke into song when his short stint as Canadiens coach ended, either.

Geoffrion actually possessed a voice good enough to get him invited onto a Canadian variety show. He lost the touch somewhat, though, after a shot hit him in the throat and kept him in the hospital for twenty-two days.

After his children grew up and began having children, Geoffrion, who had loaned some of the prized pieces representing his success on the ice to the Hockey Hall of Fame for three decades, took them back and put them up for auction, with the money going to the grandkids. Several items were revered trophies like the Hart and Art Ross. Geoffrion was also a saver who kept pucks representing milestone moments.

In his seventies, Geoffrion began having trouble with his eyesight. He lost the vision in his right eye due to age-related macular degeneration. But he lent his name to the cause to bring attention to the disease.

"A guy like me can, maybe, change the minds of a lot of people," he said. "I can sell my disease to people to prevent them from having what I have. If I can help one person fifty years old or over to avoid what I've got, I'm going to do it. They were good to me when I was playing and I don't want them to see the blindness coming into their lives."

Jacques Plante

There was a famous book made into a movie called *The Man in the Iron Mask*. The person was an anonymous French prisoner of centuries ago. The remake should be about Jacques Plante, anything-but-anonymous goalie for the Montreal Canadiens, who invented the goalie mask.

Plante was a brilliant Hall of Fame player who backstopped Canadiens' championship teams during their greatest era, but he will always be remembered as the innovator who changed the lives of all goalies for the better.

It took Plante's resolve, after getting hit in the face once too often by a puck that called for stitches, created headaches, and literally threatened his life, to introduce the mask. Initially he was considered a wimp for donning such protection. Gradually, the mask was adopted by all netminders, and it has evolved greatly since Plante first showed a simple protective mask off.

Plante was born in Quebec in 1929 and spent 20 years as a big-time professional goalie, all but one in the NHL, with his last season working for Edmonton in the World Hockey Association. His fame was gained with Montreal as he protected the goal for six Stanley Cup winners. His Number 1 jersey was retired in honor of his 11 years with the team.

A player in eight All-Star games at a time when there were only six goalies, almost all of them worthy of All-Star recognition, Plante won the Vezina Trophy seven times and became the rare goalie to capture the Hart Trophy as Most Valuable Player.

Plante first wore a mask in practice in the late 1950s, but did not try it in a regular-season game until the 1959–60 season when he became sick of risking his health by getting hit in the head by pucks traveling 100 mph.

The precipitating incident occurred in a game on November 1, 1959, when New York Rangers star Andy Bathgate fired a puck that smashed into Plante's nose. Plante went to the locker room, was stitched up, and returned to play—wearing his homemade mask for the first time. Coach Toe Blake hated the idea. But the

Canadiens didn't even have a backup goalie ready, so he had to ride with Plante.

Montreal won that milestone game, but Blake made Plante promise to give up the mask when his injury healed. When that time came, Plante, who had been helping the team win almost constantly, took it off and lost a game. After that he went back to the mask.

Plante's use of the mask was controversial and caused a sensation. Not all other goalies were instant converts. However, eventually, every goalie coming along donned the mask and the NHL made their use a requirement.

When the first game with Plante in the mask ended and he was victorious, he was surrounded by reporters in the locker room. At the time his white Canadiens jersey was still bloodstained from the nose injury.

"That's why I made this mask," Plante said of the new protective device that aided him in returning to the lineup. "Here, feel it, that's hard fiberglass. We tested it, hit the thing with a hammer and couldn't break it. It's molded to fit my face perfectly. I think it can be improved, but I don't know how."

The mask did not impair his vision, he said, but sometimes it felt uncomfortable. He predicted other goalies would start wearing masks.

Plante had already been regarded as somewhat quirky. He took up knitting to relax and relieve the pressure of being the last line of defense. He sometimes stayed in separate hotels from his teammates. Plante was outspoken. Plante said he became a goalie in the first place because he had asthma as a kid.

"If it was too cold or windy I couldn't get my breath if I skated hard," he said. "I had to play goal where I didn't have to move around so much."

Another Plante habit was traveling far enough from his net to make coaches and fans nervous. There was a reason why he developed that habit. When still an amateur Plante played on a team with a weak defense, whose players didn't clear the puck from the zone fast enough to suit him.

"It was a case of me having to go and get the puck when it was shot into our end because our defense couldn't get there fast enough," he said. "The more I did it, the farther I went. It seemed to be the best thing to do, so I did it and it worked."

The adventurous Plante almost always stopped the puck, completing his NHL years with a 2.38 goals against average. He led the league eight times with the lowest average, three of those times permitting less than two goals per game.

Plante calculated that only six times in 23 years as a goalie at various levels did he get caught off-guard and give up goals because of his roaming tendencies.

"That's not bad, eh?" he said.

Plante was the first goalie to slide behind the net to stop a puck circling the boards and he was one of the first to raise his arm to alert defensemen the referee was calling offsides.

While Plante chased the puck down he kept his head up to see if any guys were breaking loose down-ice. He loved it when he obtained a rare assist. He also insisted that in one game he should have had a record two, but the assist was given to teammate Jean-Guy Talbot.

"I asked him if he had a bonus for points and he said he did, so I said, 'Okay, you keep it,'" Plante said. "But I'd have given $100 to have two assists in the record book like that."

After most goalies adopted the mask and the Original Six era had passed, Plante was dragged out of retirement to play for the expansion St. Louis Blues. At age forty he won a last Vezina Trophy.

But he also became Exhibit A for the need for a mask. In a game against the Boston Bruins, Fred Stanfield fired a slapshot at Plante. Phil Esposito deflected the shot. It struck Plante in the head at about 100 mph, knocking him down in the crease and knocking him out. Plante suffered a severe concussion—with the protection.

"I would have been dead, no question," Plante said of his fate if he had not been wearing a mask.

Plante kept refining his masks for comfort, efficiency, and protection. He played his final pro games in net at forty-six in the WHA during the 1974–75 season.

Every bit the student of the game, Plante wrote extensively about the sport, offered goalie instruction at hockey schools, was employed as a goalie coach, and eventually moved to Switzerland. Plante, who was selected for the Hall of Fame in 1978, died from stomach cancer in Switzerland in 1986.

Canadiens general manager Sam Pollock said the player would be remembered for many reasons.

"He stands alone as the most innovative goalie that hockey has ever seen," Pollock said. "He was always several years ahead of his time."

When Plante was in his forties and was traded from Toronto to Boston many thought he would retire, but Plante felt he could still play. He felt he would know when he was no longer worthy of being a first-stringer. Talking with a sportswriter, he unwittingly may have uttered his own epitaph.

"I am a proud fellow," Plante said.

Yvon Cournoyer

Yvon Cournoyer's nickname was "The Roadrunner" because he may have been the fastest skater in National Hockey League history. Cournoyer, born in Drummondville, Quebec, in 1943, was pretty much the last great Canadiens player who became part of the dynasty years near the end of the Original Six period.

Cournoyer, who was elected to the Hall of Fame in 1982, broke in with Montreal in 1963. A low-to-the-ground 5-foot-7, Cournoyer played at 170 pounds. He said part of his speed was attributable to using longer skate blades.

"People were always telling me I was too small," Cournoyer said. "But I like the fact that I'm not big. It was always a thrill for me when somebody would criticize my size. It was like a good fight to make it to the top. As a youngster I remember a coach telling me I looked too small to play on his team. All I said to him was, 'Try me.'"

In the NHL, Cournoyer did not fight with bigger players who ribbed him about his size—he scored on them. Chicago's Jerry Korab had the temerity to ask Cournoyer what he was going to do when he grew up. Cournoyer replied that he was going to score goals and then scored one on Korab.

In 968 games with Montreal, Cournoyer scored 428 goals and accumulated 435 assists. Four times Cournoyer scored at least 40 goals in one season, his most being 47. In 1972, when he was awarded the Conn Smythe Trophy as the best player in the playoffs, Cournoyer scored 15 goals.

A Cournoyer favorite night in uniform occurred on February 15, 1975, when he scored five goals in one game against the Chicago Blackhawks.

"After I got the fifth," Cournoyer said, "I looked up at the clock and said, 'Gee, I wish there were 10 more minutes.' Everything was going so good."

Back surgery caused Cournoyer to miss the 1977 playoffs, but did not end his career as many feared. However, his back problem recurred, leading to retirement at thirty-five in 1979.

"It came as quite a shock to me when it happened," Cournoyer said. "I thought at first it was nothing more than a pulled muscle. So I went on playing, despite the pain. I had very bad feelings when I retired from hockey. After all, it had been my whole life and then it was over, all too quickly."

Cournoyer played in six All-Star games and was part of ten Stanley Cup championship teams, making him one of the most decorated players in NHL history. Cournoyer is tied for second with Jean Beliveau behind all-time player leader Henri Richard.

"When I began playing in Montreal it was like a dream come true," Cournoyer said. "As a youngster, I always dreamed of playing for the Canadiens. But as everyone else has learned in playing for Montreal, you've got to be good all the time. If you're not, there always seems to be someone to replace you. Each year we had to be number one. There is a lot of pressure in being a Canadien. But I enjoyed that pressure. It helped mold me as a person."

Cournoyer knew how stacked the Canadiens' farm system was and it took him a couple of years with the big club to earn full-time playing status. Even though Cournoyer totaled 25 goals in 1966–67 he was still fighting for PT.

"I guess I've played less than 20 games on a regular line," he said. "But I'm not discouraged by getting bumped off a regular spot."

Cournoyer played under Montreal coaches Toe Blake, Claude Ruel, Al McNeil, and Scotty Bowman and won Stanley Cups with each of them.

"Toe Blake was the hardest to play with," Cournoyer said. "But was very honest. It was a strange situation with him. As a coach you really learned to hate him. But in the same respect, you loved him more than you hated him. The more you hated him the more you loved him."

Blake, whose real first name was Hector, was part of ten Stanley Cups as a player and a coach combined. He was born in 1912 and died in 1995, long after the Original Six era ended. Some felt he was the greatest of coaches, although that label has more often been appended to Bowman's name.

As a coach Blake won the Stanley Cup the first five years he led the Canadiens between 1955 and 1960 and added three later Cups to his résumé. At the end of his life, Blake engaged in a battle with Alzheimer's disease.

Before Cournoyer retired to become a scout he had been hit enough times by bigger guys to imagine evening up the weight class in a bout after all.

"Many times," he said, "I wish I was bigger because there are some guys I'd like to lick."

Serge Savard

When Yvon Cournoyer retired, Serve Savard became captain of the Canadiens. Savard's career was almost entirely post–Original Six era, though he did break in with Montreal for a couple of games during the 1966–67 season.

He was a key player in keeping the NHL's most impressive dynasty going, playing for eight Cup championships. Savard was a bridge player, teaming with the last of the Original Six greats like Cournoyer and the first of new greats that won eight Cups between 1968 and 1979.

A Hall of Famer who is now a vice president of the Canadiens, Savard was a prototype of the new breed of bigger player at 6-foot-3 and 210 pounds. Savard was a four-time All-Star who played in 1,040 games.

"The Montreal lineup isn't an easy one to crack," said general manager Sam Pollock, "but he's so good we couldn't keep him off the team."

In 1969, barely starting his 17-year career, Savard won the Conn Smythe Trophy as Most Valuable Player in the playoffs. He was the first defenseman to earn the honor.

Savard was part of Cup titlists in 1976, 1977, 1978, and 1979, but when the Canadiens couldn't make it five in a row he turned out a winner anyway. He went to the racetrack instead of the Finals. The owner of a horse named Keith Lobell, Savard earned $19,575 when the four-year-old pacer captured the Ontario Jockey Club Maturity.

Jacques Lemaire

Jacques Lemaire, who worked his way up through the Montreal Junior Canadiens, did not play in his first game for the big club until 1967–68, the year after the Original Six doubled in size to 12 teams.

Lemaire played in 853 games, all for the Canadiens, scored 366 goals, and was elected to the Hall of Fame. He then coached 1,262 games with the New Jersey Devils and Minnesota. He played on eight Montreal Cup winners, twice scoring the winning goals, and then won another Cup at the helm of the Devils. He got a piece of credit for two other Cups as part of Montreal's front office.

With a career high of 44 goals Lemaire scored at least 20 in a season 12 times. He said he developed his whizzing shot by working out in the basement of his home. He said he was given a steel puck made by a friend in a machine shop and practiced shooting it, only to find out later Yvon Cournoyer had done the same thing.

"I still practice with the steel puck, but usually for just a couple of weeks before the start of a season," Lemaire said after he joined Montreal. "I take shots with it in the garage."

Sam Pollock

The architect of Phase II of Montreal greatness, Sam Pollock became personnel director of the Canadiens for the 1959–60 season and succeeded Frank Selke as general manager in 1963.

Montreal won nine Stanley Cups from the mid-1960s to the late 1970s on Pollock's watch.

"If you're asking if there's a special secret to winning," Pollock once told a sportswriter, "it comes down to the oldest and best thing in the world. The word is work. I get a little upset with people—especially other hockey people—when they tell me how lucky we are to have great players. . . . We didn't turn over a rock to find them. We scouted them. We assessed them. We decided they could help us, so we did our best to get them. That's not luck. That's work."

Pollock had no patience with hockey observers who felt the Canadiens were sure things.

"Sure, we've had a lot of winning teams, but we didn't win overnight," he said. "There were a lot of years when we didn't win at all. We win, and people say why should anybody be surprised? The Canadiens have the best of everything, so they should win. What about the years we don't win? What do they say then? After the 1960 season, before I was general manager, we went four years without winning a Stanley Cup."

Pollock worked as hard as he preached and was never satisfied.

"You just can't relax," Pollock said. "You can't take anything for granted. People say we're the best, but the Stanley Cup is like a new season. In horse racing, 2-to-5 favorites don't always win. You know what I mean?"

Montreal Canadiens Since

The Montreal Canadiens did not stop winning when the National Hockey League expanded to 12 teams in 1967. The Original Six era was over, but the Canadiens' era of winning Stanley Cups did not slow down for quite some time.

Who won the first Stanley Cup in the new era? The Canadiens. Who won four of the first six Stanley Cups in the new era between 1968 and 1973? The Canadiens. So it was not as if the Canadiens went into an immediate slump. Then Montreal won another four titles in a row between 1976 and 1979.

So it was not as if the Canadiens suffered an immediate talent drain when the league doubled in size and competition for players was twice as keen.

The stars kept on coming in the early 1970s, new faces of brilliance following in the tradition of the greats of the past.

Guy Lapointe made it into a lineup for the first time for five games in the 1969–70 season and went on to a Hall of Fame career. It seemed every other Montreal newcomer from this era reached the Hall of Fame.

Goalie Ken Dryden came out of Cornell University to spark Montreal to a Stanley Cup in 1971 after playing just six regular-season games.

That was the same year Hall of Fame forward Guy Lafleur, the linear descendent of Rocket Richard, broke in.

Hall of Fame defenseman Larry Robinson played his first game for the club in 1972.

Hall of Fame winger Steve Shutt played his first game for the club in 1972.

Hall of Fame winger Bob Gainey played his first game for the club in 1973.

Dryden was probably the most interesting character in the bunch, more cerebral than most hockey players. He studied to become a lawyer, later became a member of parliament and wrote a classic hockey book, *The Game*. He ended up in the Hall of Fame and also in the national cabinet while earning the Order of Canada. He was definitely an original if not an Original Six player.

It is little remembered that Dryden was originally drafted by the Boston Bruins in 1964. They traded him to Montreal, but he chose college over the pros at first.

The unusually tall, 6-foot-4 Dryden forced incumbent Rogie Vachon to the bench for the 1971 playoffs, but had not even played in enough games to lose his rookie status. So in an oddity, Dryden, who already won the Conn Smythe award as MVP of the playoffs, was also able to win the Calder Trophy in 1972, a year after being a Stanley Cup champ.

Dryden only played seven full seasons beyond his opening year cameo, not counting the 1973–74 season when he took a leave of absence because of a contract battle with the front office and to start law school. Still, he won six Stanley Cups and five Vezina trophies and played in five All-Star games. Later he became president of the Toronto Maple Leafs.

Dryden was lionized for his success, but didn't always view himself as an especially slick athlete.

"If you took 500 people and tested their reflexes," he said, "there would be 400 of them about the same [as him]." Various skills make for a good goaltender, he added. "There are other things to overcome, such as fear and uncertainty. These factors slow down a person's reactions."

Larry Robinson

There was more old-school than flash in Larry Robinson's game. The 6-foot-4, 225-pound defenseman was a good bodyguard for the Canadiens' forwards, good enough to gain admission to the Hall of Fame before starting a long coaching career.

A 20-year on-ice veteran, during Robinson's tenure the Canadiens won six Stanley Cups. He won the Norris Trophy twice. Robinson coached the Los Angeles Kings and New Jersey Devils and won another Stanley Cup as interim coach of the Devils.

Robinson wanted to be a goal scorer and became more of a hard checker. Still, he scored 207 goals in 1,384 games. When growing up he wanted to be Bobby Hull.

"I thought he was just phenomenal," Robinson said. "I still do. When I got to play with him in '76 in the Canada Cup I couldn't believe it. I got to go out to dinner with him and he impressed me so much. He's just a tremendous person."

Well into his career Robinson suffered a serious injury while participating in another sport—polo. He broke his right leg, but didn't even know it at first.

"There was a lot of pain, but then it subsided and I played the remainder of the game," Robinson said. "But when I removed my clothes the leg had swollen to an enormous size."

Robinson needed surgery and was told he would miss months of hockey, but bounced back quicker than predicted.

"The thing about rehabilitation," said Robinson, "is that it's you against the machine."

Steve Shutt

Joining Larry Robinson in a passion for polo, the two were among a few investors that founded the Montreal Polo Club. No doubt, management would have been driven nuts by two players reporting with polo injuries.

Steve Shutt, a 5-foot-11, 180-pound winger from Ontario, scored 424 goals in 930 games and 817 assists. All but his last season was played for Montreal. Shutt scored 49 goals in one season and had other years when he finished with 47 and 45. But his pièce de résistance was the 1976–77 season when he netted 60 goals.

That year the Canadiens finished 60–8–12, the best record in National Hockey League history and that was one of five Stanley Cup winners Shutt played on.

Perhaps it was being surrounded by so much talent—others on the way to the Hall of Fame, too—but when someone suggested Shutt was a pretty special player he burst out laughing.

"Superstar! Me?" Shutt said with incredulity. "You've gotta be kidding. I'm not even a star."

Some people thought so. He was chosen as a first- or second-team seasonal All-Star three times. He was not a believer in Canadiens' mystique either.

"Aura, aura, look, I don't believe in this aura stuff," Shutt said. "The only aura we have on our team is hard work. I'm not individually a good player. A lot of people don't notice me out there, I know that. But at the end of a game just look at me and I'll have a goal and two assists."

Bob Gainey

A four-time All-Star and a five-time Stanley Cup winner, Hall of Fame winger Bob Gainey succeeded Serge Savard as captain. He was chosen as the best defensive forward in the NHL four times, as well.

"I never thought in terms of being a success," Gainey said of his play. "I only thought that's what I did as what I expected of myself. It was what I was supposed to do. The compliments and the praise keep coming, but I take it in stride. I try not to think about it too much. You have to learn how to handle it."

Gainey scored 239 NHL goals in 1,150 games, all with the Canadiens between 1973 and 1989, but he played one final season of hockey in France. Currently a front office official with the St. Louis Blues, Gainey also coached the Minnesota North Stars/Dallas Stars and the Canadiens and was general manager of the Canadiens.

For all the pleasure hockey gave him, Gainey suffered two great tragedies in his life. His wife died of brain cancer at thirty-nine, and then he had a twenty-five-year-old daughter swept overboard at sea while traveling on a tall ship sailing vessel.

Gainey founded a foundation in 2008 to help others and when that was created, residents of his hometown of Peterborough banded together and organized a benefit concert to make a contribution.

It was tremendously difficult for Gainey to cope with the loss of his daughter after his wife's passing.

"It's a blow that's hard to package or describe for people," he said. "I think people who have children and are deeply connected to them can see how devastating this could be.

People will ask me, 'How are you doing this?' I really think there's two choices—either you do or you don't. And the second choice isn't a very good one."

Guy Lapointe

Guy Lapointe made his reputation as a defenseman, although he could also score more than old-style blue-liners, finishing up with 171 goals in 894 games. Three times Lapointe cracked the 20-goal mark.

When Lapointe collected 28 goals during the 1974–75 season, he set a team record for most goals in one year by a defenseman. That record still stands.

Lapointe, a 6-foot, 185-pounder who was born in Montreal, seemed to symbolize the Canadiens' acuity in finding talent. He was on virtually no one's radar screen initially, only made the team as a fifth defenseman and grew into a Hall of Famer.

Although the mark was not attributed to another NHL coach by name, when he said, "The Canadiens have guys you never heard of who can come off the bench and kill you," he seemed to be talking about Lapointe.

For the most part the Canadiens seemed to be as serious as a church service. But Lapointe gained the reputation as a guy who could keep the locker room loose. He engaged in pranks that caught teammates off guard, and in his most famous escapade smeared his hand with Vaseline before shaking hands with Prime Minister Pierre Trudeau.

Another time Lapointe made a point of greeting dark-suited general manager Irving Grundman with a pat on the back. Lapointe's hand had been lathered up in white baby powder.

Lapointe got Ken Dryden good once. Manipulating the dessert scene so there was just a single serving left for Dryden, Lapointe and teammates watched as the goalie inhaled his chocolate sprinkles spread atop . . . sour cream.

Guy Lafleur

A sniper and a scorer with flair, Guy Lafleur was the type of player Montreal Canadiens' fans not only appreciated the most, but felt was their birthright to have on the roster.

A Quebec native, the six-foot, 185-pound winger was a natural fit to become the latest god of the team, spectacular in form, talented in all ways, and flashy in the most entertaining manner when he broke in with Montreal in 1971.

Lafleur contributed to five Stanley Cup championship teams while amassing 560 goals in 1,126 games (some with the Rangers and Quebec Nordiques).

In one of the most remarkable scoring stretches in NHL history, Lafleur scored at least 50 goals and 100 points for six straight seasons between 1974 and 1980. One year he had 60 goals. One year he had 80 assists.

"The first year I had a lot of pressure," Lafleur acknowledged, "the big publicity and all that. And people were expecting me to score 50 goals in my first year."

It took a few to reach that lofty number.

The great Canadiens coach Scotty Bowman moved Lafleur to center on the team's power play and that provided more scoring opportunities.

"That's my game, going all over the place," said Lafleur, who was often referred to in the English version of his name in newspaper stories as "The Flower." "If I stand still, it's easier for other guys to check me."

Lafleur did not stand still much and stayed very dangerous. He was pretty much an offensive genius who could shake defenders and slither close to the net.

"Lafleur is the best," said Canadien Serge Savard. "He was made for this game."

He was devoted to hockey, for sure, not interested in becoming the team captain, but only in leading by example. Lafleur was so dedicated to game preparation that linemate Steve Shutt could only stare at him agape in the locker room.

"He was strange," Shutt said. "I mean, any guy who would be in his hockey uniform, skates tied tight, sweater on, and a stick beside him at four o'clock in the afternoon for an eight o'clock game has to be a little strange."

No one was going to accuse Lafleur of not being ready to play.

Although no one in Quebec saw it coming and no one could believe it when it happened, the flow of great players to the Canadiens in bunches eventually ceased. As the 1970s turned to the 1980s, Montreal was no longer a great power.

The Canadiens won a Stanley Cup in 1986 and won another in 1993. There has been an unthinkable drought between championships since. It has reached the point where fans that may have once been sick of the Canadiens winning too often even think it might be good for the sport if they at last won their 25th Stanley Cup.

2

BOSTON BRUINS

Founded: 1924
Home Arenas: Boston Arena, 1924–28; Boston Garden, 1928–95; TD Garden, 1995–present (also known as FleetCenter from 1995–2005)
Stanley Cups: 1929, 1939, 1941, 1970, 1972, 2011

Beginnings

The man who brought professional ice hockey to Boston was born in Vermont and made his money as a grocery store magnate. Charles Adams loved the sport so much he made road trips to Canada just to watch Montreal teams in the fledgling National Hockey League.

Instead of going to the sport, Adams decided to bring the sport to Massachusetts, and he was awarded a franchise for $15,000 in the NHL, which had been puttering along since 1917.

As much as he enjoyed the sport, Adams turned over primary management of the club to Art Ross. Ross became one of the pivotal early builders of the NHL, although it was always Adams's money behind the growth of the Boston hockey club. Ross named the club the Bruins after Adams told him to find a fierce mascot. Early pictures on the jersey front featured a bear. Then Adams helped obtain top-notch players by purchasing the entire Western Hockey League for $300,000 in 1926.

One might say Adams was the George Steinbrenner of his time and sport, on a reduced financial scale. Adams, who died in 1947, was ultimately enshrined in the sport's Hall of Fame. In the 1970s (although it didn't last), when the NHL sought catchy names for divisions due to team realignment, the Adams Division was named for Charles.

The first home of the Bruins was the Boston Arena, which is one of the most remarkable athletic facilities in existence. Built in 1910, and now called Matthews Arena, the structure is located on the campus of Northeastern University. In a century-plus of operation, the arena has become the oldest still-in-use indoor hockey facility in the world.

The Bruins were early tenants. But in 1911, even before the Bruins skated at the Arena, the touring Montreal Wanderers and the first Ottawa Senators of the NHL played a two-game set there.

Boston's college hockey programs all played games at the Arena over the decades. Later in life Boston Arena served as home ice for the New England Whalers when the World Hockey Association was formed in the early 1970s. Since 1979 it has been home rink for the Northeastern University Huskies. Current capacity is listed at 6,000.

Right from the start, Adams intended to create a different Bruins permanent home. He hungered for a bigger building and contributed $500,000 for five years rent as the $10 million Boston Garden was being constructed. The building, which gained additional fame from its unique parquet floor for basketball as the home of the NBA's Boston Celtics, was the Bruins' home first.

It was designed by Tex Rickard and modeled after Madison Square Garden in New York. There have been several Madison Square Gardens and Rickard built one of them. He was renowned for operating the New York Garden's boxing program and promoted heavyweight champion Jack Dempsey title fights. Adding to Rickard's lore was time spent in the goldfields of Alaska.

The first event in the Boston Garden was a fight card in 1928. Rickard designed the Garden to put fans close to the action and many visiting teams rued that idea. The Bruins became full-time tenants in 1928, in an arena that seated 13,909 fans for the sport.

In 1929, the Bruins were on their way to their first Stanley Cup championship.

The Stanley Cup is the best-known sports trophy in the world. It is 100 percent identified with the National Hockey League champion, but that was not always so.

Hockey is the national pastime of Canada and, in 1892, the Cup was created as a symbol of supremacy of the country's top amateur team. It was named for Lord Stanley of Preston, who at the time was the governor general of Canada. By 1915, two professional leagues annually vied for the rights to the Cup. Since 1926, the Stanley Cup has been the prize sought by NHL teams.

The Stanley Cup has become a beloved trophy. It is 35 inches tall and weighs about 35 pounds. It is made of silver and nickel alloy and is unmistakable. Members of winning teams have their names engraved on the Cup, and over the last twenty years players on winning teams have been permitted custody of the Cup for one day. That means the Cup travels, and thousands upon thousands of fans have seen it up close.

Another coveted NHL award is the Art Ross Trophy, named for the Art Ross who named the Bruins. He actually donated the trophy in 1947.

Art Ross was born on January 13, 1886, in Ontario. Once, someone asked him about a connection to the superstitious Friday the 13th, and he responded, "How in 'ell would I remember whether it was a Friday or not?"

Ross was born at the Whitefish Trading Post of the Hudson's Bay Company, which his dad operated. It was so far north that the nearby lake was frozen from November to May. Ross grew up speaking English and the Native dialect Ojibwe and first skated on blades pieced together by local Indians. Ross once said he grew practically immune to any hard body checking because he was protected from the cold.

"I carried so much padding an arrow couldn't pierce my armor," he said.

Those really were humble beginnings in the sport. But Ross is credited as being one of the prime movers who introduced innovations into the game and who uplifted its public profile.

Ross stood 5-foot-11 and weighed 190 pounds, with dark, wavy hair. He played defense from 1905 to 1918 and he was the spiritual ancestor to Bobby Orr. Ross was the first defenseman who rushed the puck up-ice. Before that defensemen always passed the puck to forwards coming out of the zone.

Still, Ross emphasized defense. The phrase "kitty-bar-the-door," an expression that came into vogue in the 1890s in the United States referring to the necessity of hunkering down and battening down the hatches to prevent trouble, was first applied to hockey due to a system Ross devised for a critical playoff game. In his scheme three defensemen lined up across the ice to turn away attackers.

During this era hockey players frequently stayed on the ice for all 60 minutes of a game, and Ross once scored seven goals in a game.

In 1917, Ross was suspended by his Montreal Wanderers. He was exiled to the Ottawa Senators and in his first game was greeted raucously. The ovation warmed him and as he stepped on the ice, Ross waved.

"Then on the ice I was about to stride when I went down on my seat and I couldn't get up," Ross said. "Imagine my embarrassment when I looked at my skates and saw they were both taped with the same stuff we used on the sticks. I hadn't even bothered to look at them in my excitement while getting dressed. And I had to sit there on the ice, my face as red as a beet, while I unwound the tape."

Creative and stubborn were two characteristics of Ross's off the ice. He named the Bruins and convinced Jack Adams to buy the Western League for its players. That came about because the Bruins went 6–24 in his first season coaching. Ross invented a better hockey puck that is still in use today, incorporating synthetic rubber instead of natural rubber to cut down on bouncing.

He helped modify the goalie's net in the rear, a change that remained in effect for forty years. Ross advocated and helped create the mid-ice red line.

When still active he led a player strike for more money. In the 1920s he became embroiled in a feud with Toronto Maple Leafs legend Conn Smythe. Ross and Smythe did not speak again for the last forty-plus years of Ross's life.

Ross, who coached the Bruins from 1924 through 1945, became in 1931 the first coach to pull his netminder for an extra attacker in an attempt to score a desperate goal.

Ross was the first team operator to push for minor-league connections to build a farm system. He was the driving force behind selling the Bruins to Boston when the club began and his 30 years associated with the franchise ingrained a level of hockey madness in the local fans.

A member of the Hockey Hall of Fame, three Bruins Stanley Cup championships came on Ross's watch as either administrator or coach. During World War II Ross was once taunted about Boston's poor man-advantage-play by someone saying, "Where's your power play?"

"In England, France, and Germany," Ross retorted about his men fighting overseas.

Stories were told at a testimonial dinner for Ross in Boston, 25 years into his local reign, and concurrent with his induction into the Hockey Hall of Fame. One discussed initial reluctance of a sportswriter to embrace hockey. The tale went like this: "I don't like hockey and I'm going to run it right out of Boston. What's more, I don't like Ross and before I run him out of town, I'll hit him a good punch on the nose."

A listener suggested to the blowhard that he better not miss with his first swing because Ross had been a champion amateur boxer. The antagonist said, "Well, I still don't like hockey."

Ross was not above seeking to establish a firmer relationship with hostile writers by sharing booze. He once said on a multi-city road trip in the Detroit-Leland Hotel he heard a ruckus, opened his door, and saw two scribes seeking to open rooms with keys from the Royal York in Toronto, the preceding stop. Many drinks later, Ross observed, "By five in the morning I had them convinced they really were in the Congress at Chicago."

As he aged Ross gained the nickname "Uncle Arthur" as a sort of patron-saint of the sport. At various times Ross was referred to as "Hockey's Patriarch," "Hockey's Man of Ideas," and "The Man Who Made Hockey."

Ross made it in Boston when he delivered the first Stanley Cup in franchise history in 1929. Although the phrase "Original Six" is applied to the long-lasting foundation teams of the NHL, originally there were other teams around. The weeding out process because of finances, lack of attendance, and the like, whittled the league into a group of six.

Ten franchises competed during the 1928–29 season. The Canadian division included the Montreal Canadiens, New York Americans, Toronto Maple Leafs, Ottawa Senators, and Montreal Maroons. The American Division included the Bruins, the New York Rangers, the Detroit Cougars, Pittsburgh Pirates, and Chicago Blackhawks.

Such all-time Bruins luminaries as Eddie Shore, Dit Clapper, Lionel Hitchman, and Ralph "Cooney" Weiland skated for the 1929 champions. Harry Oliver led the team in goals with 17. But no one was more integral to its success than rookie goaltender Cecil "Tiny" Thompson. Ross took a chance on Thompson, who was playing hockey for the Minneapolis Millers, but had never been seen in person by the Boston general manager.

Thompson was born in 1903 in Sandon, British Columbia. But he was not tiny. At his full height Thompson stood 5-foot-10 and another couple inches taller on skates. In fact, Tiny stood pretty tall in the nets because he played a stand-up style. You didn't catch Thompson making saves on his knees. Actually, Oliver, who was 5-foot-8, 155 pounds, was the genuine "Tiny" by pro standards.

The Bruins finished 26–13–5. Thompson played all 44 games in net and his goals-against mark of 1.15 remains the second-best in league history. It took just five playoff games, three against the Montreal Canadiens and two against the New York Rangers, to settle the Stanley Cup playoffs. Thompson collected three shutouts and surrendered just three goals.

Thompson was just starting a Hall of Fame career. His brother Paul, a year younger, was on the Rangers before spending the bulk of a 13-season NHL career with the Chicago Blackhawks.

Tiny's career goals-against average was 2.08 and he won the top-goalie Vezina award four times. He was credited with being the first goalie to catch the puck like a baseball player, as opposed to merely blocking it.

In the second-longest playoff game against the Toronto Maple Leafs in 1933, Thompson was in the Boston net for a contest that was lost 1–0 after 104 minutes, 46 seconds of overtime, 164 minutes, 46 seconds of playing time in all. Ken Doraty scored the winning goal in the sixth overtime.

During the 1935–1936 season Thompson fed a pass to Babe Siebert. When Siebert rushed down ice and scored, that represented the first time in NHL history a goalie earned an assist. Thompson's 74 shutouts remains a Bruins record since he left the team in 1939 for his final two NHL years with the Detroit Red Wings.

Eddie Shore

Even in the modern era of professional sport where kids are sometimes scouted down to junior high, families make their own tapes, massive attention is paid to college sports and the like, the occasional player slips through unknown.

Scouting was much more casual in the 1920s, if it could be said to exist in any formal way at all. It was especially difficult to get noticed if you were from a small town. Eddie Shore's hometown was a smaller than most and today is home to around 600 people.

Cupar, Saskatchewan does not take up much space on a map. Clarification was needed in describing Shore's whereabouts from birth. He is said to have come into the world in Fort Qu'Appelle. Some said he was born in Regina. Shore was there on November 25, 1902, but not taking notes. He said, "Neither! I was born in an oxcart on the road between the two places."

Shore had to build his own legend. A defenseman of ferocity and skill, Shore was 5-foot-11 and 190 pounds. He was a man of inordinate strength and crushing body checks. Shore played forward for the Regina Capitals of the Western Hockey League. Regina folded after the 1925 season and Shore surfaced with the same league's Edmonton Eskimos. In 1926 when he moved to defense, Shore gained the nickname "The Edmonton Express" because he just put his head down and zoomed up ice.

The entire league folded after that season and Boston's Charles Adams shelled out to buy the whole shebang. His biggest prize was Shore.

Between 1926 and 1940, Shore owned the blue line at Boston Garden. Anyone else passing by had to pay rent. Shore won the Hart Trophy as the NHL's Most Valuable Player four times. Although All-Star teams were not chosen during the early portion of his career, he was selected eight of his final nine years in the league.

When Shore hit you, you stayed hit. As an NHL rookie he set the league record for penalty minutes with 130. That was in 40 games, so he was a busy dude. Fans immediately embraced his wide-open game.

Shore threw his weight around and resented it when others fought back. He once clocked the Montreal Maroons' Nels Stewart, knocking him to the ice. But Stewart reached up and jabbed at him with his stick, so Shore opened up, swinging his stick at the prone Stewart. This was neither Shore's first bout, nor his last. For revenge, Maroons players jumped him three-on-one at a later date, breaking his nose and three teeth, and giving him two black eyes and a cut cheekbone. Before escaping with his life, Shore was knocked out for 15 minutes.

During his career someone keeping score said Shore took 978 stitches. Another source said 600. One source indicated Shore had his nose broken ten times and another said fourteen.

Once, during his Bruins days, Shore had an ear cut so badly the doctors at the arena said he was going to lose it. Shore refused to part with the appendage and after the game he went door-to-door looking for a doctor to save it. Shore sat through the repair work without anesthesia and told the doctor, "Just give me a mirror. I want to be sure you sew it on right."

The player said his secret plan to keep his face looking as beautiful as possible revolved around rubbing the scars every day.

"It takes five to seven years for a scar to heal and the only way to do it is to massage it," Shore said.

Shore was a party to one of the most infamous incidents in NHL history, during a game against the Toronto Maple Leafs in 1933. Shore was tripped from behind by King Clancy and in retaliation skated up and checked Ace Bailey from behind. Bailey fractured his skull on the ice and was forced to retire after his life was said to be in jeopardy.

After Bailey got well enough Toronto held a benefit for him, turning over $20,000. Bailey and Shore shook hands in public.

As if anyone doubted it, years into retirement at a hockey dinner, Shore said, "I loved to hit. But sometimes it depends on where your elbows are, where your hands are, and if your body position is right. You can hit hard, the same as football, baseball, golf, or anything else. Body position is the key for most athletes."

Shore was tough, but also talented. He was not simply a thug on ice, but a gifted player who scored in double figures for goals, and was a spirited team leader. It was once said he drew fans to their feet every time he rushed down ice because they anticipated something of great magnitude would occur.

Shore never made more than $17,500 during a season, but saved his money and in 1939 committed $42,000 to buy the minor-league Springfield Indians.

It seemed as if Shore treated many of his players with the same disdain he did puck carriers. He was often involved in salary flaps. Shore, who died at eighty-two in 1985, did not sell the Indians until 1976.

If young players thought they were going to get Xs and Os advice from the Hall of Famer, that didn't seem to happen much. He once told a player who was in a scoring slump, "Of course you're not scoring. Stay away from your wife." That was like the "Women weaken legs" advice in the original *Rocky* film.

Another player going goalless for a while was told the reason was, "You're parting your hair on the wrong side."

The Eddie Shore who grew up in rural Canada did not like seeing hockey players coddled and said it was up to them to find another career after retirement.

"I don't buy that because of this," Shore said. "The player, when he gets through playing, is not qualified to do a job for himself. If everybody does his job what's happening is that he's not using that brain of his that God gave him. God gave him an amount of brains that he should use and if he doesn't use them, what's going to happen? When he gets through playing hockey he's just another yo-yo."

The Good Guys

Sometimes it takes inner knowledge rather than obvious numbers to recognize the significance of a player. Fans may be bamboozled by statistics, and indeed those statistics may speak volumes. But occasionally the lack of statistics next to a good player's name masks his true worth.

Probably not one in fifty current-day Boston Bruins fans know a thing about a defenseman named Lionel Hitchman who toiled for the club from 1925 to 1934 and who was one of the reliables on the roster of Boston's first Cup winner.

The not-so-Tiny Thompson was the backbone of the Bruins' first Stanley Cup team, but the team had to score sometime and it had his share of players that made their stay with the franchise memorable in different ways.

Hitchman was born in Toronto, but spent the majority of his career as a blue-line companion of Eddie Shore's. That was one reason he may have been in the shadows.

Before Hitchman served his hitch with the Bruins, he was a Royal Canadian Mounted Policeman. That's not an everyday job. He traded in that stiff, bright red jacket (which was a flashier uniform), temporarily for the Boston sweater with the big B on it.

The 6-foot-1, 167-pound Hitchman was captain of the Cup-winning team while scoring just one point all season. He earned his salary by knocking down opposing forwards and stealing the puck in the zone. The Bruins gave up just 52 goals in 44 games. That was the season Thompson owned that almost invisible goals against average of 1.15.

"Without Hitch it would have been a different story," Thompson said.

While still active, Hitchman made other news in a different sport. In 1932, he caught a then-record 27-pound Atlantic salmon by a nonresident on a fly rod in the St. John's River.

Hitchman was never selected for an All-Star team. He was never a high scorer, collecting 62 points in 417 games. Hitchman spent two years coaching a Bruins minor-league club and then became Art Ross's assistant with the big club. In 1934, the Bruins retired Hitchman's Number 3 jersey.

With the exception of the admired Ace Bailey in Toronto, who retired prematurely due to injury, Hitchman was otherwise the first athlete in North American team sports to have his uniform number retired.

Later, Hitchman coached the Springfield Indians, owned by his old pal Shore.

Another player on that Boston club who was tinier than Tiny was Cooney Weiland, who measured in at 5-foot-7 and 150 pounds.

The year after the Stanley Cup championship the Bruins were almost mystically good. The Bruins finished 38–5–1 and Weiland, who scored 131 goals in an eight-year career, torched opponents for a remarkable 43 goals that season. He added 30 assists for 73 points for a team that only a year before could barely find the net with radar.

That impressive Bruins 1929–30 regular-season record was a milestone. Some eighty-six years later the Boston winning percentage of .875 remains the all-time National Hockey League record.

That year there was such a seismic shift in scoring that it almost seemed as if Wayne Gretzy caught a time machine to hang out for a season. Weiland's goal and points totals both led the league. But teammate Dit Clapper was second in goals with 41.

Some rules changes opened up play: Passing the puck forward was now allowed inside all three zones, but not across the blue line; no more than three players, including the goalie, could stay inside the defensive zone once the puck was zipped up ice; infractions were penalized; goaltenders could no longer hold and freeze the puck.

The first offside rule was also implemented, one forbidding an offensive player to enter the defensive zone ahead of the play. It was a new world for the offense and no one took better advantage of the changes more than Weiland.

Given that he retired in 1939 without winning a major NHL award and being selected for just one All-Star team, Weiland might have been lost to the mists of time in Bruins history, but for one especially important fact—he became an outstanding coach. He led the Bruins to a Stanley Cup and coached Harvard University, only a few miles from Boston Garden, for twenty-one years. So Weiland was never forgotten by Boston hockey fans and was chosen for the Hall of Fame.

That follow-up season to the Cup year, the Bruins led the American Division with 77 points. Second-place Chicago had 47 points. That year the Bruins recorded a 14-game winning streak. Although the length of seasons expanded, Boston set records for a 50-game season that were never broken. Besides winning percentage, they had most wins at 38, fewest losses at 5, home winning streak of 20, and most goals at 179.

However, in the Finals the unthinkable occurred. The Montreal Canadiens took two straight games, 3–0 and 4–3, to capture the

Stanley Cup. It was one of the great upsets in NHL history and one of the most depressing defeats the Bruins ever suffered.

Dit Clapper and the Next Generation

The bridge from past to future was Dit Clapper.

Clapper was a member of the first Bruins Stanley Cup team in 1929 and was still with the team in 1939 when they won their second Cup. Clapper, whose given name was Aubrey Victor, was born in Newmarket, Ontario. He was 6-foot-2 and 200 pounds and was the first to play 20 seasons in the National Hockey League, all with the Bruins.

After spending the first half of his career as a right wing, Clapper shifted to defense for the second 10 years of his career. He became an All-Star at both positions. As a younger player Clapper skated with Cooney Weiland and Dutch Goiner and they were called "The Dynamite Line."

If it seemed as if Clapper stuck around a long time, he was only following his heart. He got his first pair of skates at age three for Christmas. Somehow the folks understood the direction he was headed. He played in his first game at six.

Clapper was a dashing guy who liked to dress well and styled his hair in the fashion of the day with a part neatly down the middle. A magazine article at the end of his career said it resembled actor George Raft's 'do. Clapper was so well respected few challenged him to fisticuffs. He was bigger than most and he was slow to anger, but he believed in a timely extra hard check to send a message.

Clapper was a bit ahead of his time in realizing that offseason conditioning was pivotal to longevity.

"If you want to stay in it you can't let yourself go during the off-season," he said. "Conditioning and keeping in condition means everything. If you don't keep at it during the summer you might as well write *finis* to your career."

Clapper was considered a class player and only burnished his reputation in 1942 when on a Canadian duck hunting trip. Clapper saved the lives of three fellow travelers in danger of drowning. After their canoe capsized, Clapper jumped in the water, swam to shore, found a rowboat, and returned to rescue the men.

In his long career Clapper incurred a minimum number of injuries until he tore an Achilles tendon. In an upset for the ages before helmets and visors, Clapper said, "I was lucky. I never lost any teeth."

During Clapper's era, when there were only six NHL teams, all took trains. The only problem was that Clapper could not sleep on trains.

"You've just got to have one good night's sleep to be in shape for another game and you can't get it on the train," he said.

In 1944, long-serving boss Art Ross had to step away from the bench due to illness and Clapper became interim coach. Ross returned to Boston as general manager in 1945 and turned over the coaching reins to Clapper. For the last few years of his skating career Clapper was Boston's player-coach, the only one in the team's history. After retiring in 1947, Clapper stayed on as coach through 1949.

A six-time All-Star, Clapper scored 228 career goals in 833 games and was voted into the Hall of Fame in 1947.

Clapper's stature was such that when he did blow his top once and took a swing at a referee (irritating himself no end for losing his cool) nothing came of it.

"I want to apologize for saying something which caused you to lose your head," the referee told Clapper. "In my report to the league office I so stated and there will be no punishment for you."

Even more amazingly, that official was Clarence Campbell, who later became president of the National Hockey League.

Even after 20 years Clapper was a little reluctant to retire, though he believed it was time.

"Just like in any other sport, the legs finally give in," Clapper said. "In the head you're smarter than ever. You know what to do, but you can't get over there to plug up that hole or get a piece of that man. Just a question of locomotion."

At the time of Clapper's retirement, few thought any player would ever again stick with one club for 20 years or, some said, even play 20 years. Clapper had his Number 5 jersey retired as he was finishing out his career. Some years later, at the request of an incoming player, the Bruins unretired Clapper's number. In the face of numerous protests from surviving family members, Bobby Orr, and others, that decision was quickly reversed.

As a Bruin, Clapper predated the Kraut Line, the most famous trio of players working together in Boston annals. Milt Schmidt, Bobby Bauer, and Woody Dumart were all from Kitchener, Ontario, but all were of German heritage. As a line they played together from 1937 to 1947, with the exception of three years lost to World War II. All maintained a sound scoring pace and all played key roles on the Bruins clubs that regrouped.

In 1939 Boston won its second Cup by defeating the Toronto Maple Leafs. In 1941, the Bruins took their third Cup by besting the Detroit Red Wings in the Finals.

Boston was an unbelievably strong team in the 1938–39 season. Besides Clapper, Schmidt, Dumart, and Bauer, Weiland was still there. So was Tiny Thompson for part of the year. Goalie Frank Brimsek was a rookie and pushed aside Thompson. Plus, Bill Cowley. Roy Conacher, who played only about half of his career with Boston, led the team and the league with 26 goals. All ended up in the Hall of Fame. Art Ross, another Hall of Famer, was still coach.

During the regular season the Bruins finished 36–10–2. They led the league in scoring and led the league in allowing the fewest goals. A year later they went 31–12–5, but lost to the second-place New York Rangers in the playoffs.

However, the Kraut Line went 1-2-3 in the scoring race: Schmidt, Dumart, and Bauer, in that order. As an aside, the trio shared an apartment in a Boston suburb.

Bauer, born in 1915, was a four-time All-Star and won the Lady Byng Trophy three times. Bauer, Schmidt, and Dumart met in juniors on the Kitchener Greenshirts. In the minors the threesome played together and an opposing coach named them "Sauerkrauts." The nickname was shortened to the Kraut Line.

Bauer scored 20 goals as a rookie and during this period the Bruins finished first in the standings four straight years, starting with 1938–39. Dumart once said of Bauer, "He was the brains of the line, always thinking, and a very clever playmaker."

When the Bruins topped Detroit to win the 1941 Cup, Bauer scored the winning goal. The team and the players' careers were disrupted by World War II. All three Bruins joined the Royal Canadian Air Force. Given that the opponent in the war was Germany it was no longer thought to be a clever idea to call them the Kraut Line. For several years that appellation was dropped in favor of either the Buddy Line or the Kitchener Kids. After World War II, the nickname reverted to the Kraut Line.

Bauer was a small player at 5-foot-7 and 160 pounds, but Schmidt said he made up for his lack of size by being "a brainy player."

Bauer played seven full seasons after being brought up by the team for one game (he scored a goal in it) at the end of the 1936–37 season and one game during the 1951–52 season. That was a special one. Bauer had retired at thirty-one, but returned to the Bruins for a single appearance at thirty-six.

Schmidt was retiring and chasing his 200th career goal. Bauer suited up for a one-day reunion of the Schmidt-Dumart-Bauer line. Sure enough Schmidt scored the coveted goal and the other two received assists. The occasion was actually Schmidt and Dumart's special night at the Boston Garden. Among gifts received were gold watches, sterling silver service, radios, bicycles, and movie cameras. Bauer's cameo made the night complete.

Bauer coached young players in Canada for years after retirement and also coached Canada's entry in the 1956 Winter Olympics in Cortina d'Ampezzo, Italy.

In 1964, Bauer was stricken by a heart attack while playing golf and died. In 1996, he was elected to the Hockey Hall of Fame.

Woody Dumart was born in 1916. He grew to be 6-feet tall and 190 pounds and spent 16 seasons in the NHL, from the time he was nineteen until age thirty-seven, with time off during World War II. Every minute of his NHL ice time was spent in a Bruins jersey.

Dumart, who scored 211 goals in 772 games and was a three-time All-Star, was remembered for one off-ice habit. He was a last-minute dresser. He waited until 8 p.m. exactly to pull on his Bruins top. It was a personal preference, but also a signal to other players it was time to hit the ice. The other peculiarity of Dumart's ritual was requiring a trainer's help to pull the jersey over his head. This was habit that became superstition.

Dumart's nickname was "Porky." He recorded 11 seasons of double-figure goal-scoring, five of them hitting the 20s, with a high of 24 goals in one year, although he was better known for his defense.

Dumart retired after the 1954 season. In 2001, as he was headed to the Fleet Center for a special night the Bruins were throwing for defenseman Ray Bourque, Dumart felt ill, and a heart attack killed him at age eighty-four, less than two weeks later.

"Woody was one of the truly great Bruins and one of the best players in the NHL in his time," said Boston team president Harry Sinden.

The third member of the Kraut Line was Schmidt, who as of March 2016 was the oldest living former NHL player at ninety-eight.

One of Schmidt's grandest memories was the final game he, Bauer and Dumart played together before leaving for World War II and an uncertain future. The Bruins won, 8–1. Honoring the trio, Montreal's players lifted up Schmidt, Dumart, and Bauer onto their shoulders and carried them off ice as Boston fans saluted them.

"I will take it to my grave," Schmidt said. "What a great night. I will never forget it. First, the game we had—Bobby, Woody, and I had about 10 points that night. And then to be carried off the ice by the Montreal Canadiens? That's something that never leaves you."

No one has been so closely identified with the Bruins for as long as Schmidt. As recently as New Year's Day 2016, Schmidt appeared at the Winter Classic game between Boston and

Montreal in Foxboro, Massachusetts. That's after breaking in as a player in 1936 and skating with the big B on his sweater through 1955. As an illustration of change, Schmidt's first contract was for $3,500.

Before the Classic, Schmidt reminisced about the many battles his Bruins played against the Canadiens.

"Oh, it was really high-strung," Schmidt said. "It didn't matter the time of the year, whether the season just began or what. We looked forward to it because you could get away with high-sticking and some good body-checking."

Of playing against the legendary Montreal star Maurice "Rocket" Richard, Schmidt pointed to his teeth and joked, "I can take these out and show them to you."

Schmidt coached the Bruins from 1954 through 1966, as well, and in the middle of that run was elected to the Hall of Fame in 1961. He also served as general manger of the team. As a player Schmidt competed for the 1939 and 1941 Stanley Cup champs and scored 229 goals for Boston in 776 games. Schmidt touched all the bases with the Bruins as a player, captain, coach, and general manager in the 1970s. The combination of duties put Schmidt's name on the Stanley Cup four times. His Number 15 jersey was retired, too.

"Boy, how lucky can you get," Schmidt said of those four Cup engravings. "There are so many great hockey players in the league that never ever got to play on a Stanley Cup team. And that's a shame.

Art Ross, the extraordinary figure in early Bruins lore, once anointed Schmidt the best player at his position he ever saw.

"Milt Schmidt at center," Ross said, "greatest in hockey history, anywhere. Schmidt on top, all the way."

Ross was in charge of the Bruins when he discovered Schmidt's playing ability. He was wary of his small stature. Schmidt eventually grew to be 6-feet tall and 180 pounds, but as a teenager was small.

Still, Ross wrote to Schmidt and invited him to attend Bruins training camp. The naïve Schmidt wrote back and said he sure would like to attend, so he was going to work hard all summer to save money to pay his way. Ross told him that would not be necessary since the Bruins would pay his way from Ontario.

Schmidt picked up other admirers, including a testimonial from an unlikely source.

"I'd take five Milt Schmidts, put my grandmother in the net, and we'd beat any team," said NHL referee Red Storey.

Schmidt stayed up to date with the Bruins and got to know greats young enough to be grandsons. One was defenseman Ray Bourque.

"For me it was getting to know a guy like Milt Schmidt and becoming a part of that history that is called the Boston Bruins," Bourque said. "Those players built something that we ended up playing in. To be part of so much history and the Original Six is a pretty neat feeling."

Just about all anyone needs to know to understand how good the goalie was for those two Stanley Cup winners of '39 and '41 is to hear the nickname. People called Frank Brimsek "Mr. Zero."

Brimsek was a twenty-three-year-old rookie when he shoved Tiny Thompson out of the net during the 1938–39 season with one of the most spectacular Bruins seasons in history. Ironically, Brimsek was on the tiny side at 5-foot-9 and 170 pounds. Thompson suffered an injury in preseason and never got his job back.

That year in net Brimsek's record was 33–9–1 with a 1.56 goals against average. He won the Calder Trophy, the Vezina Trophy, and was a first-team All-Star. He was also an American, of which there was a limited supply at the top level of the game, coming from Eveleth, Minnesota.

Brimsek became an eight-time All-Star in nine years with the Bruins and won two Vezina trophies. As a rookie Brimsek collected 10 shutouts, which got him that flashy nickname. Brimsek broke in with six shutouts in his first eight games and was initially called "Kid Zero." That was later amended to "Mr. Zero."

Although Brimsek's career was interrupted by Coast Guard service in World War II, he was inducted into the Hall of Fame and was in the inaugural class of the American Hockey Hall of Fame, which opened in 1973. Brimsek set records for wins and shutouts by an American goalie and was not displaced in the record books for four decades.

When Art Ross found Brimsek he gave him a personal tryout. Ross laced up, took the ice, and shot 25 pucks at Brimsek without getting a single one past him. "I knew then that Brimsek was as quick as I thought he was," Ross said. "His hands were like lightning—the fastest I ever saw."

Brimsek felt the responsibility of being the Bruins goalie keenly and was often nervous. Sportswriters pumped him for information on his background, commenting on his muscular arms.

"You work in a field from sunup to sundown swinging a scythe and your arms will be muscular, too," he said.

Many thought he was a hard guy to read. He definitely wasn't boastful about his ability.

"Goaltending is mostly luck," Brimsek said.

Around that time the Great Depression took a toll on the financial health of NHL franchises and it took until 1942 to shake out.

The Pittsburgh Pirates became the Philadelphia Quakers and folded. The Ottawa Senators became the St. Louis Eagles and folded.

The Montreal Canadiens flirted with moving to Columbus, Ohio, but refrained from taking such a drastic step.

Tough times produced fallout that ended up with only the Boston Bruins, Chicago Blackhawks, Detroit Red Wings, Canadiens, New York Rangers, and Toronto Maple Leafs representing the National Hockey League beginning with the 1942–43 season.

There were no franchise changes or shifts again until 1967, and that era of 25 years was the period defined by the six-pack of teams termed the Original Six. They were the six teams left of the original ones dating back to 1917 and their roots stemmed from an era of hockey predating the existence of the later twenty-four teams.

Hard Times

It was a long time between Stanley Cups for the Bruins after 1941 and after a while even they, too, stopped coming close.

In 1943, in an NHL diminished by players off competing in World War II instead of on the ice, Boston lost the Finals to Detroit. Right after the war, when teams were reassembling, Boston lost a Finals to the Montreal Canadiens. In 1953, 1957, and 1958 they also reached the Finals and fell to Montreal in all three of those cases.

Pretty soon those five almosts qualified as the good old days.

Between 1960 and 1967 the Bruins were the worst team in hockey. They did not reach the playoffs in any of those seasons. Boston finished last six out of those eight seasons and last five times in a row.

The Bruins ran dry of players, particularly top-notch goalies. During the 1961–62 season the Bruins scored 177 goals and surrendered 306. Five times in the 1960s in 70-game seasons, the Bruins failed to win more than 18 games.

Pretty much with the exception of what amounted to borrowing legendary goaltender Terry Sawchuk for two years in the mid-1950s, none of the players well-remembered from this time period were netminders.

The player always called Fernie in Boston was named Ferdinand. He first skated in a single game for the Bruins in 1944 and except for a minimal detour with the Maple Leafs he stayed in Boston through 1961. The best part of those three seasons was that Fernie Flaman got to play on a Stanley Cup–winning team.

A tough defenseman, Flaman was popular both with teammates and fans. He was captain of the team and scored more with checks than with goals. Yet Flaman was eventually selected for the Hall of Fame in 1990. He remained in Boston after retiring from the NHL and coached Northeastern University for 19 seasons through 1989.

Flaman got into enough fights on the ice that the 5-foot-10, 190-pounder was once compared to former heavyweight champion Rocky Marciano, another Boston sports hero. A sportswriter asked Flaman if he went looking for trouble and if he liked fighting.

"I wouldn't say I go looking for trouble," Flaman said. "Sometimes it can't be avoided. I won't say I dislike it."

Even the biggest stars were careful around Flaman. The Canadiens' Jean Beliveau said, "Any other player I do not worry about. But when I go near that fellow, believe me, I look over my shoulder."

Flaman scored just 34 goals in his playing career while amassing 1,370 penalty minutes. Boston observers, and later, the *Hockey News*, contended that Flaman never lost a fight in the NHL.

Detroit superstar Gordie Howe said of Flaman, "He's the toughest defenseman I ever played against."

In some ways defenseman Leo Boiven was like Flaman. Boiven played in the NHL between 1951 and 1970 and became a Hall of Famer. He was an undersized defender at 5-foot-8 and 183 pounds, but one of the rugged guys who understood it was his primary job to protect the goaltender. His build gave him the nickname "Fireplug." The majority of Boiven's career was with Boston—12 seasons, worth—and for four of those he was captain. Boiven's talent was hitting opposing guys so hard they didn't even remember they had been carrying the puck.

"I just wanted to play so badly that I wasn't going to let anything stop me from getting to the NHL," Boiven said. "I knew I was short, but I didn't let that bother me. Instead, I decided to use my size and weight to my advantage. I became more of a hitter . . . and got more into the physical part of the game."

Boiven was from Prescott, Ontario, and his first few seasons in the league were with Toronto. His long Boston sojourn followed. Most of Boiven's career was concentrated in the Original Six era, but he hung around long enough to squeeze out some bonus seasons with the Pittsburgh Penguins and Minnesota North Stars.

"I really had to work hard to keep my job, as well," Boiven said. "You have to remember that I played most of my career in the old six-team league. There were only 120 jobs available during those days and I consider myself to be fortunate to have played in the league as long as I did under those circumstances."

Overall, Boiven played in 1,150 games and collected 1,192 penalty minutes. Only once did Boiven score as many as 10 goals in a year. He was not a tough guy with a bad temper. He was a tough guy who knew what he had to do to prevent opponents from scoring.

"As long as they wore a different sweater and were hittable, I'd hit them," Boiven said. "Of course, they'd bide their time and come back and hit you in return."

Echoing Flaman, Boiven said the toughest guy to steer away from was Gordie Howe. Howe seemed to have plenty of respect for Boiven, too.

"When Leo stepped on the ice, my game would change," Howe said. "If he caught you at the angles of eleven o'clock or one o'clock, he'd kill you—and not by having the stick on you. He made you think. You'd never cut into the hole against him. He made players extra cautious and a step slower. There was always the fear of getting hit by him. He'd lift you into orbit, or put you on the trainer's table."

One Bruins coach during the hapless years was Phil Watson. One day Watson was trying to teach young forwards how to check a defenseman. Watson made the mistake of demonstrating on Boiven.

"He went at Boiven," said Bruins star Johnny Bucyk, "hit him, bounced off him, and fell flat on the ice. The whole team cracked up laughing."

Normally, goalie Eddie Johnston appreciated Boiven's assistance more than anyone else. He once described Boiven as "a cement truck and strong as an ox." Bobby Hull, the wicked slap-shooter of the Chicago Blackhawks, was in his prime and everyone estimated the speed of his shot traveling roughly as fast as the fastest fastball pitched in the major leagues. Once, Hull nearly parted Boiven's hair with a bullet and scared Johnston. Johnston charged out of the net yelling at Boiven that he was supposed to stop those rockets.

"'Me?'" Boiven said. "'You're the one wearing the equipment.' I had blocked a Hull shot the year before from about fifteen feet away. It hit me on the back of my glove and broke two bones in my hand."

Bronco Horvath's NHL career spanned 1955 to 1968, and just four of those years were with the Bruins. But they were his most productive seasons and he was a fan favorite at the Boston Garden.

Horvath's family moved to Canada from Eastern Europe after World War I. The 5-foot-11, 185-pound skater bounced around quite a bit, playing for five of the Original Six teams and playing 200 more games in the American Hockey League than he did in the NHL.

However, Horvath excelled with Boston, leading the league in goals with 39 in the 1959–60 season. His 80 points were one point shy of Bobby Hull's leading mark that year. Horvath made his only All-Star team that year, as well.

"That was a very frustrating season for me," Horvath said. "I really wanted that scoring title."

The scoring title slipped away on the last night of the season when the Bruins were hosting Chicago. Hull scored and Horvath didn't. Bronco came oh-so-close to netting a goal on Glenn Hall, though.

"I took the shot and it hit one post, slid behind Hall, hit the other post, and came back out," Horvath said. "The thing I'll never forget about that game is that the fans gave me a standing ovation after it was all over. That was a nice consolation to the whole thing. But I was miserable for a week after that season was over with. I wouldn't talk to anybody because I had lost that scoring title."

During his one All-Star game Horvath played on the same line as Howe and Hull.

"It was a dream of a lifetime for me," he said.

Although they did not spend an inordinate amount of time together with the Bruins, Horvath, Vic Stasiuk, and John Bucyk shared the same line. They first played together with Edmonton in the minors, and with all of them being of Ukrainian heritage, the line was called "The Uke Line."

Stasiuk could not get a break during his early years with the Red Wings. He was up with the big club and down in the minors for the first half of the 1950s until he was swapped to the Bruins. When coach Milt Schmidt put the Ukes together they clicked right away. During the 1957–58 season Stasiuk, Horvath, and Bucyk, who would long outlast the others and go on to bigger stardom later, became the first line where all three players scored 20 or more goals.

During his six seasons with Boston Stasiuk topped 20 goals four times, with a high of 29. The core of Stasiuk's NHL career was with Boston. After retiring he was the beneficiary of the expanded NHL when he coached the Philadelphia Flyers and California Golden Seals.

Stasiuk wondered a bit about the younger generation when he headed those teams.

"You have to have enthusiasm and a love of this game to play," Stasiuk said. "You must keep interested and not get distracted. I can't understand a player who isn't enthusiastic. If you're not enthusiastic you've got no business on the ice."

While the Bruins were struggling, Don McKenney was not. McKenney joined the club in 1954 and finished as runner-up and rookie of the year. During the fallow years of the late 1950s into the early 1960s, McKenney was one guy who could lift the spectators out of their seats at the Boston Garden. He was considered a clever stick-handler and a classy player like a Jean Beliveau.

Among other achievements, McKenney won the Lady Byng Trophy during his nine seasons with the Bruins and one year led the league with 49 assists. Seven times he scored at least 20 goals for Boston with a high of 32.

McKenney played in seven All-Star games.

"It was just a pleasure to play in them," McKenney said. "I just think it's an honor to play in them."

McKenney drifted to a few other teams after his service with Boston, winning a Stanley Cup with Toronto in 1964.

"Toronto was going for the Stanley Cup and they just wanted to reinforce their chances," he said.

McKenney returned to the Boston area to raise a family. He became an assistant coach to Fernie Flaman at Northeastern University and after he retired from that job the school named a coaching award after him. In the 1980s, one of McKenney's sons played for Northeastern.

When Tommy Williams broke in with the Bruins for the 1961–62 season, the native of Duluth, Minnesota, became the first American player in the National Hockey League since Frank Brimsek retired in 1950. During that era, big-time hockey was almost the sole preserve of Canadians.

"It was pretty tough," Williams said of scouts looking down on American prospects. "The biggest knock against Americans was that they didn't play the hard-hitting type of hockey Canadians did."

Butch Williams later followed Tommy into the pros and they became the first American brothers in the history of the NHL. In 1966, Williams appeared on the television show *I've Got a Secret*. His secret was being the only American-born player in the NHL at that time.

When still an amateur, Tommy Williams represented the United States in the Winter Olympics of 1960 at Squaw Valley. Much like the more publicized US entry at Lake Placid in 1980, that group of skaters captured the gold medal in an upset.

"I was only nineteen and we were picked to finish last," Williams said. "Canada outshot us 45–20, but we beat them 2–1 in the semifinal." Williams assisted on the winning goal by Billy Christian in the 3–2 gold-medal championship over the Soviet Union.

Williams's performance in the Olympics got the Bruins' attention, but he went to training camp with misgivings.

"I had always wanted to play in the National Hockey League," Williams said. "That had been my dream. But the money wasn't that good and I was getting myself beat up pretty good in training camp. I didn't think I was good enough to play. But I must have done something right."

Williams played for the Bruins for eight years in the 1960s. He later played for other NHL teams and the New England Whalers of the World Hockey Association. He scored a career-high 23 goals in 1962–63 for Boston, but at the end of his career scored 22 goals for the expansion Washington Capitals. All told, including the minors, Williams played 17 seasons professionally.

Along the way Tommy Williams acquired a dramatic nickname. He was called "The Bomber" and that would have been a compliment if he had received it for owning a wicked shot. Not so. He made the mistake once of telling Toronto customs officials he was carrying a bomb in his suitcase. These days that would have set off major criminal proceedings. Even then Williams was slapped with a one-game penalty by the league.

Off the ice Williams's life was pockmarked by tragedy. In 1970, his wife was found dead in their car. A son from his second marriage died at twenty-three in 1987. And Williams died of a heart attack at fifty-one.

Willie O'Ree

The first black player in National Hockey League history had a challenging go of it when he broke the color barrier at the top level of professional hockey. As the years passed Willie O'Ree gained more fame and respect and has since become known as the Jackie Robinson of hockey.

O'Ree first suited up for the Boston Bruins in 1957, ten years after Robinson became the first African American player in Major League Baseball in the twentieth century.

But O'Ree struggled to maintain a spot on an NHL roster and spent most of his long career on skates in the minors. O'Ree was born in Fredericton, New Brunswick, and played two games for the Bruins during the 1957–58 season. He returned to Boston for the 1960–61 season, appearing in 43 games with four goals and 10 assists that year.

In 1950, Art Dorrington, another black player, signed a contract with the New York Rangers, but he was never promoted out of the minors. Larry Kwong, a Canadian player of Chinese descent, played one game for the Rangers in 1948. It was not until the 1974–75 season that the second black player competed in the NHL. Mike Marson, then nineteen, made his debut with the Washington Capitals that year and played five seasons in the NHL.

"I had wanted to become a pro hockey player from the time I was fifteen years old," O'Ree said. "I began skating at three and played my first organized hockey at five. I fell in love with the sport and was obsessed with playing it. I couldn't get enough of it."

Most of the rest of O'Ree's career was focused in the Western Hockey League with the Los Angeles Blades and San Diego Gulls where he was a very popular player and nine times scored at least 20 goals. In his best years, twice O'Ree notched 38 goals. In all, O'Ree played pro hockey for 21 years.

The milestone moment in O'Ree's career was the night he first took the ice in a Boston uniform. The date was January 18, 1958, and the Bruins beat the Montreal Canadiens, 3–0. That was the first appearance by a man of color in an NHL uniform.

His linemates that game were Don McKenney and Bronco Horvath, and Milt Schmidt was the man who inserted O'Ree into the lineup.

"I remember that first game like it was yesterday," O'Ree said forty years after the occasion. "It was a Saturday night and I was no stranger to Montreal fans because I had just played there the week prior as a Quebec Aces player."

That two-game stint had to satisfy O'Ree for the moment, but he was glad he was recalled for a longer time on the roster.

"Being the first hockey player to break the color barrier stands out," O'Ree said. "I was excited about being there, maybe even more so the second time up."

The late 1950s and early 1960s were a tumultuous time in race relations across the United States. Many of the rights blacks were being denied were in the forefront of demonstrations.

As of the fortieth anniversary of his special break-in game O'Ree had not yet met the younger generation of black players, but said he wanted to do so.

"I'd like to tell them about 1958 and how we've progressed since then," O'Ree said. "I think it would be good for the league and good for hockey."

Not all opponents were kind to O'Ree on the ice, singling him out for verbal abuse, and there were rude fans to contend with.

"Someone threw a black hat on the ice to poke fun at me," O'Ree said of a minor-league game. "There were always racial remarks made to me by other players after the whistles. I just learned to let them go in one ear and out the other."

Although he had long been retired and actively worked in hockey with youths in West Coast cities, O'Ree enjoyed a resurgence of attention. He began working with the NHL's diversity task force, as well. Books were written about his experiences and he was able to speak in more forums about his time in the NHL. A film was made about his life, titled *Echoes in the Rink: The Willie O'Ree Story*.

Among those recognizing O'Ree on that fortieth anniversary was President Bill Clinton, who wrote a congratulatory letter to him. The letter read in part, "You remind us anew that we must work together to create a society where all of us are free to live out our dreams. Both on and off the ice, your spirit and determination have set a strong example of leadership."

Little-remembered was how tremendous an all-around athlete O'Ree was as a young man. The Milwaukee Braves baseball team sought him and convinced him to attend a tryout camp in Waycross, Georgia. O'Ree told the Braves he planned to play hockey, but they said he should come anyway.

When O'Ree flew into Atlanta, his first trip to the American South, he was confronted by white-only and colored-only signs for the restrooms, another first for him. He was then informed he had to sit in the back of the bus for the journey to Waycross. O'Ree said even training camp was segregated for him and another half-dozen players of color from other parts of the globe.

The group went into a drugstore to buy postcards and soft drinks and while O'Ree dallied with the postcards others ordered. White men at the counter began issuing insulting racial remarks. Baseball did not seem so inviting.

There were also days when hockey was not so free of prejudice, either.

"Teammates, by and large, accepted me," O'Ree said. "The worst came from the fans. A lot of them were bigoted. I guess they'd look out on the ice and see a dark face and couldn't cope with it. There were a lot of names. I wasn't much of a fighter on the ice, but I did a lot of fighting. Not because I wanted to, but because I had to. Somebody was always saying something about my color. I felt it was my duty to stand up for myself. I just wanted to be accepted as a hockey player."

As the years passed from his too-short time on skates in the NHL, O'Ree gained more recognition for being a pioneer. He was awarded a Doctor of Laws degree from Saint Thomas University in his hometown of Fredericton. The San Diego Gulls retired his number 20 jersey. He was inducted into the New Brunswick Sports Hall of Fame. The city of Fredericton named a sports complex after O'Ree.

In 1984, Grant Fuhr became the first black player to have his name engraved on the Stanley Cup. Numerous other black players have competed in the NHL since, including Mike Grier, Anson Carter, and Jarome Inigla.

O'Ree said he always fit in well as a Bruins player. He scored his first NHL goal against the Canadiens and had praise for the Bruins stars of the time.

"Fernie Flaman has gone out of his way to help me and so have others," O'Ree said at the time. "It was Bronco Horvath who gave me a shooting tip that led to my first goal."

Although the description of being the Jackie Robinson of hockey has followed O'Ree for some time, he thought the appellation exaggerated because Robinson suffered more bias.

"There was never that kind of pressure or problems that Jackie went through," O'Ree said. "The only pressure I felt was that which I put on myself to be good enough to stay in the NHL."

Still, as far back as 1955 when O'Ree joined the Quebec Frontenacs junior team, the coach, Phil Watson, who later took over the Bruins, was wise enough to provide advice.

"Phil told me I'd be in for a rough time," O'Ree said, "that I'd take a ride from the other players. But he told me, too, that if I kept my head and paid no attention to the jibes, I'd be okay and that I could become the Jackie Robinson of hockey. His encouragement, his counsel, and his coaching really helped me."

Much later O'Ree said when he played, "I heard the N-word so often I thought they were paying me a compliment."

The NHL began taking notice of O'Ree and his pioneering history on the fortieth anniversary of his debut with the Bruins. That was magnified for the fiftieth anniversary in 2008.

O'Ree operated the NHL's diversity program, and kept repeating there should be more blacks in the player ranks. In late December 2008, at age seventy-three, O'Ree was recognized with the Order of Canada by his home country.

"I was at a loss for words, really," he said.

Life and Death for Ted Green

For many years during Original Six days games could be wars. A skater headed out to score goals and do battle. It was like trying to tame the frontier for 60 minutes every night.

One of the most frightening events in hockey history occurred on September 21, 1969. It was not even a regular-season game, but Boston defenseman Ted Green and St. Louis left winger Wayne Maki engaged in a vicious stick fight. The game was being played in Ottawa and resulted in Green nearly being killed in the altercation. Green was coming off his only All-Star season and feeling optimistic about the new campaign.

It is regarded as one of the ugliest confrontations in league history and helped generate discussion about players wearing helmets.

Green was a hard-nosed defenseman from Manitoba and had enough of a reputation for toughness that he was nicknamed "Terrible Teddy." Green broke into the National Hockey League with the Bruins in 1959, and he was twenty-nine when his battle with Maki broke out.

Maki had been around the league since 1965 and was the younger brother of better-known Chico Maki.

The skirmish between Green and Maki, who died at age twenty-nine from brain cancer only five years later, began as so many NHL fights do. A little jawing. A little checking. A little elbowing.

Maki was trying to skate past Green and Green grabbed his jersey. In retaliation Maki speared him below the belt. Green was not going to accept that, so Green whacked Maki across the arm with his stick. Things escalated. The stick swinging did not last long. Maki connected with Green's head and drove him to the ice.

Green lay helpless. He began experiencing convulsions and his head jerked back and forth. Green was soon rushed to the hospital where he was diagnosed with a fractured skull and paralysis on his left side. The NHL was outraged. Maki was suspended for 30 days. The NHL said Green would be suspended for 13 games, "If and when he returns to hockey."

Survival was Green's immediate concern. He underwent surgery for a brain injury and had a plate inserted in his head. Even when he went home Green was not right. He said he once answered a phone he heard ringing, only to be greeted by a dial tone. The ringing was in his head. He could not handwrite at first. Green sat out the entire season, but came back for 1970–71. For the rest of his career he wore a helmet to protect his head from any further injury.

"I came back way too early," Green said. "I spent a whole year with no physical guidance and was on anticonvulsive drugs that inhibited my stamina. I had some side effects. On the ice I didn't have the same awareness and comfort zone. Things were more of a panic for me. I had the shakes a lot and constant headaches."

Green returned to the Bruins, but switched to the New England Whalers and Winnipeg Jets of the World Hockey Association for the last seven years of his career. In all he played until he was thirty-eight. Green later coached the Edmonton Oilers.

However, twenty years after his head was bashed Green admitted he had never been 100 percent again.

"I drop a pen or a knife sometimes because the feeling isn't right in my left hand," he said. "And I still have headaches. Sometimes it's like there's a guy banging to get out from under the plate in my head."

Old-time hockey fans remember that plate being inserted in Green's head as a lifesaver, but he said most believe it is steel when it is really plastic.

"I kid people that I can't play golf because I'm a lighting rod and I don't play in the rain because the rust will run down my neck," Green said.

The next night in another exhibition game after Green was leveled, Boston defenseman Don Awrey wore a helmet.

"Last night when I saw the look in Ted Green's eyes as he was lying on the ice, I decided to wear a helmet from now on," Awrey said.

After the awful sight of their teammate being left prone and helpless on the ice, there was some consideration given by Bruins management to see if players would regularly play with helmets. Coach Milt Schmidt ordered two dozen of them, but when he brought them to practice the players refused to wear them. Awrey did not stay with his helmet.

The first NHL player to wear a helmet was George Owen during the 1928–29 season and he was playing for the Bruins. Owen, who was a football player for Harvard University and was later enshrined in the College Football Hall of Fame, used the same leather helmet he wore on the gridiron when he skated in the NHL.

The defenseman spent five years with Boston. No one else showed much interest in wearing a helmet on the ice.

That changed briefly in the 1930s after Eddie Shore's devastating hit on Toronto's Ace Bailey. While Bailey was forced to retire, Shore returned from his injury, though he wore a helmet when he played. Some other NHL players donned head protection for a little while, but except for a handful of players such as Boston's Dit Clapper, the habit died out.

In January 1968, Minnesota's Bill Masterson was hit in the head during a game against the Golden Seals. Masterson was charging up ice when he was cut off by two players, Larry Cahan and Ron Harris, who checked him. It was concluded that Masterson was unconscious before he hit the ice and began bleeding from his nose ears and mouth. Despite being rushed to surgery Masterson died less than a day and a half later from a brain injury. He is the only NHL player to die as a result of an in-game injury.

That sparked discussion about players being required to wear helmets, and the Green incident followed quickly. But the players resisted the safety advancement. It may have surprised many, but Green was among those who lobbied against the imposition of a helmet rule, even when his injury was still fresh.

Admitting he knew he would have to wear a helmet to play again, Green said, "Given the choice, I would not put one on." He said he did not see why his situation should influence anyone else's decision.

Before the 1979 season began, NHL president John Ziegler decreed that helmets would be mandatory for players coming into the league from then on. Veterans were grandfathered in and could make their choice, but had to sign a liability waiver. Craig MacTavish was the last player to compete without a helmet, during the 1996–97 season.

This plan more or less tracked the thinking of Phil Esposito, who noted that kids were wearing helmets and then gave them up when they turned pro. Esposito said he did not want to start wearing a helmet, but if he had worn one all along he would have stuck with it.

Although he paid a high price for it and he did not relish his role in the proceedings, what happened to Ted Green in 1969 contributed to the league's change of policy.

Bobby Orr and a New Stanley Cup Era

The pursuit and signing of Bobby Orr by the Bruins was more akin to a courtship and marriage than a professional sports deal.

Rarely are even the greatest of players (and many believe Orr may have been the best of all) able to project a future so bright at such a young age. By the time Orr was thirteen, Bruins management knew who he was and salivated over what an adult Orr could bring to the team.

Orr was born in 1948 in Parry Sound, Ontario, and by 1961 Bruins officials had seen him play. Before that year was over, Boston curried favor with Orr by investing $1,000 in his local hockey team. Although it sounds insane, even by his early teens Boston general manager Wren Blair described Orr as a combination of Doug Harvey and Eddie Shore. The kid was, well, still a kid. The others were on their way to the Hall of Fame. Yet Blair was correct.

As Orr worked his way through junior hockey the Bruins angled to make sure that when he turned eighteen he was going to be Boston property. By that age, Orr was not only a member of the organization, he was already starting. Orr won the National Hockey League Rookie of the Year award in 1966–67, the last season when the Original Six constituted the entire league. He was an All-Star, the first of nine straight selections before knee injuries began taking a toll in derailing his career.

As he morphed into one of the game's legendary players, Orr won the Norris Trophy as the NHL's best defenseman eight times and revolutionized the sport by how he played the position.

In memory, Orr will always be the crew-cut kid who came to town, put an entire franchise on his shoulders, and taught the adults surrounding him on the ice how to play this age-old game.

Most defensemen of prior eras were not thought of as scorers. Their job was to guard the zone and protect the goalie. The 6-foot, 197-pound Orr had the talent to play defense as well as any, but also to carry the puck out of his zone, evading squadrons of defenders and bring it all of the way in on the opposing netminder.

Orr's up-ice rushes left fans breathless. He stick-handled around would-be checkers, skated past stationary defensemen, and flicked shots into the net. What Orr did was turn defense into offense. No one had seen a player quite like Orr. He bamboozled foes and made admirers out of teammates.

He scored more goals than any other defenseman and he set up teammates with brilliant feeds after drawing opponents to him like moths to a light. Defensemen used to be like stay-at-home housewives, expected to take care of housekeeping work mostly out of the limelight.

Orr led the NHL in scoring twice, led in assists five times, and won three MVP awards by the time he was twenty-three. Defensemen did not lead the league in scoring. They left that flashy work to forwards. Orr topped 100 points in a season six times, with a high of 139 in 1970–71.

It was often said Orr was hell on goalies, but one time he whipped such a hard shot in practice that he nearly killed a Bruins goalie. During his early days with the B's, an Orr shot struck Eddie Johnston in the head. Johnston, who was not wearing a mask, went down as if shot and doctors feared for his life when blood clots materialized in his head.

"They figured it was all over for me," Johnston said. "Someone called a priest and he stayed with me for the next two weeks."

Johnston survived and returned to the Bruins. Except for his recurring knee woes, Orr only thrived from then on.

The funny thing was that Orr, who was often heralded as performing ballet on ice, once said, "I'm a terrible dancer. Oh, I'm an awful dancer."

He was a force of nature, the indispensible man, the player no other team could match. After missing out on the playoffs those eight years in a row—with Orr as a cornerstone before the end of the 1960s the Bruins were on the rise. They were being built into a Stanley Cup contender.

In unfortunate foreshadowing, Orr did not make it through his rookie season unscathed, suffering the first of what would be several knee injuries. In the long run Orr's career was ruined by knee problems, forcing him to retire by thirty.

"Bobby Orr was better on one leg than anybody else was on two," said Maple Leafs star Darryl Sittler.

Johnston, who recovered from that shot to the head, once scoffed at anyone who suggested Orr's defense suffered because he raced up ice. Heck, Johnston said, Orr was playing 40 minutes a game and controlling the puck for 20.

"What better defense is there?" Johnston said.

One of Orr's coaches was the estimable Don Cherry, before he gained greater fame as a *Hockey Night in Canada* broadcaster. Cherry said he never actually coached Orr—that nobody could because he was too good. Cherry called Orr the best player of all.

As Orr faded in skill because of the constant battering his knees took the Bruins made the horrifying public relations decision to trade him to the Chicago Blackhawks. Orr never wanted to go, but he told Cherry his contract negotiations were going poorly: "They're treating me like I'm a horse ready to be shot."

Years before, Orr became a very large foundation piece on a club that ended the Bruins' playoff failures and brought two Stanley Cups to Boston in 1970 and 1972.

The Bruins were the most colorful and devastating team around. There was Orr, of course, but Milt Schmidt orchestrated what is often called the greatest trade in NHL history when he acquired Phil Esposito, Ken Hodge, and Fred Stanfield from the Blackhawks for Gilles Marotte, Pit Martin, and Jack Norris.

What a crew. Johnny Buyck had matured into a Hall of Famer. The flashy Derek Sanderson was on the club. So was Wayne Cashman. Gerry Cheevers, who scratched in every faux stitch on his mask that the goalie believed would have cut his face, shared the net.

The era of the Original Six had passed. In the most daring expansion in the history of professional sports, the National Hockey League doubled in size by adding six new teams at once for the 1967–68 season. The new teams played in their own division and the winner of that division met the winner of the other division with the older, established teams. In 1970 that team was the St. Louis Blues.

Harry Sinden, who worked in the Bruins organization as coach, general manager and president, was the coach for the Blues showdown. The Bruins dominated the first three games, but the teams went into overtime at 3–3 in the fourth. Orr, who led the league in scoring with 120 points, netted one of the most memorable goals in NHL history to capture the Cup.

As he fired the puck into the net, Orr was tripped. Flying through the air horizontally, he realized the shot was good and he let a broad smile crease his face and raised his arms in the air, stick included. The image was captured by a Boston photographer. The picture is one of hockey's most famous pictures.

"Honestly, I don't know how it went in," Orr said later.

Esposito, later an executive, played 18 years for the Blackhawks, Bruins, and New York Rangers, but his time with Boston made him a Hall of Famer. A six-time league-leading goal-scorer, once with a then-record 76, all with Boston, Esposito was an eight-time

All-Star and won two MVP awards. That same year Esposito added 76 assists for 152 points.

When Esposito notched his 75th goal in 1971, Boston fans gave him a standing ovation. Esposito didn't expect it and said afterwards for the first time in his life he was embarrassed.

"It's the greatest moment an athlete can experience," Esposito said. "That kind of recognition, that kind of ovation for an achievement. It moved me a little bit all right. The people here are just terrific."

At 6-foot-1 and 205 pounds, Esposito was a sturdy character. He made his living feasting on short rebound shots in the crease in front of the goalie. At one time there were bumper stickers on cars in Boston reading, JESUS SAVES . . . AND ESPOSITO PUTS IN THE REBOUND. Other teams threw big men at Esposito, but he was anchored like a tree in the face of constant assaults.

In his prime with Bruins Esposito got about as much fan mail as anyone in the United States. He averaged 1,200 letters a week during the season and 40,000 pieces of mail a year. Although they were fan letters and letters expressing dislike for him, the majority were autograph requests. It was some challenge to keep up, but Esposito did visit an office twice a week to sign requests and spent $20,000 a year keeping up with the correspondence.

Once, Esposito telephoned a little old lady who wrote from Saskatchewan. Another time he visited a little old lady in a Boston suburb and had tea and cookies with her. Now that's fan appreciation.

The Bruins also skated the inimitable Derek Sanderson. Sanderson was an exceptional fore-checker, talented scorer, and could put female fans in the seats. Sanderson developed the image of a party animal and playboy who was the hippest guy in hockey. Sanderson was always where the action was, on and off the ice.

A center with dashing good looks, Sanderson was 6-foot-2 and weighed 200 pounds. He was scrappy on the ice, but seemed to play with a wink at the seriousness of it all. He broke in during the 1965–66 season and won the rookie of the year award.

Sanderson also had a knack for making news off the ice.

"The square hockey world could use a change," Sanderson said. "I'm the guy to change it."

Sanderson inspired newspaper headlines like "One of the New Breed" and "Females by the Thousands Seek Date with Dashing Derek." A Boston radio station ran a contest asking females to write in and say why they wanted a date with Sanderson. Apparently, women wrote in from thirty states and all over Canada, ranging in age from eight to sixty-three. One envelope was covered with Xs and Os, and they weren't about playing tic-tac-toe.

One letter said the writer had just left a convent and felt this would get her back in "the swing of things." Another said she would do anything for a free meal. One kid wrote in on behalf of her mother because "daddy doesn't take her out."

Sanderson modeled bell bottom trousers when they were in, ruffled shirts and even scarves. When he violated Bruins policy by refusing to wear a tie his response to club officials was, "Fine me. Cool. Groovy. Just don't lecture me."

Another Sanderson comment may not have made "Bartlett's quotations," but it should have. "I can't decide which I like best, sex or hockey," he said.

Sanderson did not gain allies in the league office by referring to President Clarence Campbell as "a stuffed shirt."

Sanderson was constantly asked to explain himself to a core of sportswriters that could have been a gathering of his fathers and uncles.

"Some people act as though I was a freak," he said. "All I am is my own man. I think my own way, say what I think. The writers love me because I'm outspoken. What's so freaky about that? I like luxury. I like pretty girls. I like to swing. Most people do. People envy me."

Sanderson often battled conservative management over money and when the fledgling World Hockey Association came along he became a rich guinea pig. Sanderson jumped to the Philadelphia Blazers for $2.6 million, then the richest sports contract ever.

However, Sanderson ended up the victim of alcohol abuse, blew through all of his money and at one time was so broke he slept on a park bench in New York. His long-time friend Bobby Orr paid to send him into rehab and ultimately, as a white-haired senior citizen Sanderson was sober and active in the business world.

There were extreme highs and lows in an adventurous life, but Sanderson made it through the tunnel.

Boston Bruins Since

In 2011, the Bruins won the Stanley Cup. When they defeated the Vancouver Canucks in seven games it was the first time Boston players had hoisted the precious trophy since 1972.

Between 1968 and 1996, Boston qualified for the playoffs every season. That was a National Hockey League record 29 straight years. The only two Cup victories, however, during that stretch were those early 1970s triumphs.

The captain of the 2011 Boston champions was defenseman Zdeno Chara who, at 6-foot-9, is the tallest player in the history of the NHL. He also played at 250 pounds, which means he packed a wallop when he checked someone. Chara is from

Slovakia and joined the NHL in 1997, playing for the New York Rangers and Ottawa Senators before signing as a free agent with the Bruins in 2006.

Given Chara's size the NHL granted him a waiver to use sticks that are two inches longer than what is otherwise the maximum length.

At the All-Star game skills competition in 2012, Chara unleashed a shot clocked at a record 108.8 mph. Chara is a seven-time All-Star and a winner of the Norris Trophy as best defenseman in the league.

"Could I top 110 mph?" Chara said. "We'll see. It's always my motto . . . I want to be better every season."

On January 8, 2016, the Bruins became the second team in NHL history—behind another Original Six franchise, the Montreal Canadiens—to win 3,000 games.

"When you look at 3,000, it means the team's been around for a while," said coach Claude Julien, "so I've always been proud of being part of an Original Six team. This team has done a lot of things in the past and we hope we can follow that up in the future."

3

NEW YORK RANGERS

Founded: 1926
Home Arenas: Madison Square Garden, 1926–68; Madison Square Garden, 1968–present
Stanley Cups: 1928, 1933, 1940, 1994

Beginnings

The least successful of the Original Six teams was the New York Rangers. They started with high hopes, great fanfare, and as the gem in the eye of famed sports promoter Tex Rickard. They even won a Stanley Cup almost immediately after starting play.

New York won another Cup in the 1930s, and one in the 1940s, but then began the enormous patience-draining drought that did not produce a fourth Stanley Cup title until 1994. As the end of another quarter of a century approaches, the Rangers have yet to win another Cup.

What the Rangers did have going for them in their early days, and as the days stretched to years and decades, were members of the Patrick family, one of the most esteemed in hockey history.

Lester Patrick, born in 1883, along with his brother Frank and father Joseph, not only founded the Pacific Coast Hockey Association, but helped establish the rules of professional hockey. Some twenty-two rules he wrote remain part of the sport. For the most part Lester played on West Coast clubs. But when the Rangers were founded he became the team's first coach.

At that point Patrick had played for more than 20 years, though his career essentially concluded before the National Hockey League was founded.

Lester took the reins in 1926 and held them until them until the end of the 1938–39 season. Under Patrick the Rangers won two of their four Stanley Cups. The "Silver Fox" was even forced into action in goal on April 7, 1928, when he was forty-four.

New York had an outstanding goalie in Lorne Chabot, but in the second game of the Stanley Cup Finals, with the Rangers down 1–0 in games to the Montreal Maroons, Chabot was injured. He was hit in the eye with a stick, bled profusely, and had to be carried off the ice. He could not resume play.

As was typical of the times, the Rangers did not have a backup goalie on the ice. The team was given ten minutes to put a player in the net or forfeit the game. A top minor-league goalie was present at the game and Patrick, who was also general manager, asked the league president, Frank Calder, if he could suit up Alex Connell.

There was a rule against using any player not under contract to the club, however. Calder said if the Maroons did not object he would allow the Rangers to use Connell. The Maroons, who had the foresight to bring a backup goalie, were not sympathetic. They basically said, "Tough luck."

Team officials turned to Patrick, amazed at the request. He agreed to play and told the trainer, "I want you to get me a dry set of underwear. Strip off Lorne's skates and uniform and I'll use his equipment."

Responding to the responsibility, Patrick became defiant when he skated onto the ice, shouting, "Let them shoot!" Odie Cleghorn, who agreed to run the bench while Patrick defended, said, "For God's sake, don't let them shoot!"

Patrick did botch an easy shot, letting the puck go through his legs, but the game went into overtime at 1–1. The Rangers won it with Patrick making 16 saves in 23 minutes of action. Chabot remained sidelined and the Rangers signed Joe Miller of the New York Americans to fill in for the remainder of the series. Despite this odd and seemingly depressing situation, New York rallied and won the Cup.

Lester Patrick remained general manager of the Rangers until 1946 and stayed on as vice president of Madison Square Garden until 1950. A Hall of Famer, he spawned several other Patricks that made a mark in the NHL. Some call the Patricks hockey's royal family.

Lynn Patrick, one of Lester's sons, played ten years in the NHL, all with the Rangers, and also became a Hall of Famer. Lynn coached with the Rangers (for two years), the Boston Bruins, and was named the first coach of the expansion St. Louis Blues as the Original Six era came to an end. He was also general manager of the Bruins.

At first, Lester did not want to sign his son for the Rangers' organization, but some of his assistants convinced him it was the right idea. A member of the 1940 Stanley Cup team, Lynn scored as many as 32 goals in one season for the Rangers.

Lynn's brother Murray, or Muzz, was a member of that same Stanley Cup team, but when World War II broke out he joined the army. Serving from 1941 to 1945, he became a captain. This Patrick returned to the Rangers for one season after the war and then pursued a coaching career. After his apprenticeship in the minors Muzz Patrick coached the Rangers for parts of two seasons in the mid-1950s, briefly became their interim coach in 1959–60 and coached the team one last year in the early 1960s.

Eventually, Lynn and Muzz met as coaching foes when the Bruins and Rangers played. While they battled things out by-proxy then, apparently when they were younger exuberant fights were more personal.

"When we were kids growing up in Victoria [British Columbia] we used to fight just for the hell of it," Muzz Patrick said. "I understand Lynn claims he out-punched me then by a 15–1 margin. Maybe he's right. All I know is that after I was sixteen or so, I was the one that did all the clobbering in the family."

Muzz did have plenty of boxing experience. He fought in the amateurs and it was said he had potential as a professional heavyweight.

"I had a lot of offers to turn professional," Muzz Patrick said. "I had a big yen for boxing, but a nose injury I got while playing rugby helped me decide to quit. Then, about that time, I had a chance to get into professional hockey, so I took it."

In that game when Lester Patrick had to fill in the winning goal was scored by Frank Boucher. Boucher also became a future Rangers coach and general manager. Boucher played professionally from 1921 to 1938 and he dressed again for a season in the 1940s. His nickname was "Raffles." Boucher won the Lady Byng Trophy seven times in eight years.

It was in Boucher's first year as coach that the Rangers won the Stanley Cup. He led the team for parts of 11 seasons, but after reaching the heights right away he endured a stretch of five straight seasons without making the playoffs. Boucher, who was from Ottawa, is the one who hired both Patrick brothers to coach the Rangers at different times.

During the 1945–46 season Boucher broke precedent as coach by using two goalies regularly. Charlie Hayner and Jim Henry alternated every other game. Sometimes Boucher used them interchangeably within games. While the idea struck some as being all right, it did not pay dividends for the Rangers. They finished 13–28–9.

Boucher was one of the most important Ranger figures in history. He played for the team's first two Stanley Cup champs and coached the club to its third.

The interesting thing about Chabot in goal for the Rangers during that Stanley Cup when Lester Patrick filled in was that he only played two seasons for New York. During his NHL career from 1926 to 1937 he moved around constantly. Rather peculiarly, he played for six teams before there was an Original Six. In addition to the Rangers, Chabot played for the Montreal Canadiens, Chicago Blackhawks, and Toronto Maple Leafs, plus the Montreal Maroons and New York Americans.

Chabot, who was only forty-six when he died, played goal in the two longest games in NHL history. He was the losing goalie to Detroit's Normie Smith in the six-overtime epic in 1936. But he was the winning goalie in the previously longest game in 1933. He won that one, 1–0, over Boston after 104 minutes, 46 seconds.

Chabot certainly was a realist about what it was like to play goal long before anyone used a face mask.

"I stitch better when my skin is smooth," he said of shaving before every game.

The Rangers were trying hard to sell hockey to residents of Manhattan in their early days and someone in the publicity department said Chabot should change his name to "Chabotsky" to make it sound more Jewish so Jewish fans would be lured to watch him in net. The change did occur, but it did not last.

Another time the overheated Rangers publicity team suggested to Lester Patrick that the team's best player, Bill Cook, be kidnapped and the story leaked to the newspapers to promote the upcoming season three days away.

"I've got an idea that's sure-fire stuff," said Johnny Bruno to Patrick. "Strictly buildup. So tomorrow we get Bill Cook kidnapped."

"Out!" declared Patrick, urging Bruno to vacate his office.

"But of course we locate him in time for Cook to make it to the game," Bruno said.

Cook, who was elected to the Hall of Fame, led the NHL in goals three times for the Rangers and twice in points while making four All-Star teams during his 1920s–1930s career. Cook did not break into the NHL until he was thirty after playing several years in the Western Canada Hockey League.

His rookie year of 1926–27 was the squad's first. Known as "The Original Ranger," Cook posted an unusual scoring line. He blasted home 33 goals, but had just four assists. During the 1931–32 season Cook scored 34 goals in 48 games.

However, the year the Rangers won their second Cup, 1932–33 he scored 28 goals and led the league in points with 50.

The third time around in 1939–40 the Rangers gave up only 77 goals all season. Goalie Dave Kerr's goals against average was a stupendous 1.54. Both Patrick brothers played on that title team. So did Bryon Hextall, the first of several Hextall family members to play in the NHL. He led the league with 24 goals that year.

Another Patrick came along later. Craig, who served as assistant coach for the United States' gold medal–winning hockey club in the 1980 Winter Olympics in Lake Placid, New York, couldn't have been a surprise hire as Rangers' coach in the 1980s. His grandfather was Lester Patrick and his father was Lynn Patrick. Muzz Patrick was his uncle.

As a player, Craig competed for the Minnesota Fighting Saints in the World Hockey Association, and for eight years with the California Golden Seals, St. Louis Blues, Kansas City Scouts, and Washington Capitals.

Patrick, who also became Rangers general manager just like his grandfather, coached New York before winning two Stanley Cups as GM of the Pittsburgh Penguins.

Ironically, after the 1999–2000 season, Craig Patrick won the Lester Patrick Trophy, for outstanding service to hockey in the United States.

Emile Francis

They called him "The Cat" because his reflexes in goal were so quick.

Emile Francis was born in 1926 in North Battleford, Saskatchewan, and was most closely identified as a player and especially a coach and general manager with the New York Rangers, although he did play for and lead other teams.

He made his National Hockey League playing debut in 1946 and he first played for the Rangers during the 1948–49 season. Mostly, though, Francis was a career minor-leaguer on the ice during the Original Six era when teams swore allegiance to one main goaltender for the entire season and usually didn't even have a backup around.

Francis took over as coach of the Rangers for the 1965–66 season. By then the Rangers had gone a quarter of a century without a Stanley Cup. They had been blessed with some individual talent in the intervening years, and New York still had some stars under Francis. They made the playoffs in nine of the ten seasons Francis was in charge, although the club could never win a Cup. The closest the Rangers came under Francis was losing in the Finals to Boston in 1972.

New York played some exciting hockey during this period and Francis's career regular-season mark with the team was 342–209–103. The Rangers were good enough to tease the fans, but not good enough to win it all. Francis made the Rangers winners day-to-day, but not in the big picture.

You might say he wasn't always able to put the best players on the ice all of the time. One year a huge blizzard struck the New York metropolitan area shutting down most avenues of transportation. The Rangers were scheduled to play a game against the Philadelphia Flyers that night. Several key players, including the starting goalie, did not make it to Madison Square Garden in time.

Anticipating a possible situation, Francis knew he was going to start second-string goalie Don Simmons. But what if he got hurt? So Francis, then forty-four, signed himself to a playing contract for $1. Just in case.

Francis began each season believing his Rangers would finally win a Cup. Given the defeatist attitude in the city, keeping an optimistic outlook could do no harm. Even if this was a time period when the Boston Bruins with Bobby Orr were dominant, Francis believed anything could happen.

"Remember, this game is slippery," he joked. "It's played on ice."

Francis was known for his heavy smoking of Lucky Strikes and for being a very nice guy. But he took pride in making his players sweat hard in training camp.

"We run the toughest camp in the league," Francis said. "These guys have been skating three hours a day and then taking special classes at night for seven days."

While Francis's NHL playing career was limited he played all over the North American map in the United States and Canada. Unlike some players with charmed careers, he didn't win much wherever he traveled. In 1969, when the Rangers moved into first place in the standings, even if it was going to be brief, Francis was happier than most hockey observers might have guessed.

"I never played with a professional team that spent even one day in first place," Francis said. "I don't even remember being with a first-place team when I was in school. Hey, correction! When I was coaching the Guelph Juniors in the 1961–62 season we won 18 consecutive games and we led the OHA [Ontario Hockey Association]. But they didn't give me a medal or anything like that."

During the 1973–74 season some hockey people considered the Rangers favorites, but they were not playing that way. Rumors surfaced about the future of the coach, as they always do. In this case it was assistant coach Larry Popein, who had been elevated to the top spot.

"That is a lot of baloney," Francis said of the likelihood of Popein being fired. "It's not true. It's ridiculous. There's no thought whatsoever about him continuing to do that job."

Popein was ousted after 41 games.

In the end, although Francis put together a résumé good enough to get him elected to the Hall of Fame as a builder, he was fired by the Rangers. Still, he made Rangers World a better place, winning

60 percent of his games and enhancing the image of the product enough to entice 14,500 season ticket holders to the new Madison Square Garden.

"I have no regrets about my record," Francis said. "We made the playoffs for nine straight seasons, so I must have done something right."

Andy Bathgate

If Andy Bathgate is not the greatest of New York Rangers, then he's definitely on the short list. Born in 1932 in Winnipeg, Bathgate played 17 seasons in the National Hockey League and his finest years were with the Rangers.

His career spanned some bad times, but also included a period when the Rangers seemed on the rise and likely to break their Stanley Cup drought. The 6-foot, 183-pound right winger broke in with New York in 1952 and retired with Pittsburgh in 1971, although near the end of his career he did some minor-league time.

Bathgate scored 973 points in 1,069 games and when he joined the New York club he represented a hopeful future. He overlapped with other great Rangers stars, but they could not capture another Cup together despite his and others' Hall of Fame credentials.

The only thing Bathgate might love as much as hockey is golf. Besides playing that sport all of the time in retirement, he owned a driving range. Perhaps he had the same swing in both games.

Bathgate scored 40 goals for the Rangers during the 1958–59 season and that year won the Hart Trophy as Most Valuable Player. Bathgate accidentally contributed to the greatest equipment innovation in hockey history. A shot he fired on net hit Montreal goalie Jacques Plante in the face on November 1, 1959. Bleeding and stunned, Plante skated off in need of medical treatment. When he returned to play he was wearing a mask to protect his face.

Another time Bathgate got considerable attention for bringing the issue of violence in hockey to the forefront. A story appeared in *True*, a men's magazine, in which Bathgate told the world that spearing was so dangerous it could lead to tragedy. In the story he said, "unchecked brutality is going to kill somebody."

The headline read "Atrocities on Ice." Bathgate named six players who stood out for spearing and criticized them. In an example of how hockey has changed since the Original Six era, some of them replied that spearing was part of the game, but they only used the stick poking tactic to defend themselves. One thing that motivated Bathgate to speak out was a spleen injury to teammate Red Sullivan. He also harkened back to an incident when a Fernie Flaman stick caught him in the eye in a game against Boston.

Boston owner Walter Brown defended Flaman.

"I've had Flaman since he was fifteen years old," Brown said, "and I'll tell you this: There isn't a mean bone in his body. Of course he's rough. You can't be a pantywaist and play defense in the National Hockey League. They separate the men from the boys early around those points."

NHL fined Bathgate for making inflammatory comments that it said were bad for the game.

"They changed the rule at the end of the year, but they still didn't give me my $1,000 back," Bathgate said. "It burns my [butt] at times, but you have to stand up for it."

Bathgate had as many as 35 goals a few years after his 40-goal year and recorded five more New York seasons with at least 20 goals. Bathgate knew how to score.

"The main thing in shooting is your grip on the stick," Bathgate said. "You don't have to be big and you don't have to be strong, but you have to have the right grip. People talk a lot about my slap shot—that's an arm shot, you don't break the wrists. But my best shot is a wrist shot with no follow through. I know exactly where it's going and I can get it off pretty fast."

Other teams grew to fear Bathgate in the Rangers' lineup, and Chicago Blackhawks coach Rudy Pilous was a key member of that club.

"Andy operates with that soft lamplighter effect," Pilous said, groping for metaphors to describe Bathgate's scoring prowess. "But he puts on all the lights for the Rangers. He's the best electrician they've got."

Most of Bathgate's youth was spent in Manitoba. Playing hockey outdoors could be like skating in a big ice box. Sometimes temperatures dropped to minus 50.

"I remember it was so cold one day that your breath froze in front of you, like the jet stream," he said.

Bathgate's father died when he was thirteen. Bathgate's widowed mother moved the family to Guelph, Ontario, when he was sixteen. His brother Frank, who played just two games for the Rangers in his only NHL showing, was playing juniors there for the Guelph Biltmores. Andy Bathgate teamed up with such future pros as Dean Prentice, Harry Howell, Lou Fontinato, and Ron Murphy. The early influences involved with that team convinced him never to drink or smoke as the team won the Memorial Cup. Also while with that team Bathgate suffered the first of several haunting knee injuries that long-term slowed his career.

"Before my knees went bad I could keep the puck all day," Bathgate said.

Bathgate, much as Stan Mikita and Bobby Hull did together, stumbled on the value of a curved stick. Bathgate said he invented the curved stick. Mikita got the credit on the international stage, but Bathgate said he knew all about curved sticks as a kid in the 1940s.

"I had a curved blade playing road hockey when I was a kid," Bathgate said. "I thought, 'Geez, with this big hook I can raise pucks. This is wonderful.'"

Bathgate said his junior coach broke his curved sticks as a way to break him of the habit of using them. Bathgate said he resumed counting on curved sticks when he turned pro.

"I would heat the blade up with hot water and then I could bend them," he said. "I would put them in the [locker room] toilet stall door and leave them overnight. The next day they would have a hook in them."

Bathgate said over the course of a game the sticks straightened out, but he got a stick manufacturer to insert fiberglass into his sticks to make sure the sticks stayed curved. Bathgate said Mikita actually borrowed some of his curved sticks from the Rangers trainer, but Mikita said he didn't know what Bathgate was talking about.

"Andy is getting up there in age," Mikita said. "I keep telling him the mind is the second thing to go. Maybe he's thinking about his nine-iron."

Although Bathgate did not play at as high a level for the Leafs he became a member of a Stanley Cup championship team.

As popular as Bathgate was with the Rangers—and for the most part he was viewed as the most popular player on the roster—he said he could blend in on the bustling streets of Manhattan in a way he never could in Toronto or Montreal, where hockey players are kings of the heap.

"I'm very seldom recognized on the streets," Bathgate said. "People have so many other things to do in New York. Everybody's in a big hurry. Everybody's going somewhere."

He was the highest profile Ranger in the 1950s and into the 1960s. He once scored goals in 10 straight games. That brought some attention. The 10th goal came off Jacques Plante and it wasn't a rocket.

"It dropped suddenly by a foot," Bathgate said. "It was falling like crazy when it got to Plante."

Plante was handcuffed and agreed with the description of the movement on the shot.

"That shot had pepper on it," Plante said.

In a 180-degree opposite circumstance, Bathgate once fired a shot so hard at Boston netminder Harry Lumley that it tore the glove off of Lumley's catching hand.

"That never happened to me before," Lumley said. "It was like trying to catch a brick."

Although Bathgate was a first or second team All-Star four times, he was also playing right wing when Gordie Howe and Maurice Richard held down the position, making it impressive he was able to break through at all.

Bathgate served the Rangers as captain of the team, albeit reluctantly at first. General manager Muzz Patrick informed Bathgate the team wanted him to become captain, but his first reaction was "I don't know."

Bathgate pictured himself as a leader by scoring and wondered how he would fare as a vocal leader.

"I don't want it just because I've scored more points than some of the other guys," he said. "I'm not going to go around squawking about every little thing."

There was also some joking along the way. Players in the Original Six era did not make big bucks and often worked off-season jobs. One year defenseman Lou Fontinato, the team tough guy, worked construction, and a New York newspaper, apparently to show how strong Fontinato was, ran a photograph of him hefting three bags of cement. Behind him was an empty wheelbarrow.

Bathgate took one look at the picture and called Lou "Dopey Looie."

"Whaddya mean by saying Dopey Looie?" Fontinato asked him. "Can you lift three bags of cement?"

"Anybody who lifts three bags of cement with an empty wheelbarrow behind him is dopey," Bathgate replied.

Eventually, Bathgate and the Rangers split when he was traded to Toronto after a dispute with New York general manager Muzz Patrick.

"Muzz and I didn't see eye-to-eye," Bathgate said. "One time Muzz told me, 'You're just getting too big for your britches. I think it's time you got out of here.'" It did not help matters when Bathgate retorted, "I don't think we're ever going to win and that's what we're here for, to win a Stanley Cup." Bathgate says, "I got traded shortly after that."

At the very end of his skating career, at age forty-one, after leaving the NHL, leaving the minors behind, playing in Europe for a year, and after coaching the team for a season, Bathgate surfaced in the World Hockey Association with the Vancouver Blazers. He wasn't certain how that was going to go.

"If I'm not making it Joe [coach Joe Crozier] will tell me and if he doesn't, my wife certainly will," Bathgate said.

Ultimately, the Rangers retired Bathgate's Number 9 jersey, but not for many years. That honor came along long after Bathgate was inducted into the Hall of Fame in 1978. In between, another Rangers star, Adam Graves, wore the number. So the team essentially retired Number 9 twice for both of them. Graves graciously called Bathgate "the greatest Ranger to ever wear the number 9."

Jim Neilson

His nickname was "Chief" as much because Jim Neilson played a professional sport during an era when just about any athlete with Native-American blood in the United States was called that. It applied to Canadian athletes, too.

Neilson was born in 1941 in Big River, Saskatchewan, the son of a Cree mother and a Danish father. He broke into the National Hockey League with the Rangers for the 1962–63 season and remained with the franchise through the 1973–74 campaign. He then finished his NHL career with the passing-through-the-league Cleveland Barons and the California Golden Seals before making a one-season cameo with Edmonton in the World Hockey Association. A strong and tough defenseman, Neilson stood 6-foot-2 and weighed 205 pounds.

Not a big scorer, but a hard hitter, Neilson appeared in 1,058 big-league games with 69 goals and 299 assists. He also accumulated 908 penalty minutes.

In a less-enlightened time Neilson was frequently insulted because of his heritage. It was as if there were still frontier battles going on between cowboys and Indians.

"I used to hear a lot of 'You blankety-blank Indian' stuff," Neilson said near the end of his NHL career. "It got me into my share of scraps when I was a rookie. Now it's different. It's just a joke when the other guys call me 'You blankety-blank Chief.' It's the same as saying 'You blankety-blank Westerner' or 'You blankety-blank Newfie.' I think it's finally all behind me. With all of the civil-rights legislation of the past few years I think they think of me as just a native-born Canadian like everybody else.

"But when I came up in New York they were always wanting to play it up big, put a headdress on me for pictures, that kind of thing. I never wanted anything to do with that Big Chief stuff."

Another thing Neilson encountered early in his career were fans shouting Indian whoops when he rushed up ice, as if he was making a charge on horseback. Not that many such occasions arose because he was a stay-at-home defenseman who always thought more about preventing goals than scoring them.

"I always felt that it was the forwards' business to score goals and that I had done my job when I got them the puck," Neilson said.

Neilson said his only aspiration when he came into the NHL was to stick around a long time. He was shooting for 20 years and played for 17, counting the one WHA season. He was shooting for 1,000 games and he reached that milestone.

Neilson never had it easy and it wasn't only prejudice against natives. When he was four years old his parents split up. His mother returned to the reservation. His father, a mink rancher, traveled extensively. Neilson and his two sisters were sent to an orphanage in Prince Albert, Saskatchewan. The girls eventually went elsewhere, but Neilson was happy there and stayed, saying he was well-treated and got a good education.

Neilson did not forget the place when he became a professional hockey player, returning to give pep talks to the residents.

"I guess I'm a little bit of a hero to the youngsters now in the orphanage there," he said.

Later, when Neilson was with the Rangers, his Long Island house burned down and he had to rescue his family. Neilson was able to react promptly when he smelled smoke because he had trouble sleeping that night. A visit to the dentist left him with residual pain and he wasn't resting well.

"I smelled something foreign," Neilson said. "I had an idea and when I saw the reflection of light flickering on the wall, I knew."

Neilson and his wife Donna darted into the bedroom of his five-year-old daughter Darcy and pulled her to safety even though there were flames shooting several feet high nearby. The Neilsons also aggressively attacked the fire and mostly put it out before the fire department arrived, although some materials were still smoldering.

A short circuit in an extension cord had sparked and set the child's blankets on fire. Neilson suffered third-degree burns on his hands, but only missed one game before returning.

"I was able to hold on to the stick with just a couple of fingers," he said. "But the burns are healing nicely. It could have been worse."

Neilson said he had a lot to learn as a young player joining the Rangers, but defensemen like Harry Howell and Doug Harvey taught him a lot. Later in his career, Neilson was the elder statesman. He helped break in Brad Park and others.

"I guess there is quite a difference in my play since I broke in with Doug Harvey way back in 1962–63," Neilson said. "Now they put the kids with me and I have to do the thinking and the little extras if they make a mistake."

Even though Neilson ended up with so many penalty minutes, they added up over a long period of time. He never once broke 100 minutes in the box in a single season.

"Sometimes I deliberately try to play a hitting game," Neilson said, "but I don't go out of my way looking for trouble."

Neilson enjoyed the bustle of New York when he was a player, but spent off-seasons in a quieter environment in Saskatchewan.

"I still prefer the open spaces, the lakes and fields," Neilson said. "I prefer fresh air and clear skies. I hunt and fish."

In those summer days he spent considerable time with his father, who lived alone in a wilderness environment.

"He was never a hockey fan," Neilson said. "I know that he is proud that I have made it in hockey because that is what I wanted, but I think he is prouder of me as a son than as a hockey player. I have no hard feelings for him. He was left alone with us and simply couldn't care for us himself, but he cared and did what he could and I feel close to him."

Harry Howell

During his time with the Rangers, Harry Howell was the great protector. Any opposing player crossing the blue line was considered to be trespassing and Howell let him know it. Howell skated 17 years for New York between 1952 and 1969, but he did not retire when he departed the Rangers. He kept on going, Gordie Howe–like, playing five more NHL seasons with the Seals near San Francisco and the Los Angeles Kings. And then he stuck around some more, playing three more years in the World Hockey Assocation.

Howell could practically qualify for a pension when he retired. In 25 seasons, which led him to a spot in the Hall of Fame, Howell played 1,411 games in the NHL and another 170 in the WHA. He was no scorer, notching just 94 goals in the NHL and another four in the WHA. But Howell's value was measured in intangibles.

Howell got used to scoring five goals a season or so, except for the 1966–67 season when out of nowhere he scored 12.

"The puck had eyes for me in '66–67," he said. "Everything I threw at the net went in."

Howell, who in the latter stages of his career when his hair was graying was described as resembling President Richard Nixon, won the Norris Trophy as the best defenseman in the league that year.

Howell was thirty-five and looking his age when the retirement question popped up.

"At my age any year could be a year of decision," Howell said. "But honestly, I feel fine and think that I can play at least four or five more years."

He was right about that. Playing for 25 seasons meant that Howell was asked about hanging around many times over many years.

The only regret of Howell's career was that he never played on a Stanley Cup winner. The Rangers were the team on the outs for decades and that overlapped with Howell's entire career.

It might have in 1962 when the best chance slipped away. In a double overtime game against Toronto, New York goalie Gump Worsley made a save, but didn't know where the puck was. He was lying on top of it and the Rangers felt the whistle should have been blown for a face-off, but it wasn't. When Worsley arose, the Maple Leafs' Red Kelly poked the puck in the net to win the game.

"That was a very discouraging moment," Howell said, "because that was one of the years that we had a good chance of winning it. That was tough."

In 1972, Howell felt the Rangers could go all the way, but were eliminated by the Boston Bruins.

"The teams were perfectly equal, except for one guy, Bobby Orr," Howell said, "and he's the guy who beat the Rangers that year."

Howell was the last defenseman to win the Norris Trophy before the Original Six teams saw the league double in size through expansion. He said he was glad he got the award when he did because he predicted young Orr was going to pretty much own it for a while. Howell was correct. Orr won the Norris the next eight years in a row.

That same season the Rangers threw a special night to celebrate Howell's career. He called that the biggest thrill of his career.

"And, of course, that same year, I won the Norris Trophy," he said. "And that is something they can't take away from me."

Camille Henry

One of a group of young stars who joined the New York Rangers in the early 1950s and seemed likely to lead the squad to a Stanley Cup, but couldn't, Camille Henry was a diminutive player at 5-foot-9 and 150 pounds. When he dipped to 145 he was the lightest player in the NHL. He was swift afoot, but had to skate around defenders rather than through them.

A native of Quebec City, Henry won the rookie of the year award after the 1953–54 season. His promise was unbounded, especially since he beat out Jean Beliveau for the Calder Trophy. Henry scored 24 goals that season.

During his New York prime Henry scored 37, 32, 29, and 28 goals in individual seasons. He also won a Lady Byng Trophy.

When Henry was playing he was also involved in a celebrity marriage with Canadian actress/singer/comedienne Dominique Michel. Their only problem was competing careers during the winter when they saw one another barely more than once a month. Henry said that kept things fresh.

"It's like a honeymoon always," Henry said.

That was Henry's heyday. After retirement things did not go quite as well. The couple eventually split up, and although Henry briefly coached in the World Hockey Association in the 1970s he later had trouble finding a good job. In the early 1980s he was working as a security guard for $245 a week, mostly on night shifts. Although Henry remarried, he faced some health problems stemming from diabetes.

During part of his siege with the disease Henry dropped to 116 pounds. Then he fell into a coma. Rebounding from that he was happy to have the security job.

"There aren't many jobs I can do, so I'm happy I got this," Henry said. "I'm proud to be taking home money. What I make might not be a lot for most people, but it's quite a bit for me. I don't have any debts. I'm able to take my wife out to dinner once in a while. What more could I want?"

Still, during his worst of times, unemployed and unhealthy, Henry said he contemplated suicide.

"I'm fifty-three years old and my only qualification for anything is that I'm a hockey player," Henry said in 1987. "All I ever thought was, 'I want to be a player.' When you're finished you still want to be a player. You don't know what else to do. I've thought about doing something drastic, ending it. You know . . . I'm not proud of what's become of me."

In 1996, after he had dipped deeply into poverty, Henry won a court-ordered payment of $85,000 from the NHL Players Association. A year later he died from the effects of his diabetes at age sixty-four.

Dean Prentice

Another of the terrific crop of young New York Rangers that came along at about the same time, Dean Prentice made his debut in New York for the 1952–53 season and played for 24 years. The first 11 were for the Rangers.

Primarily a left-winger, Prentice's highest scoring year was the 1959–60 season when he scored 32 goals. In all, Prentice tallied 391 goals in 1,378 games during his lengthy career.

Born in Ontario, as of early 2016, Prentice, then in his eighties, was still living in that province. A brother, Eric, managed to play five games with the Toronto Maple Leafs. Prentice also had a nephew who became the premier of Alberta.

On one occasion when Prentice was playing for the Boston Bruins, Chicago's Stan Mikita brought him down from behind, earning him a penalty shot. The only problem was that the fall knocked Prentice unconscious.

He slowly revived, only to hear Blackhawk Bobby Hull taunting him with, "Come on, Dean, you're not going to let one of your dummy teammates take the penalty shot for you, are you?"

That is exactly what Prentice should have done. Angered by the message, Prentice got to his feet and took his turn. He charged down ice, faked Blackhawks goalie Denis DeJordy, and scored.

The only problem was that after Prentice returned to the Boston bench and his line shift was called again he could not stand up.

His feet and legs failed him. He had to be carried out of the building on a stretcher and it turned out he had a broken back.

As a player Prentice made sure he had a good time—too good of a time. He sometimes returned from road trips hung over. His wife berated him. Prentice straightened up his act and began Bible study.

"For me, it was like skating around with a piano on my back and having it lifted off," Prentice said. "The heavy weight of my sin was gone and I felt a new sense of freedom. I felt physically younger and stronger as I relied on Christ to give me strength. There was no letdown in my game. I was playing for Christ."

Vic Hadfield

A 6-foot, 190-pound wing from Ontario, Vic Hadfield was one of the tough guys of the Rangers during his time with the club between 1960 and 1974 before concluding his National Hockey League career with the Pittsburgh Penguins.

Hadfield played in 1,002 games and his tough-guy credentials were established with 1,154 penalty minutes. Hadfield did also score 323 goals.

"Right from the start I felt my only chance in the NHL was to be aggressive," Hadfield said. "That's the way I played junior hockey. I know it was a good decision because a lot of players who were better scorers than I was in junior hockey have failed to make it in the NHL."

Hadfield was one of those forwards who loved the curved stick and was dismayed when the league cracked down.

"It was like trying to walk again after years of hopping," Hadfield said.

Hadfield was known as the practical joker of the Rangers. One of his specialties was telephone teasing, calling up teammates and pretending to be other people. He called Rangers star Andy Bathgate and imitated a Toronto executive, faking a desire to bring Bathgate back to the Maple Leafs. Only in reality the two men were more likely to spit in each other's direction than to team up. Another time Hadfield called Boom Boom Geoffrion and faked being a sportswriter. He engaged Geoffrion in a lengthy "interview." Although it did not come out during that chat, Geoffrion did once say, "I wish I had ten Vic Hadfields on my team."

"I think it helps to keep a team loose," Hadfield said. "I don't kid around on the ice."

It was an interesting role to assume for a hockey team captain.

During a playoff series against Toronto Hadfield became infuriated, stole Maple Leaf goalie Bernie Parent's mask, and threw it into the stands at Madison Square Garden. After the series ended in Toronto Hadfield said he was approached by a woman who asked where Parent's mask was.

"Lady, it looks like you've got it on," Hadfield said in what was not a compliment. "And that's all I heard."

Gump Worsley

In a 22-year career which took him until age forty-four, Lorne "Gump" Worsley won the Calder Trophy as rookie of the year, two Vezina trophies, and was elected to the Hall of Fame. For a time he also had an enthusiastic fan club that produced "Gumper Grams."

Worsley, who was born in 1929, minded the nets in New York for 10 years, and he is probably most closely identified with that franchise despite later-in-career team shifts.

Worsley picked up the nickname "Gump" from what some believed was a strong resemblance to a comic-book character named Andy Gump. The nickname was employed so often most fans probably did not even know his given name.

Gumper Grams were a hoot. They were barely more sophisticated than child's play. Sometimes they included poems. Sometimes they included rudimentary drawings, of the Vezina Trophy. Membership cards in the Gump Worsley Fan Club were accompanied by Gumper Grams. Also, a Gump Worsley coloring book could be obtained.

One Gumper Gram contained the following message: "This is the Vezina Trophy. Great Goalies win it. Glenn Hall would like it. So would Johnny Bower. And Terry Sawchuk. And Roger Crozier. And Ed Giacomin. And Caesare Maniago. And Ed Johnston. And Bernie Parent. But . . . they are all good goalies, not great ones. In fact, some of them are not even good. Gump Worsley is a great goalie. The greatest. This is the Vezina Trophy. Color it Gump."

Worsley made his National Hockey League debut with the Rangers for the 1952–53 season. His salary was $7,500 and when he asked management for a $500 raise the next year after winning the Calder Trophy he was sent to the minors, apparently for insubordination.

The Gumper was one of a terrific group of contemporary goaltenders during that decade and into the 1960s, most of whom ended up in the Hall of Fame. During the Original Six era most teams turned over the most pressurized role in hockey to one man and only sparingly carried a spare. That was when Worsley was in his prime.

He stood just 5-foot-7, but was a sturdy 180 pounds. One season, 1955–56, Worsley played all 4,200 minutes of all 70 games.

Other years he stood between the pipes for 68, 67, and 65 games. Worsley had the misfortune to play for several Rangers teams that either did not qualify for the playoffs or that were eliminated early. He had his best luck later with the Montreal Canadiens when he did not have to play every game, recorded his best goals against average at 1.98 and made two All-Star teams.

The determined goalie made up for the lean years with Montreal when he backstopped the club to four Stanley Cups. His Vezina awards were shared with Charlie Hodge once and Rogie Vachon the other time as a new era of using multiple goalies was ushered in.

Worsley gained a following throughout the league wherever he played. It was such a tight-knit group of teams for most of his career that each city knew him. But he was almost surely most popular during his New York days. Worsley, who kept a book on opposing players, taking notes on their shooting and skating tendencies, did experience some of the Rangers' bad old days.

Once, a questioner, who no doubt thought Gump was going to refer to his special book, asked which team in the league gave him the most trouble.

"New York Rangers," he said of his defense. "Just the other night in a game I looked up and there the opposition was coming at me—three on nothing."

Displaying a naturally round face, Worsley did not have a sculpted body. Once, Rangers coach Phil Watson threw this accusation at the Gumper: "Gump's not in shape. He's got a beer belly." Worsley recoiled. "Beer belly!" he retorted. "I don't drink beer. You tell Watson that I only drink V.O."

Years later, when he was turning fifty, Worsley ran into Watson and Watson said, "You're still fat." Worsley said he weighed 183 pounds, about the same as he did during his play-ing days. Sportswriters actually often referred to Worsley in stories as "chubby."

Worsley never thought he should be open to criticism for drink-ing screwdrivers and other hard liquor like Scotch. He said of other athletes known for party habits, "I was drinking it when they were still on formula."

For a man who could be so tense he might pop a blood vessel on a plane or in a net, Worsley tried to stay loose with teammates. He even made fun of his build to them.

"He'd walk through the room past guys with perfect builds," said Gilles Tremblay, "and he'd say, 'I've been in the league a lot of years with this belly, so I hope you guys can do as well as I did.' He always made us laugh."

After becoming part of four Stanley Cup champs later in his career, Worsley was not always nostalgic about his Rangers time.

"We didn't win many games and we didn't make much money," he said. "Muzz Patrick used to throw money around like a man with no arms."

Despite being booed sometimes, Worsley did like New York fans.

"Ranger fans are great fans," he said. "They used to boo me, they used to yell, 'Go get a lunch bucket.' But when my wife Doreen had a baby they sent me a present."

There were periods when Worsley was not as grateful to Rang-ers fans. One game when he returned to Madison Square Garden as an opponent in a Montreal uniform someone threw a knife his way onto the ice.

On that occasion, Worsley said, "They should tear the place down. And they should lock up all the animals."

A traditionalist, Worsley initially disdained the idea of donning a mask. Worsley called the risk of a speeding puck conking him "an occupational hazard. When I played there was pretty much only one goalie. If he'd get hit in the face they'd stop the game, stitch him up and twenty minutes later the game would get started again."

Worsley played in the NHL until he was forty-four and resisted using a mask until 1974, right before the end when he competed for the Minnesota North Stars. He wore the mask for just six games. He said he avoided using any mask for so long because "they were too warm and I was too stubborn." Worsley experimented with the mask, but couldn't get comfortable. "I hated them," he said. "It was too hot and I couldn't see the puck between my legs."

If some describe goalies like Worsley as fearless for facing down those hard shooters, that would not be quite accurate. He was terribly frightened of flying. Once he suffered enough anxiety to leave the Canadiens in mid-road trip home. It was bumpy from Los Angeles to Chicago and he said that was it. Worsley got off the plane and took a train the rest of the way home.

"If we still had train travel like the old days, I'd probably play until I was a hundred," Worsley said two decades into his career. "I love the ice. I hate the air."

On one turbulent flight with the Canadiens coffee spilled all over star Jean Beliveau. The flight attendant was mortified, wiping him off and telling him that taking his suit and tie to the cleaners would be on the airline.

"Hey, lady," Worsley said in an illustration of the type of fright such incidents gave him. "What about my shorts?"

After fifteen years of coping with flying, Worsley did take a break from goaltending and pondered whether to retire. He decided to stick with it even if he had to fly.

"The Canadiens sent me to a shrink and he told me the only cure was to change occupations," Worsley said much later. "I had to forget it. I still hate flying."

Worsley said goaltenders like him, Johnny Bower, Glenn Hall, and Jacques Plante were able to play successfully for so long because of expansion and lack of young competition.

"Kids don't want to play goal much anymore," he said in the early 1970s right after the Original Six era ended. "The kids don't think there is much glamour in tending goal. They feel all the action is in being a forward or defenseman."

Worsley believed he would be a Ranger for life. When rumors about his future spread, he asked general manager Muzz Patrick what was up.

"He said, 'You'll be a Ranger for the rest of your career,'" Worsley recalled.

The next day he was traded to Montreal. Worsley was inducted into the Hall of Fame in 1980 and died from a heart attack at age seventy-seven in 2007.

Jean Ratelle

Over 22 seasons, 16 of them with the New York Rangers, Jean Ratelle scored 491 goals and amassed 776 assists in 1,281 games. He won the Lady Byng Trophy twice, won the Bill Masterson Trophy and the Lester Pearson Award.

A smooth skater, the Quebec native who was raised speaking French, teamed with Rod Gilbert and Vic Hadfield on one of the most famous of Ranger lines, the GAG line. The name stood for Goal A Game.

Ratelle was not from big-city Quebec, but from a more rural area 300 miles north of Montreal. Although he began skating at five he didn't own his own skates.

"I wore my father's skates, size ten, and wore them over my socks, shoes, and galoshes all at one time so they'd fit," Ratelle said. "We'd go out on the frozen lake every day and just play for hours and hours."

In later years when he told the story of wearing the oversized skates, Ratelle said they helped build extra strength in his ankles. However, that didn't help when a shot dinged him and broke one ankle.

The family moved to Montreal when Ratelle was sixteen and moving up in the hockey world. A youthful teammate was Gilbert, and they played on the same line way back then. Playing in Ontario could be challenging for a French speaker. Ratelle learned to speak English from a girlfriend who gave him lessons on weekends and eventually married him.

There was one point early in Ratelle's Rangers stay when it appeared his career might be in jeopardy. Back pain came and went over a period of a couple of years until it became too much to ignore and not treat.

"The doctor said he thought it was a strain," Ratelle said. "But I felt that there was something really wrong with my back. The pain went all the way down to my legs." Even after a season ended his health did not improve. "I had trouble sitting in a car and I couldn't walk too fast."

Although just twenty-three, it turned out Ratelle needed a major spinal cord operation, a spinal fusion. He underwent surgery.

"I knew that the only thing that would fix me up was an operation," he said. "The decision was up to me and I wanted to get it over with."

Ratelle slowly regained full strength. He played in fewer than normal games the next season and fewer than normal minutes within those games. It was unclear if he would be able to bounce back. But his best years were ahead of him.

A Hall of Famer, the 6-foot-1, 175-pound Ratelle's finest year was the 1971–72 season when he scored 46 goals and 109 points. He had other seasons with New York when he scored 41 goals and three times collected 32 goals. Ratelle was hard to stop around the net. But he wasn't fancy, either on or off the ice.

"He's our straight arrow," said teammate Brad Park. "Ratelle is, without a doubt, the model hockey player, totally dedicated to the sport and the team. He plays hockey according to rule book and would never think of elbowing or smashing a guy or doing anything physical. He's just a beautiful player."

Ratelle had to be one of the cleanest hockey players of all, totaling just 276 penalty minutes in those 1,200-plus games. Some called him "Gentleman Jean."

Although he had always been a reliable player Ratelle seemed to improve as he hit his thirties and was at his peak with Hadfield and Gilbert. It also helped that the Rangers obtained some more up-front talent so other teams could not always key on that trio's line.

"Making things happen very quickly is the key to scoring goals," Ratelle said. "I know exactly where Vic and Rod will be at all times. I don't have to look. I just know they'll be there and can make my move to that spot. They do the same with me."

Although he was more Ranger than Bruin, Ratelle did complete his NHL career with six strong seasons in Boston. He twice topped 30 goals in seasons once again and five times overall reached 25 or more.

"He's like good wine," said Boston coach Fred Creighton when Ratelle was thirty-nine. "Some people are thinking of what they're going to do after they get the puck. He's thinking all of the time. He's half a stride ahead of other people with his knowledge of the game and his anticipation."

After he had been around the league for 20 years Ratelle was esteemed by teammates and foes alike.

"Jean Ratelle is THE special player in the league because he brings so much dignity to the game," said Bruin Wayne Cashman. "He's the man we'd all like to be because he has such peace in his life. He's never wasted fifteen seconds in his life being petty or small."

Ratelle was aging gracefully at the same time that Gordie Howe came out of retirement and was playing first-rate hockey in his fifties.

"Me? I'm just playing them one at a time," Ratelle said. "Of course, he probably said the same thing when he was my age."

Ratelle was forty when he retired and he was in the NHL's all-time top ten in goals, assists, and points at the time. He was elected to the Hall of Fame five years later in 1985.

Rod Gilbert

He may have been Canadian, but Rod Gilbert was born for Broadway. They could have written the song "I Love New York" for him.

Handsome and debonair, the 5-foot-9, 180-pound Gilbert with a knack for finding the net was viewed as a New York playboy at times during his stay with the Rangers between 1960 and 1978. He spent his entire career in a New York uniform, competing in 1,065 games with 406 goals and 615 assists. That was good enough to get him elected to the Hall of Fame in 1982.

Few players in Rangers history excited the Madison Square Garden fans the way Gilbert did bursting up ice. In 12 seasons Gilbert scored at least 24 goals, with a high of 43 in the 1971–72 season when he totaled 97 points.

Early in his career Gilbert was diagnosed with a perennially bad back. He was given the option of immediately undergoing an operation and missing the entire season or toughing it out. Gilbert played with a special upper body suit of armor made of steel and leather. It was strapped so tightly on him that he sometimes had difficulty breathing. It was not the best way to go into athletic combat.

"When you love hockey as much as I do," he said of why he chose to play under such circumstances rather than going under the knife, "there really was no choice. I had to play and take my chances."

Gilbert's spine was cracked in two places. He eventually underwent a bone graft with part of the tibia of his left leg being transplanted. More problems ensued and Gilbert needed additional surgery.

With his dashing good looks and fun-loving demeanor propelling him to live life to the fullest in New York City, Gilbert was often compared to the New York Jets football star Joe Namath, who had claimed the "Broadway" nickname before Gilbert's behavior warranted it.

In 1974 Gilbert was profiled in a men's sex magazine of the time called *Genesis*. The reporter even interviewed girlfriends about Gilbert's prowess as a lover and made him sound like the late-night king of singles clubs. Sportscaster Sal Marciano, who appreciated both Gilbert's maturity and class, said "He is the epitome of the male fantasy, the guy who presumably lives the way most guys think they want to. He's the masculine dream."

Yet for all of that party buzz stuff, Gilbert fell in love for the first time when he was basically a toddler and first skated.

"I was just three when I first glided out and promptly fell on my ass," he said. "By five, I was so hung up on skating that I'd forget to come home for lunch. At night, after five or six hours sleep I'd try to sneak out of the house to practice."

He also did not deny a strong attraction to females developing at the same time he was showing promise in hockey.

Girls, he said, as so many young men might echo, "proved to be one helluva discovery. They were not only nice to look at, but nice to touch."

Despite his "swinging" image, teammates saw a different Gilbert. He was a player who always worked hard and constantly sought to improve.

"During the season no chick interferes with Rod's game," said defenseman Brad Park. "He not only feels his responsibility as a player, but he enjoys it, thrives on it. He loves the game and his role in it."

While teammates ogled the women that approached Gilbert and he sometimes turned his back on them in order to rest up for hockey, Gilbert maintained perspective about what many would consider to be a go-go 100 percent glamorous lifestyle.

"A lot of any professional athlete's life is a drag," he said. "The airport scene, the different cities, time zones and temperatures. After a while they all combine to worry your head about digging in and getting the rest you need for a game. Only another hockey player knows the amount of energy needed for peak performance. Only he experiences that total exhaustion after a game."

Gilbert was a Montreal native, but didn't dream of playing for the Canadiens.

"As a kid I realized the Canadiens were overstocked with talent and that I would probably get lost in their farm system if I signed with them," Gilbert said. "New York then was in trouble. They needed young skaters. When I first came to the team they were losers. I was part of a rebuilding program."

Gilbert did not know the rebuilding program would never result in a Stanley Cup title.

"From the beginning, the Rangers made me feel as though I were a part of their future," Gilbert said. "They have continued to make me feel that way. The same is true of the Ranger fan. He may not be the most knowledgeable, but he certainly is the most avid. The New York fan lives for a Ranger win."

Gilbert recognized the link between sport and show business and knew the people in the seats wanted to be entertained.

"When I'm at center ice, see the crowd, I feel like a performer," Gilbert said. "I like recognition. I don't skate to the crowd, but I skate for them. When I feel their affection, I skate harder. The entertainer in me comes out. The fans have more power over me than I do over them, I think. Without their applause, a lot of the kick goes."

Gilbert was a man of his time, a smart dresser for the period, a man-about-town in the midst of the nightlife, often with a dazzling young lady with a hold on one arm.

"There's no other place to play but New York," he said.

Gilbert felt that deep down in his soul. Gilbert got an apartment in Manhattan after one year spent in New Jersey.

"You just couldn't ask a girl to come back to Weehawken," he said.

Gilbert appeared in his 1,000th NHL game in 1976 and received a standing ovation that night. He scored three assists in the game, to boot. He did think back to his first back injury in juniors and how much he would have missed if he had not recovered.

"I thought I'd never play one game in the NHL, let alone 1,000," he said.

Gilbert was thirty-six when he retired after the 1978–79 season. The Rangers then retired his Number 7 jersey, the first set aside by the team in its history.

Ed Giacomin

It took until he was twenty-six for Ed Giacomin to win a goalie spot in the National Hockey League with the New York Rangers as the tail end of the Original Six era approached. That was symptomatic of the challenge for a young goaltender before the league expanded. There were six starting slots, period.

And this was a guy who as soon as he began playing regularly made All-Star teams, won a Vezina Trophy, and eventually was chosen for the Hall of Fame.

The 5-foot-11, 180-pound Ontario native spent years in the American Hockey League before he got a break seeing any action for the 1965–66 season in New York. Early on, before playing five years in Providence with the Reds, Giacomin had to overcome some burn injuries incurred in a kitchen accident.

Once he got in the lineup, Giacomin didn't want to come out, and for four years running he appeared in 68, 66, 70, and 70 games in a 70-game season. In 14 seasons in the NHL, 11 of them with the Rangers, Giacomin compiled a 2.82 goals against average. By age thirty-one Giacomin was prematurely gray and some people thought it was because he played in too many games. He didn't buy that.

"No doubt it's a long season," he said. "Everyone wears down some. It's more the mental pressure than the physical thing."

When Giacomin joined the Rangers he wanted to join many of his teammates where they lived on Long Island, but was stunned by the length of the commute. It probably took ten minutes to go end-to-end in Providence, but the driving distance was different on the Long Island Expressway.

"Even with no traffic it took us an hour and fifteen minutes to drive to the Garden," he said. "The guys told me it might take twice as long in traffic. In Providence we lived about a mile from the rink and if I wanted to I could get to it in a couple of minutes. In New York it's an all-day trip."

Giacomin was in Providence long enough to register to vote in Rhode Island, but said he enjoyed the owners and the fans, and the game action gave him a chance to grow up on the ice.

"Sure, we had our troubles winning, but the way I look at it, I had a chance to learn the business in which I've found experience means so much," Giacomin said. "I might not have gotten that chance with another team."

It wasn't as if all of Giacomin's numbers sparkled with the Reds, either. New York general manager Emile Francis looked beyond the stats to basic talent when he plucked Giacomin from the minors.

"I don't go by records," Francis said. "This fellow is good mechanically and he has all kinds of determination."

Giacomin came along when the NHL was changing and growing and most goalies had adopted the mask introduced by Jacques Plante. Giacomin did not want to wear one, but a few years into his major-league career he tried it out. He did not like the Plante-style mask and looked for an improved model.

"The one I am wearing is not adequate, as far as I am concerned," Giacomin said.

Giacomin excelled at clearing the puck to defensemen to get it out of the offensive zone.

"I've seen plenty of goalies in my day, but there aren't many who move that puck out of their zone the way that kid does," said future Hall of Famer Johnny Bower, nearing the end of his career in 1965.

However, Giacomin raised eyebrows due to his habit of roaming far from the net to cut down angles on shooters. Once in a while he got beat on that maneuver and fans didn't like it. But Giacomin three times led the NHL in shutouts, once with nine and twice with eight.

Like all goalies, Giacomin took a beating from the puck and opposition players. Once, sitting in the locker room after a game he commented on what hurt: "My hand, my face, and my knee. They haven't missed much."

The knee was hurt when two opposing players crashed into him simultaneously, one from the front and one from the back. Giacomin was creamed by a puck in the face—lucky for him after he donned a mask—by a Dennis Hull slap shot. The force of the shot dented the mask, cut Giacomin's nose through the mask, and knocked him over backward. A trainer said he might have been killed if not wearing the mask.

Another time Bobby Hull fired the puck at Giacomin. He blocked it, but was lying on the ice as Hull skated in prowling for a rebound. He skated over Giacomin's hand, cutting through his glove and cut him above the knuckles.

"I could feel the skate cut into my hand," Giacomin said. "There was a burning sensation and a lot of blood inside my glove."

Giacomin did not even leave the game. He had the hand bandaged and played on.

"It made me sick to look at it," said teammate Brad Park. "The bandage kept coming loose and Eddie's glove was all bloody. The cut must have been a quarter-inch deep and the skin was ripped and hanging loose. Isn't he something?"

After all of those rough patches, Vic Hadfield, another Ranger teammate said, "Somebody ought to give Eddie a Purple Heart."

Giacomin was thirty-six when the Rangers let him go. The Detroit Red Wings picked him up for the $30,000 waiver price. At first he was stunned, but he adjusted and played three more seasons.

"I was amazed . . . and shocked . . . and disappointed," Giacomin said. "But as time went on and when I put on the Red Wing uniform I came to my senses and said to myself, 'This isn't too bad.'"

When Giacomin returned to play at Madison Square Garden, fans greeted him as a friend and chanted, "Eddie! Eddie!"

It may be that because Giacomin was such an accomplished passer that he set an NHL record of two assists in one game for a goaltender. It was rare enough for a goalie to obtain one assist in a season, but in a game against the Toronto Maple Leafs in April 1972 he collected two assists.

"I would trade them for a goal," Giacomin said. He also said he ranked third in his own family in scoring since his eight- and six-year-old sons scored in their leagues. "So I know where I stand."

Actually, much later Giacomin got his goals. He began playing wing in a thirty-and-over league in the Detroit area at thirty-eight and scored three goals in a single game before even announcing his retirement from the NHL. He joked about going against the amateur goalie, saying, "I feel bad about him. He's got to stop me tonight."

Brad Park

One of the greatest defensemen of all time, Brad Park played his first eight seasons in the National Hockey League for the New York Rangers and even though he played an equal number of years with the Boston Bruins he is more closely identified with his inaugural team.

Park, who was from Toronto, was an offensive defenseman. Despite his many achievements he never won a Norris Trophy because he was in the shadow of Bobby Orr during their simultaneous playing years. He was the consistent runner-up for the honor. Still, Park played in nine All-Star games and was an easy selection for the Hall of Fame.

Drafted in 1966 at age seventeen, Park broke into the NHL for the 1968–69 season at age twenty, just as the Original Six era passed. Park was teammates with almost all of the Ranger stars who came along a few years ahead of him and began their careers during the six-team era.

In 1,113 games, the 6-foot, 200-pound Park scored 213 goals and assisted on 683 others. He managed those totals in 18 seasons, playing until he was thirty-six.

As slick as he could be, some believed Park was superior to Orr on the defensive end.

"Park is a tremendous defenseman," said Ned Harkness, the Detroit general manager at the time. "He moves the puck well, he rushes it and he's sound defensively. He's a great one. By comparison, Orr is more offensive-minded."

Park was always considered special in his own way, combining the new-style offensive skills with old-fashioned toughness and defense. Park, slightly younger than Orr, said he watched Orr closely and learned from him.

"Bobby has had a definite influence on my play," Park said. "One thing that impresses me is that he never panics. He slows play down and then, when he's drawn guys in, he'll bust out with his great skating speed."

One of the biggest surprises in Park's career was being plucked from the amateur ranks by New York. He always thought the Maple Leafs would grab him.

"The idea of being picked by any team other than the Leafs never occurred to me," Park said. "The Leafs were always my favorite team."

Park began playing hockey at five as a goalie. But he developed quickly enough as a skater to move. Park was committed to the sport from the time he was a youth, sometimes driving his parents crazy with his devotion, practicing his shot even in the most inconvenient of places.

"By the time we decided to move to another home there were more dents in the wood paneling than there were nails," said Park's mother Betty.

Park's seasonal high was 25 goals, but he also scored 24 and 22 in other years. This gave him a role in the revolutionary change of thinking allowing defensemen to carry the puck up ice more.

"That kid means as much to our club as Bobby Orr does to Boston," said New York general manager Emile Francis. "His very presence on the ice does something for the rest of the guys."

In 1972, Park scored two hat tricks in one season, the first time in 30 years a defenseman had done that. That year, when Park passed 20 goals on his way to that 24 he became only the third defenseman in league history to top 20.

Orr, the man Park was always compared to, had his career cut short because of bad knees. Park, who was traded to Boston after eight seasons in New York in a shocking deal, even though it brought Phil Esposito to the Big Apple, also had chronic knee problems, although he outlasted Orr.

Park was acquired by Boston after playing 13 games for the Rangers in the 1975–76 season. Orr appeared in his final 10 Boston games that year. With Park as the new king of the defense, the Bruins reached the Stanley Cup Finals twice, but lost both times to Montreal. Park never played on a Stanley Cup winner.

Strangely, since everyone says New York is the place to be seen as a celebrity, Park felt he was better known in Boston.

"No one recognized me on the streets when I played in New York," he said. "You had Broadway and actors and actresses. When I came to Boston it was different. My wife would walk with me and say I looked distracted. I was. I thought people were looking at me."

Later in life he moved to remote Sebago Lake, Maine, with his family, a quiet place he fell in love with. Once, he was asked to drive the pace car at a NASCAR race in New Hampshire and waved to the crowd. He did not keep many keepsakes from his career in a prominent home location.

"It's bad enough my kids had a hockey player for a father," said Park, the father of five. "I didn't want to have them live in a shrine."

As terrific a player as Park was, he did not have a king-sized ego. He felt something might always happen to humble a person.

"When you get punched in the face in front of 17,000 people, you better have some humility," Park said.

It hurt Park not to get his name engraved on the Stanley Cup.

"I remember after a game we lost in a preliminary series I was so upset I had to go off by myself," Park said. "I went to a bar for a beer. I hadn't been sitting for more than a minute when a fan came up and accused me of being a fat cat who was making so much I didn't care if I made the extra money in the playoffs."

The fan was lucky Park didn't bodycheck him into the boards. Park always said he didn't care about the playoff bonus, but hungered for a Cup championship.

"I donated my playoff money to charity to prove that point," he said.

New York Rangers Since

When the New York Rangers at long last won a Stanley Cup in 1994 the celebration was loud and prolonged. It had been fifty-four years since the franchise won its last title.

The road had been long and torturous with many stars highlighting numerous years, but leaving the Rangers unfulfilled.

New York tried everything to win it all, but always fell short. One bold stroke was hiring Herb Brooks. Brooks took a band of inexperienced collegians to victory over the juggernaut Soviet Union and to a gold medal in the 1980 Winter Olympics in Lake Placid, an achievement that ranks as one of the greatest in hockey history and in all of American sport.

Trying to bottle that magic, the Rangers hired him as head coach in 1981 and he stayed through 1985. While Brooks's teams finished 131–113–41, he went 12–12 in the playoffs and became just one of many New York castoffs in the coaching box who could not bring a Cup home.

Before Brooks was killed in an automobile accident at age sixty-six, he gave an interview which sounded very unlike the often-pugnacious coach.

"You know, Willy Wonka said it best," Brooks said of the movie character. "We are the makers of dreams, the dreamers of dreams. We should be dreaming. We grew up as kids having dreams, but now we're too sophisticated as adults, as a nation. We stopped dreaming. We should always have dreams. I'm a dreamer."

Mike Richter

The Philadelphia-area born goalie Mike Richter, who played his entire NHL career with the Rangers between 1989 and 2003, accomplished something that neither Gump Worsley nor Ed Giacomin could—he won a Stanley Cup with the New York Rangers.

With a 2.57 goals against average, the 1993–94 season was Richter's best and he was the man between the pipes when New York ended its championship drought.

Richter also won gold and silver medals at various levels of international play representing the United States. As a youth Richter's favorite goalie was Bernie Parent of the Philadelphia Flyers, and he took the University of Wisconsin up on its scholarship, though he did not stick around long enough to graduate, playing instead for Team USA in the 1988 Olympics, then going pro.

So possessed with the idea of succeeding in hockey when he was young, Richter admitted he was somewhat of an odd stay-at-home duck, doing exercises when friends went to movies.

"I was fairly shy," he said. "In some ways, having so much to do was a relief for me. I never went to a prom. I never had an ordinary growing up."

Adam Graves

While he played with three other NHL teams and even was part of a Stanley Cup winner with the Edmonton Oilers, Adam Graves's greatest moments came with the New York Rangers. He helped bring a Cup to New York after a half-century and scored 52 goals that season of 1993–94, as well as topping 30 goals in a year three other times.

"The last time I had 50 goals?" Graves echoed a question on the occasion when he reached that milestone in the NHL. "I dunno. Maybe back when I was ten years old."

It was a one-time thing for Graves, with his next-best Ranger year being 38 goals. Someone told him he was the first ex-Edmonton star to score 50 goals elsewhere, something not even Wayne Gretzky had done.

"Hey, don't even mention me in the same sentence with Wayne," Graves said.

Brian Leetch

Hall of Famer Brian Leetch was the rock of the New York defense throughout most of his long New York Ranger career. He twice won the Norris Trophy and the year the Rangers won the Cup in 1994 he was the Most Valuable Player in the playoffs. He scored 34 points in 23 playoff games that year.

NHL rookie of the year Leetch became one of only a handful of defensemen to ever top 100 points in a season. Leetch played in 11 All-Star games.

An unusual fact about Leetch is that he was born in Corpus Christi, Texas, not exactly a hockey hotbed. That was because his father Jack was stationed there as a navy pilot. Even as young as eighteen months old, when he was first learning to talk, Leetch imitated TV broadcasters. He shouted, "Score, Bobby Orr," or "Score, Esposito."

The family moved to Connecticut and dad took a job managing a skating rink. That's how Leetch got exposed to skating by age five. Leetch's dad was an All-American defenseman for Boston College and so was Leetch. By then Leetch had chosen his sporting path, ignoring opportunities in baseball that stemmed from a 90 mph fastball and the achievement of striking out 19 in a high school game.

Although he did finish his career with other teams, Leetch was the mainstay of the Rangers for so long the team retired his Number 2 jersey. The applause from fans on that occasion moved Leetch.

"I have felt this building shake," he said of Madison Square Garden, "starting in the blue seats and filling this arena."

Mark Messier

For all of the stars that the Rangers raised or acquired, the finishing touch for the roster was adding Mark Messier, the five-time Stanley Cup winner with Edmonton. Messier, one of the NHL's all-time greats who played for a quarter of a century, won the Hart Trophy as league MVP his first season in New York.

The shaved-head, 6-foot-1, 210-pound Messier was just showing the Rangers what it took to be a winner. He played 1,756 regular-season NHL games, scored 704 goals, won two

MVP awards, and was selected for 15 All-Star games. He was known as much for his leadership, the type of hockey player called a born captain.

What few people remember about the square-jawed Messier, who looked tough enough to fight for the heavyweight championship, is that as a teenager he actually played in the World Hockey Association with the Indianapolis Racers and the Cincinnati Stingers.

Messier was not quite thirty-one when the Rangers pried him loose from Edmonton. General manager Neil Smith said he didn't even believe obtaining Messier was attainable.

"To trade for a Mark Messier seemed like a fantasy when we first started talking in July," Smith said of the 1991 deal. "It took us a lot of slaps in the face for us to realize this could be true."

Messier made friends right away in New York.

"I'm starting my so-called second career," he said. "I have every confidence my second career will be every bit as good as the first."

Not quite, but playing a critical role in bringing a Stanley Cup to New York in 1994 made him a forever-hero in the city. Eventually, Messier, who was chosen for the Hall of Fame in 2007, had his Number 11 New York jersey retired. As tough a guy as Messier was on the ice, he cried the night officials shelved the number.

"It's something you can't describe unless you've actually lived in New York," he said of his affinity for the largest city in North America. "It becomes a part of who you are. I love New York. I love the area. I love, obviously, the team."

4

CHICAGO BLACKHAWKS

Founded: 1926
Home Arenas: Chicago Coliseum, 1926–29; Chicago Stadium, 1929–94; United Center, 1995–present
Stanley Cups: 1934, 1938, 1961, 2010, 2013, 2015

Beginnings

The founder of the Chicago Black Hawks (as it was spelled until 1985 when combined into one word) was actually a Boston gentleman named Huntington Chadwick, in the sense that he was awarded the expansion franchise in 1926.

Hardwick bought the Portland Rosebuds of the Western Hockey League for $100,000. But he flipped the franchise the way real estate moguls quickly turn around houses. Chadwick sold out to Frederic McLaughlin within a month and it was McLaughlin who actually gave the team its nickname.

McLaughlin was born in Chicago in 1877 and was a coffee magnate, running a business he inherited from his father after he graduated from Harvard. McLaughlin favored bow ties in his dress. His favorite sport as a youngster was polo.

One of McLaughlin's biggest achievements with the team was naming it. During World War I McLaughlin served in the 333rd Machine Gun Battalion of the 86th Infantry Division. The unit was called the Blackhawk Division after Sauk Native-American tribal chief Black Hawk. McLaughlin emerged from the service as a major and he regularly used that rank as a title for the rest of his life.

The Sauks were originally centered near the St. Lawrence River in upstate New York, but migrated westward to the current-day US Midwest because of tribal conflicts. Black Hawk lived between 1767 and 1838. He was a prominent warrior, although during the War of 1812 he fought with the British against the Americans. In a rarity for his time, Black Hawk participated in the writing of a book about his life. He died in Iowa, probably at the age of seventy.

The iconic Native American face and head symbol on the front of Blackhawks' jerseys honors the link between the hockey team and the chief. However, it was not created by McLaughlin, but by his actress wife, Irene Castle.

The original home arena of the Blackhawks was the Chicago Coliseum. The first Coliseum was built in 1866, but the hockey team played in the third one, constructed in 1899. The arena held 6,000 people and the Blackhawks played there until 1929 when the much larger (17,000 seats) Chicago Stadium opened.

McLaughlin was no sit-on-the-sidelines owner. He ran the team for 18 years and employed 13 coaches. This overlapped with the Great Depression, but job security for the Blackhawks was no more reliable than life on Wall Street when the stock market crashed.

During various stretches over the decades almost no Americans could be found suited up in the National Hockey League. Yet McLaughlin periodically ordered his coaches to obtain as many Americans as they could. One year the Blackhawks won the Stanley Cup with eight Americans on the team.

For sure McLaughlin could be a demanding boss. He fired his first coach Pete Muldoon after one year and although Muldoon's utterance did not compare to the impact of the Billy Goat Curse on the baseball Chicago Cubs, the departing coach said he put a curse on the team stating the Blackhawks would never finish in first place.

"Fire me, Major, and you'll never finish first. I'll put a curse on this team that will hoodoo it until the end of time," Muldoon said.

McLaughlin also had strained relations with some NHL owners, in particular James Norris in Detroit. Conn Smythe, the Toronto Maple Leafs honcho, once said of McLaughlin, "Where hockey was concerned Major McLaughlin was the strangest bird, and yes, perhaps the biggest nut I met in my entire life."

McLaughlin may have been hard to work with, but the Blackhawks won two Stanley Cups on his watch before he died in 1944. The 1934 and 1938 titles were the first two in franchise history.

Dismissing Muldoon was not the problem. Chicago finished 19–22–3 under his leadership, but the Blackhawks were truly horrible the next two years, going 7–34–3 and 7–29–8. Chicago's first winning season came in its fourth year of experience.

One of Chicago's first stars was Johnny Gottselig. He was born in Russia in 1905 although his family left that country for Canada when he was an infant. Gottselig stood 5-foot-11 and weighed less than 160 pounds, but notched 176 goals in 17 seasons between 1928 and 1945 with the Blackhawks.

Later in life he returned to the team and was a member of the front office in 1961 when the club earned its third Cup. Gottselig skated for both of the 1930s Cup winners and was captain of the second one.

Gottselig recalled some shenanigans that went on in 1932 when McLaughlin hired still another coach, Godfrey Matheson, to run the show. At the first practice Matheson went out on the ice in street clothes. Over his clothes he wore yellow elbow and knee pads.

"Not under his clothes," Gottselig said, "over them. He looked weird."

When it came time for shooting practice, Matheson, acknowledging how important a figure goalie Charlie Gardiner was, did not let the team fire pucks at him. Instead, he bought a dummy, dressed it in a hockey uniform, and placed it in goal.

During a practice Matheson was on his hands and knees on the ice tossing pucks right and left to skaters as if he was a pitching machine throwing batting practice. Frock Lowery, pretending he missed the puck, brought his stick down lightly on the back of the coach's neck. Or so he thought.

"He must have tapped him harder than he intended," Gottselig said, "because the guy was knocked out and had to be carried off on a stretcher. 'Carry on, men,' he says from the stretcher. 'Captain Wentworth will be in charge until I'm able to resume.'"

That was practically never. Matheson coached only two games for the Blackhawks.

In 1934 the Blackhawks bested the Montreal Canadiens, the Montreal Maroons, and the Detroit Red Wings to capture their first Cup.

Goalie Charlie Gardiner was the captain and Matheson was right about him being the most important Blackhawk. In the regular season Gardiner played every game in net and posted a 1.63 goals against average.

If Americans were rare in hockey, rarer still were players from overseas when Gardiner joined the Blackhawks in 1927. He was born in Edinburgh, Scotland, although he was a bit older than Gottselig when his family moved to Winnipeg in 1911. Gardiner did not learn to skate until he was eight and soon was pigeonholed as a goalie.

That turned into a fortuitous move. Gardiner was one of the greatest players of his time, a four-time All-Star and a two-time Vezina Trophy winner during his seven seasons with Chicago. Gardiner showed athleticism and gymnastic tendencies in net. Gardiner was a good all-around athlete, a standout at rugby, and a good baseball player.

He was better at hockey. Gardiner was so good in net he managed to excel even when the rest of the Blackhawks did not. During one of those horrendous losing seasons of the late 1920s Gardiner's goals against average was 1.85. Four times Gardiner recorded sub-2.00 averages.

During the Stanley Cup playoffs of 1934, when Chicago won it all for the first time, Gardiner surrendered 12 goals in eight games. Unimaginably, Gardiner would never play again. In the off-season he became ill and died at age twenty-nine.

Gardiner had been fighting off illness for quite some time and ended up with an infection in his tonsils. This nagging problem began in 1932 and by the end of the year Gardiner was seriously ill, although trying to shield his circumstances from the public. In a December 1932 game against the Toronto Maple Leafs, Gardiner made 55 saves and Chicago won, but the goalie was running a high fever and sprawled on the locker room floor to rest between periods. After the game he was taken to a hospital.

Even after the season ended the player was never cured, and in January 1934, Gardiner was discomforted by pains in his throat

The Montreal Hockey Club won the first Stanley Cup awarded in 1893. It was named for Lord Stanley of Preston—the Governor General of Canada.

The Stanley Cup went to the Ottawa Hockey Team in 1911, going back to the days before the National Hockey League was founded.

A brilliant net-minder for the Montreal Canadiens, Georges Vezina had the trophy for goal-tending excellence named after him.

Montreal Canadiens star Howie Morenz was one of the great early players in NHL history. Morenz died from complications that set in when he was in the hospital after suffering a broken leg in a game at the early age of thirty-four.

Montreal goalie Jacques Plante was one of the game's great innovators, introducing the mask to help protect goalies' faces.

Two of the great Canadiens stars of the Original Six era were Hall of Famers Maurice Richard (left) and Jean Beliveau (right), here shown together after they helped claim the 1958 Stanley Cup.

(Left to right) Eddie Shore, George Owen, and Lionel Hitchman worked together on a line for the Boston Bruins during the 1928–29 season.

One of the best net-minders in Boston Bruins history was Frankie Brimsek, who helped lead them to world championship status.

The famed Boston Arena, one-time home of the Bruins, which is still hosting college hockey games more than a hundred years after it opened in 1910.

The most famous photograph in the National Hockey League portrays the great Boston defenseman Bobby Orr scoring the Stanley-Cup winning goal over St. Louis at the Boston Garden in May 1970.

A group of New York Rangers pictured together as they prepared for the 1928 season. (top row, left to right) Billy Boyd, Butch Keeling, coach Lester Patrick, Ching Johnson, Myles Lane, Taffy Abel, and Paul Thompson. (bottom row, left to right) Trainer Harry Westerby, Murray Murdock, Frank Boucher, Bill Cook, John Ross, Leo Bourgault, and Bunny Cook.

A family affair of Rangers. (from left to right) Neil and Mac Colville, and Lester, Lynn, and Muzz Patrick.

Interior of Madison Square Garden at Night

Interior of Madison Square Garden at night

Bobby Hull was one of the greatest goal scorers in NHL history. When Hull broke in with the Chicago Blackhawks in 1957, he looked even younger than his eighteen years.

Until the 2000s, the Chicago Blackhawks did not take home many Stanley Cups. On this occasion in 1938, Bill Stewart received the Cup. Shaking Stewart's hand was Chicago Cubs manager Gabby Hartnett.

Inside the Chicago Coliseum, between 1910 and 1915.

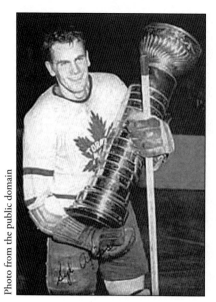

Toronto Maple Leafs star Syl Apps.

(left to right) Maple Leafs players Vic Lynn (the only man to play for all Original Six teams), Gus Morrison, Ted Kennedy, and Bud Poile in their dressing room during the 1946–47 season.

Toronto goalie Turk Broda makes the save off New York's Tony Leswick in a 1950 game as New York forward Edgar Lapgrade went after the punk.

Red Wings hero Gordie Howe, who died in 2016 at age eighty-eight, is often called the greatest hockey player of all time.

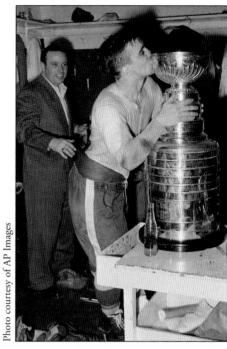

Winning a championship is special, and Detroit's Ted Lindsay demonstrates his joy by kissing the Stanley Cup. (The other man pictured was unidentified).

Coach Jack Adams hugs Johnny Sorrell (left) and Scotty Bowman after Detroit won its first league title in 1936.

This was the appearance of the first Stanley Cup from 1893, which some said resembled a silver salad bowl. This original Cup now rests on the top of the much taller Cup that is familiar to modern hockey fans.

A reproduction of a studio photograph of the Stanley Cup that was presented to the Ottawa Senators in 1921.

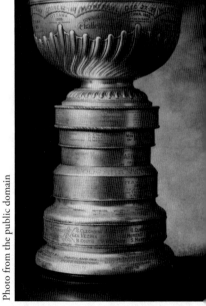

The Stanley Cup as it looked in 1930.

and kidneys. Occasionally, Gardiner had vision problems. He experienced a uremic convulsion.

After that season, Gardiner returned home to Winnipeg, but his health only deteriorated and he passed away on June 13 of that year. That was only a short time after the Blackhawks won the Cup in a 1–0 overtime game over the Red Wings.

Tommy Gorman, the coach of the Blackhawks' Stanley Cup winners, called Gardiner "one of the most colorful figures that ice hockey has ever produced. Chuck Gardiner was taken away at the peak of his hockey career. Never in the history of hockey has a better exhibition of goalkeeping been given than that which 'Gardiner the Great' put up against Detroit in that championship final."

Gorman continued to laud Gardiner. "Gardiner was a born showman," Gorman said. "Every move was a picture. He made bad games look good. Dull matches he transformed into fascinating ones."

The 1937–38 Blackhawks may be the worst team to win a Stanley Cup. They had no business being in the playoffs, never mind winning playoff series. It was a season that made no sense.

Under another new coach, Bill Stewart, the Blackhawks finished 14–25–9 during the regular season. They didn't even have a winning record at home. Somehow Chicago managed to eke out a spot in the playoffs two points ahead of Detroit. The Blackhawks scored just 97 goals all season, the lowest number of any team. They also gave up 139 goals, second-most of any team.

Losing netminder Gardiner was a blow Chicago found difficult to recover from, and the 1938 starter, Mike Karakas, played every game. Teams averaged 2.80 goals against him, which wasn't bad considering his limited support.

In the playoffs the Hawks outlasted the Canadiens and New York Americans in tight series to advance to face the Maple Leafs. Things got worse, however. The Blackhawks were without an injured Karakas, who had a broken toe. Chicago tried to get minor leaguer Paul Goodman to Toronto on time, but travel snafus intervened.

Instead they used another minor leaguer, Alfie Moore, in the first game and won. Moore wasn't even in the arena when he was proposed as a fill-in. The Maple Leafs had to okay his appearance because he wasn't on any team roster. Gottselig found Moore in a bar.

"He'd had about ten or a dozen drinks," Gottselig said. "We put some coffee into him and put him under the shower. By game time he was in pretty good shape."

Moore gave up one goal in 60 minutes to give the Blackhawks the series lead. Chicago won 3–1; players carried Moore off the ice on their shoulders. Even Toronto fans cheered "The Goalie From Nowhere." Despite a long minor-league career, Moore played in just 20 NHL regular-season games between 1926 and 1942.

Toronto's Conn Smythe refused permission to use Moore again because Goodman, who was affiliated with the team, showed up in town. Smythe was angry about losing to Moore, a "hung-over, minor-league goalie." In Game 2 the Blackhawks used Goodman and lost. Karakas returned after that. Still, the Blackhawks won the Cup in four games.

Not even Chicago players expected to win that title. Before the Finals began defenseman Roger Jenkins made a bet with Karakas. If the Blackhawks won the Cup, Jenkins said, "I'll push you down State Street in a wheelbarrow." Many witnesses turned out when Jenkins paid off in downtown Chicago.

The grateful Blackhawks did not overlook Moore, either. They rewarded him with a gold watch and $300.

The Wirtz Family

Arthur Wirtz, born in 1901, was involved in the National Hockey League from 1929 until his death in 1983, first with the Detroit Red Wings and then as owner of the Chicago Blackhawks.

The team has been in the family since 1954. William Wirtz succeeded his father as owner and when Bill died in 2007 son Peter briefly ran the team before turning the reins over to brother Rocky. Rocky is the current face of the franchise and under his control the Hawks have won three Stanley Cups in the 2000s.

Arthur Wirtz and partner James Norris did originally covet the Blackhawks, but Major McLaughlin had a hold on the club in 1931. After McLaughlin died in 1944, Wirtz was approached about buying the Chicago team, but he was ingrained with Detroit and couldn't extricate himself right away. It was not until after Norris died that Wirtz pulled away from Detroit and bought the Blackhawks.

At various times the Wirtz family has owned the Chicago Bulls basketball team, the Ice Follies skating show, Chicago Stadium, large amounts of Chicago real estate, a liquor and beverage company, and co-owned the United Center.

Arthur Wirtz once sailed a yacht across the Atlantic Ocean to Holland, and when asked by a sportswriter about the safety of such a journey replied, "The new yacht is 10 feet longer than the *Santa Maria* was and Columbus didn't have a telephone."

The Blackhawks won one Stanley Cup, in 1961, under Arthur Wirtz's tutelage, and he was inducted into the Hall of Fame in 1971.

Bill Wirtz was president of the Blackhawks for forty-one years and succeeded his father as chief of the team as well as head of the family businesses. The younger Wirtz had a reputation for generosity in the community, but not with his team.

This Wirtz was viewed as tightfisted, blamed for superstar Bobby Hull departing for the World Hockey Association, and in latter years refusing to put Blackhawks games on television. By the 2000s Chicago had gone forty-six years of his life without a Stanley Cup triumph. He was elected to the Hockey Hall of Fame anyway, but upon his death, Bill Wirtz's son Rocky immediately revamped the team, front office, roster, and television policies and promptly built a champion.

Rocky Wirtz shook up the team and restored strained relations with former stars Hull and Stan Mikita with a special night in 2008. Wirtz downplayed the use of an organ during games in favor of songs appealing to a younger audience and "Chelsea Dagger" by the rock group the Fratellis became a team anthem.

Attendance, which had fallen drastically, perked up swiftly, and Blackhawk games were once again automatic sellouts.

"Rocky has done an amazing thing here in Chicago," said coach Joel Quenneville even before the team won a Cup.

In 2010 Chicago won its first Stanley Cup in forty-nine years. Rocky Wirtz teams were perpetual contenders and added two more Cup victories within five years. His efforts completely revived the status of the Blackhawks in the community.

When the Blackhawks celebrated the third Cup after beating the Tampa Bay Lightning, Rocky Wirtz spoke at the rally.

"Did anyone notice we had a little bit of rain Monday night?" Wirtz said. "I didn't see any lightning."

The Bentley Brothers Shine

Between 1939 and 1958, the two-time Stanley Cup–winning Chicago Blackhawks missed out on the playoffs in 14 seasons out of 20. Only once, in 1944, did the Blackhawks reach the Finals, losing in four straight games to the Montreal Canadiens.

None of that was Max Bentley's fault.

Bentley played organized hockey from 1937 to 1962, from 1940 to 1954 with the Blackhawks, Toronto Maple Leafs, and New York Rangers. He was pretty good for everybody, but very good for the Hawks. Some seasons in Chicago produced goal-scoring totals of 31, 29, and 26, the three highest totals of his NHL career.

Those seasons helped propel Bentley, who grew up on a farm in Delisle, Saskatchewan, into the Hall of Fame in 1966.

The 5-foot-9, 158-pound Bentley was not very big, but he was quick and he had a knack for finding the net. When Bentley tried out for the Boston Bruins they cut him with the admonition he wasn't big enough to play in the NHL. When he tried out for the Canadiens the team doctor told him he had a heart condition and that he must retire or die within a year.

Bentley kept playing hockey at lower levels, but concerned about the medical diagnosis, took multiple kinds of medication. Teammates teased him for being a walking drugstore, and he worried excessively about any type of minor ache or pain.

In the meantime, Bentley's older brother Doug hooked on with the Blackhawks in 1939 and put in a plug for Max.

"I have a kid brother at home who's twice as good as I am," Doug Bentley said. "You should give him a chance." Doug Bentley played 13 seasons and scored as many as 38 goals in one year for the Hawks, so even if the message was hyperbole, the Hawks thought they should check it out.

Doug was even smaller than Max at 5-foot-8 and 145 pounds, but Chicago listened, scouted Max, and signed him. That was despite him looking sickly and pale. In fact, co-owner Bill Tobin said, "He's the first walking ghost I have ever seen."

The one time Max became really discouraged is when he was sent to a Blackhawks affiliate in Kansas City for seasoning. His first reaction? "I won't go. I'll quit hockey and return to Delisle."

Coaching KC was old Blackhawk star Johnny Gottselig and he talked Max out of premature retirement.

"You come down here, Max and I'll look after you like a father," Gottselig said. "You can live with me and use my car. I'll make sure you're never lonely. Take my advice, Max, you're going to be a hockey star and I can help you."

Bentley scored 11 points in a week and was on his way back to Chicago because of Blackhawks injuries.

Max scored his first goal in his first game in 1940 and a couple of seasons later scored 70 points and a couple after that he scored 72. Bentley became so good eventually the Maple Leafs traded five players for him, although Chicago threw in another guy.

The 72-point season was in 1946–47. Max Bentley was tied with the great Maurice "Rocket" Richard at 71 points. The Canadiens were done. Bentley had a game to play against the Rangers.

Bentley put the puck past netminder Charlie Rayner after being set up on a pass from Bill Mosienko. Score! And scoring title.

Doug, too, won a scoring title, in 1943, and he too was on his way to a Hall of Fame career. He once had four assists in one period. Max scored 245 goals and Doug 219. They ended up together again with the Rangers in the early 1950s.

Max's trademark was speed and stick-handling and he gained the nickname "The Dipsy-Doodle Dandy From Delisle."

"Max was one of the very few players who could make a fantastic play while still going at high speed," said Boston's Milt Schmidt.

At times Max Bentley's wrist action on his shot was attributed to strength built as a youngster milking cows back home on the farm. That was one theory, at least.

After Doug Bentley's recommendation of Max proved out, Max was asked by an NHL coach if there were any more prospects back in Saskatchewan. He said, "It's just too bad all our seven sisters are married and settled, for they too were pretty good hockey players."

For a time Max and Doug Bentley played on the same line as Bill Mosienko, called "The Pony Line." This was the Blackhawks' best-scoring trio. Mosienko was from Winnipeg and he too was selected for the Hall of Fame.

During the 1943–44 season Mosienko scored 32 goals and collected 70 points. His greatest claim to fame is an achievement that has held up as an NHL record for more than 60 years. In a March 23, 1952 game against the Rangers Mosienko scored three goals in 21 seconds, record speed for a hat trick.

At 5-foot-8 and 160 pounds Mosienko was another small guy, and despite all of his other accomplishments the number-one thing hockey fans recalled about him was the swift hat trick. In retirement Mosienko owned a bowling alley and said the record was constantly mentioned.

"All these years have gone by and people still come up to me on the street and at the lanes wanting to know about it," Mosienko said thirty-one years after the super-speed goals. "Of course, I'm so involved with the public every day of the week. Even some of the ladies who bowl here mention it and they don't really know much about hockey today or thirty years ago. I hope it's one record that stays in the book."

Another thirty years later it is still in the book, although Mosienko passed away at seventy-two in 1994.

Max Bentley was such a slick skater and puck handler that years after his retirement when someone else came along of supreme talent it was sometimes said among old-timers that he reminded them of the young Bentley. Wayne Gretzky, the greatest scorer in hockey history, was one such player. Famed and prolific hockey writer Stan Fischler said Bentley was his favorite player of all.

Fischler interviewed Bentley five days before he died at age sixty-three in January 1984. His heart lasted much longer than that Montreal doctor predicted.

"To be compared with Wayne Gretzky is a tremendous honor," Bentley said. "I did play like him. I carried the puck a lot. My idea was to try to set up somebody. I'd beat two or three guys and then make a pass."

The biggest scoring star in the game during Bentley's time was Maurice Richard and he definitely respected the Rocket.

"He scared me," Bentley said. "He wanted you to keep backing up and when he was at point-blank range he would let it go."

Once, after Bentley had been swapped to Toronto, he was in a tight game with the Maple Leafs in dire need of a goal. An inspirational pitch came from an unusual source. A rich local fan beckoned to Bentley from the lower seats. This wealthy man was involved in horse racing.

"Get me a goal and I'll give you a race horse," he told Bentley.

Bentley skated back into the action and scored.

Eric Nesterenko

It only seemed like Eric Nesterenko played in the National Hockey League forever. But people who think he only played for the Chicago Blackhawks were late to the party. Nesterenko broke in with the

Toronto Maple Leafs in 1951 and did not retire until 1974 after 21 NHL seasons and one World Hockey Association season thrown in.

Nesterenko, born in Flin Flon, Manitoba in 1933 of Ukrainian extraction, stood 6-foot-2 and weighed nearly 200 pounds. He spent from 1956 through 1972 with the Blackhawks. As a hard-checking forward, Nesterenko played in 1,219 NHL games and scored 250 goals. He reached at least 10 goals in a season 15 times, including his time in Toronto. Once only, during the 1957–58 season, Nesterenko hit the 20-goal mark.

There was a reason why Nesterenko's nickname was "Elbows." Opponents knew what to expect when they skated into the corners. Not only was Nesterenko tough on foes, his two decades in the NHL were at times tough on him. Doing battle with the other guys resulted in more than 600 stitches. He also had to overcome battles with drugs and alcohol. His other nickname was "The Flin Flon Flash" and occasionally he was referred to as "Eric the Great." That gave Nesterenko a hat trick of nicknames.

Nesterensko excelled as a penalty killer.

"I can't say enough good things about him," coach Billy Reay said. "What Nesterenko does will not show up in the scoring column, but he's just as important to this hockey club as a goal-scorer. He's a tremendous defensive player. You can pit him against anybody in the league."

What few knew about Nesterenko was that he was a sharp, articulate, and sensitive man who aspired to go to college and major in English. Nesterenko may well have become a college hockey player, but turned down a scholarship to the University of Michigan to accept an NHL offer.

Nesterenko had a falling out with the Maple Leafs, feeling they restricted his game. When Toronto traded him to Chicago

Nesterenko had already enrolled in the University of Toronto. Somehow he figured out how to play hockey full-time and go to college.

When Nesterenko and the Blackhawks reached a contract impasse once, he showed up at the training camp of the Toronto Argonauts Canadian Football League team. Nesterensko was even offered a contract, but the Hawks feared they would lose him, so they upped their salary offer and he stayed with the NHL.

Among other careers Nesterenko tried later in life was disc jockey, teaching at a hockey school, and freelance writer. His mind was always working. That thirst for knowledge may have been inherited from his father, who was fluent in six languages.

He also saw a difference between illegal violence on ice and violence in the context of the hockey and other sports.

"Ballet doesn't come close to the grace and elegance of violence as it is played within the rules—remember I said, the rules—of sports," Nesterenko said in 1979. "Believe me, it is beautiful and that's the art of it. But today, at least in hockey, it's a gang fight."

When he was forty-five Nesterenko acted in a Canadian Broadcasting Corporation series and called sports, "the theatre of the common man." Nesterensko also had a part in the 1986 hockey movie *Youngblood*. For those who wonder, he played Rob Lowe's father.

At the time Nesterenko was working on a ski patrol and as caretaker of a lodge in Colorado. That was after a stint coaching in Switzerland right after he hung up his skates. Consistent with his love of skiing, Nesterenko said that was a lure.

"They must have twenty ski resorts within an hour of where I'll be working," he said, "and I've made sure they'll let me do plenty of that."

At the time Nesterenko was also offered the coaching job with the Chicago Cougars of the WHA. He spent a year in Lausanne, Switzerland, and then suited up for the Cougars in 29 games at age forty.

Truthfully, Nesterenko's job in Colorado came with its share of life-and-death adventure.

"We did mountain rescue work," he said of his Colorado experiences, "brought injured people down the slopes and worked at avalanche control. I hope to go on skiing the rest of my life."

Nesterenko said when he retired from hockey he was pretty much at loose ends. It was a midlife crisis and skiing filled the void. Nesterenko was tired of the spotlight and the big-time hockey world. He felt he had grown as a person and the game had not really advanced.

"I was burned out with hockey, mentally and emotionally," he said. "The NHL game seemed for little boys. The trend appeared to be towards violence, head-hunting. The elegance, flow and continuity were fading. I was on a downer towards competitive sports. I liked the idea that you could ski and not have to beat anybody."

Nesterenko's comparison of the NHL to a little boys' game was not quite apt. Perhaps immaturity was a better description because the little boy in Nesterenko never died when it came to hockey. When he was with Toronto Nesterenko sometimes went out by himself and skated on a local pond.

A couple of decades later Nesterenko was driving on a highway near Chicago and spied an outdoor rink. Nobody was skating because it was intensely cold and windy. Nesterenko drove up to the rink—he just happened to have a pair of skates in the trunk of his car—and spent 45 minutes alone on the ice.

"It was like when I was a kid in Flin Flon," he said. "Nobody was there and all I could hear was the wind. In Flin Flon back then the lakes would often freeze by early October. The snow wouldn't come till much later so you could skate for miles. I was free. You know?"

Practically every Canadian youngster knows the joys of outdoor skating and pond hockey.

As for Nesterenko, the people who made those beer commercials featuring a character called "The Most Interesting Man in the World" should have hired him.

Stan Mikita

In many ways Stan Mikita is viewed as "Mr. Blackhawk," playing for the franchise from 1958 to 1980. He was a key member of the 1961 Stanley Cup champions, played 1,394 games with Chicago, and scored 541 goals with 924 assists for 1,467 points.

An eight-time All-Star, Mikita led the NHL in scoring four times and during the 1966–67 and 1967–68 seasons he consecutively won the Hart Trophy as Most Valuable Player, the Art Ross Trophy as leading scorer, and the Lady Byng Trophy as the most sportsmanlike player. One of his nicknames was "Stosh."

Mikita had been a rougher player when he was younger despite his 5-foot-9, 169-pound frame, but decided to clean up his game after his wife told him his young daughter watching on TV asked why he was sitting down (in the penalty box) so much during a game.

The remake was dramatic. One year Mikita totaled 154 penalty minutes and two years later he totaled 12.

"I found out I couldn't fight," Mikita said. Of his daughter's comment, he said, "That kind of got through to me."

Born in the Slovak Republic in 1940 during World War II, Mikita's name at birth was Stanislav Guoth. Czechoslovakia was under Communist rule and as troops belonging to Nazi Germany rampaged across Europe, the boy's parents decided to send him to Canada to live with an aunt and uncle for safety. He was eight years old at the time. When he moved to Canada he became Mikita.

Mikita learned to skate in the neighborhood from other kids who were pretty much born on blades.

"I was a street kid and a rink rat," Mikita said of how he ended up as such a hard-nosed player at first. "There was a language difference and being taunted and ridiculed shaped my personality. I thought I had to fight the world and, in a sense, had something to prove."

He quickly developed into a superior hockey player. Mikita gained stature in the 1950s as the Blackhawks improved from an always-miss-the-playoffs team into a Stanley Cup contender.

One of the top lines of the period was "The Scooter Line." It featured Mikita at center with Kenny Wharram at right wing and first Ab McDonald and then Doug Mohns at left wing. That high-scoring trio was a critical complement to the production that came from the flamboyant, devastating goal-scorer Bobby Hull.

Mikita never resented the "Golden Jet" image and his garnering of bigger headlines.

"It was all fair," Mikita said. "Look, I played hard and got the job done. But I didn't lift fans out of their seats doing it and the other guy did."

Mikita was a fair goal-scorer himself, notching 40 one year and topping 30 in a season eight other times. He collected as many as 67 assists in one season, although interestingly not in one of the four years he led the league in scoring. It was Mikita's playmaking as much as any other skill that players admired.

Fascinatingly, Mikita and Hull pioneered the use of curved sticks, a utensil so effective that the National Hockey League had to regulate the number of inches the blade could curve. However, this was not an intentional adjustment. Mikita discovered the advantage of the curved stick—more oomph behind the shot—by accident.

The precipitating event occurred during the 1960–61 season. In the middle of a practice, Mikita's stick cracked, but did not break all of the way through. He kept using it and realized each time he took a shot the puck took a jump. Hull also noticed this development. They had a discussion after the practice and thought to purposely curve sticks.

Since nobody was manufacturing them at the time, Hull and Mikita had to make their own as if undertaking a high school science project. To make what became nicknamed "the banana blade" they placed sticks under a door and gradually bent them. As Hull and Mikita, already dominant players, scored even more, others watched with dismay. It took most of a decade, but the NHL stepped in for the 1967–68 season and ruled that a stick could not be curved by more than one-and-a-half inches. In 1970 the limit was reduced to one inch.

Hull said, "I've been trying different sticks and haven't found one I like yet. I also can't adjust to shooting the puck." Mikita said, "I'm used to shooting that curve and I can't seem to find the right lie with a straighter stick."

Mikita became such a solid citizen after coming to Canada without any knowledge of English that in 1973 he was honored with an honorary doctor of laws degree from Brock University in

St. Catherines, Ontario. And yes, Mikita did wear a gown and a mortarboard for the ceremony.

"It's like winning the Stanley Cup or the scoring championship," Mikita said. "I can't tell you how much I appreciate it since the honor came from the city where I grew up. It's always nice to know you're not forgotten."

When Mikita was rewarded, the university commented that he was "a man devoted to his art. Mr. Mikita has been an exemplary hero, the team leader, a role model for young people to admire, to meet, and we hope, to emulate."

Ironically, Joe Mikita, Stan's uncle-adoptive parent, worked in construction, and helped build the first structure on the campus.

One of the most controversial developments in Blackhawks history occurred when Bobby Hull jumped to the World Hockey Association for a huge raise. Hull made the new league's legitimacy. Mikita, too, had an offer in 1972.

"I decided to stay in the NHL," Mikita said. "At my age it's a little risky to change. Besides, the National Hockey League has a pretty good track record for more than fifty years, while a good many of the WHA clubs seem to be having trouble."

When Mikita scored the 500th goal of his career, in his 18th season, he was the eighth player in NHL history to do so. He collected it in the third period of a 4–3 loss to Vancouver, but at least it came in Chicago and the fans roared.

"It was a thrill and a relief," Mikita said after going goalless for two games. "What an ovation. I've been calm outwardly, but cranky inside. Instead of yelling at my wife and kids I decided to come down early and take a nap. Instead, I watched golf on television."

When Mikita missed considerable time with the Blackhawks due to injury one season Philadelphia Flyers coach Fred Shero said it wasn't the real Chicago team on the ice "because the brains of the operation is missing." Mikita laughed at that suggestion, saying he had more guts than brains "or I'd have gotten out of this sport a long time ago. I just hate to go."

Mikita often made fun of himself that way.

"I should have stayed in school and become a brain surgeon," Mikita once joked about his aches and pains. "It would have been easier."

When Mikita retired in 1980, his back finally doing him in, he was third in NHL scoring and third in playoff points. Praise came from many quarters.

"To me Stan Mikita is the greatest player to ever wear a Blackhawks uniform," said team owner William Wirtz, who promptly announced that the team was going to retire Mikita's Number 21 jersey.

Mikita moved into the Blackhawks' broadcast booth as a color commentator, but made fun of himself in that role, saying, "Putting me on TV is like putting earrings on a pig." Known for playing jokes within the team, Mikita appeared in the movie *Wayne's World* and was the key character in a children's book.

Mikita was inducted into the Hall of Fame in 1983, and after a period of estrangement from the Blackhawks, the new regime in 2006 wooed him back into the fold. Mikita became a team ambassador to the community.

That came to an end as Mikita turned seventy-five. In January 2015 it became known that Mikita was suffering from a progressive form of dementia and could no longer remember his playing days.

Bobby Hull

Before the National Hockey League became the province of super luminaries who played in the television age, Bobby Hull was a legend.

When he arrived in Chicago for the 1957–58 season Hull was the possessor of a slap shot so powerful it seemed likely he might break the boards at Chicago Stadium. Hull reached exalted status in the NHL when he broke Maurice "Rocket" Richard's and Boom Boom Geoffrion's record of 50 goals in a season.

Hull received an eight-minute standing ovation when he collected the 51st during the 1965–66 season. The applause and adulation was so loud and long, Hull said he was embarrassed by it.

"I wanted it to stop," he said surprisingly. "I wanted to crawl into the boards."

The next year he scored 52. A few years later he scored 58. After he jumped to the Winnipeg Jets of the World Hockey Association he scored 77 goals in one year. Hull was a goal-scoring machine. He loved that part of the game, being the man who put the puck in the net so often.

"Hell, I just enjoy scoring goals," Hull said. "That's what I play hockey for—to score, the kick I get out of scoring goals. If I set records, fine. But the goals themselves, they give me all the satisfaction I need. Yeah, well there is pressure, of course, but hell, anything that is worthwhile doing, it has its bad things, its problems."

Coach Billy Reay was one of Hull's champions, touting his star's talents. He once compared him to both Richard and Gordie Howe.

"Bobby is a combination of both Richard and Howe," Reay said. "He has the explosive potential and the strength and durability of Howe. He can skate better and faster than either one and he shoots harder."

If Hull was going to leave Chicago at all—and most fans believed management should give him any amount of money to stay—it was appropriate he transfer to a team named the Jets since his nickname was "The Golden Jet." The combination of Hull's blond hair and his furious up-ice rushes bestowed the moniker on him.

Hull, born in Ontario in 1939, played big-time hockey from 1957 to 1980, and although it was not part of his Original Six legacy, his switch to the WHA in 1972 added the kind of credibility to that upstart hockey league as Joe Namath's signing with the New York Jets did for the American Football League.

Standing 5-foot-11, Hull was no frail flower who needed protecting by his defense. Even though he weighed slightly less than 200 pounds he was a rugged player, a man of great strength, as well as skating speed. He had a knack for making the great play and the big goal, with style. Newspapers began mentioning that Hull's slap shot traveled at 119 mph.

"I don't know where they got that," he said, "because I know that no one ever measured it. But if they say a pitcher's fastball goes at a hundred miles an hour, then I'm sure the puck goes at least 119 mph because when I shoot a puck from 60 feet it gets to the cage faster than any pitcher's fastball."

Just how fast was fast for Hull was open to interpretation since there was no accurate way to measure the speed of his shot. But teammate Glenn Hall, one of the greatest goalies of all time, certainly faced that shot in practice innumerable times and claimed Hull's shot was "the hardest ever in hockey."

How much muscle did Hull pack on his frame? Once, a tailor made some sports jackets for Hull. He forgot to measure his forearms when fitting him and when they came back, Hull couldn't get his arms into the sleeves because his biceps were too large.

"He was built like Popeye," the man said.

As gifted as Hull was, he had an innate work ethic that permeated his life, even away from the ice. Yes, he worked hard at hockey, but he worked hard at everything he did. He couldn't relax on vacations, once cutting a Hawaiian trip short by more than half because he couldn't stand lying around doing nothing. When he had a hockey day off, Hull, who lived on a ranch raising cattle, was up early to look over the beasts.

Hull wore Number 9 during his career with the Blackhawks to pay tribute to his most admired hockey player, Gordie Howe. The irony of that was that the two men often battled for league supremacy as the best player in the NHL. In the end, Howe outdid Hull in points and longevity, but Hull had bigger goal-scoring seasons than his idol.

When general manager Tommy Ivan signed Hull to his first contract in 1957 he compared the teenager to Howe.

"When I think of Hull, I think of Gordie Howe," Ivan said in a bold statement for a then-untried player.

Bobby scored 610 goals in 1,063 NHL games, all for Chicago. Then he added another 303 goals in 411 games with the WHA. He was a key player on the 1961 Blackhawks Cup championship team, but he was also on three AVCO Cup champions with the Jets. Hull was a 12-time NHL All-Star and a five-time WHA All-Star. In the NHL he won three scoring titles and two Most Valuable Player awards.

Hull was eighteen as a rookie, but stayed around long enough to lose those curly golden locks and play nearly bald. He was handsome enough to obtain endorsement opportunities that had him posing for all sorts of merchandise, from dandruff prevention medication to bathing suits to automobiles. Some of those modeling deals dropped off a little when he repeatedly had his nose broken. Hull proved adaptable. After he began losing his hair he endorsed a company that opened hair salons around Canada called "Plus Hair."

"I'm not sensitive about losing my hair," Hull said. "At least, I don't think I am. If you ask whether I'd prefer to have my hair back, there's no doubt what the answer would be, but I don't sit around worrying because it's getting thin."

Sure enough, though, Hull did have a hair transplant.

"What man in his right mind wouldn't rather have hair instead of a cueball?" he asked. (Michael Jordan was more than a decade away from making the scene in Chicago).

For many years Hull was the most dangerous man alive with the puck on his stick, the skater most likely to make a goalie's knees shake as he approached and fired a shot that broke the sound barrier. Hull was voted the NHL's best player of the 1960s by the Associated Press.

Early on he carried the Hawks and sometimes had two full-time shadows from opposing teams on him. He hated that and needed every bit of muscle he possessed to fend off the strong men that constantly sought to ride him out of the play. He did not make friends with those foes.

"The less said of some of them, the better," Hull said as he neared the end of his NHL tenure.

Tommy Ivan, the Hawks general manager, eventually began complaining out loud to the league office and to the newspapers about how defenders illegally abused Hull.

"The referees don't call a quarter of the penalties they should against the players trying to check him," Ivan said. There was some gamesmanship involved, naturally, but there was truth in Ivan's lament. "He's hooked and held and tripped more than any man in the league because he's as great as he is and the refs ignore what these guys do to him. Holding is holding and hooking is hooking, no matter whether the man being hooked or held is Bill Smith, Tom Jones, or Bobby Hull."

One thing Hull revealed to a magazine writer was that he sweated almost as much before a game getting ready, from the adrenaline flowing, as during a game. He kept a towel close at hand in the locker room to wipe down his chest before putting on the Blackhawks jersey.

Gradually, as the Blackhawks improved, they displayed a more diversified offense. Hull's scoring totals dropped, but the team win totals rose, and so did his assist totals.

"Let's just say it's now a twenty-man operation and I'm not getting as many hurts," Hull said.

One reason Hull was so popular in Chicago beyond his superb on-ice performance was the way he interacted with fans and sportswriters.

"If people think enough of me to want to shake my hand or talk to me or interview me, then time must be made for it," Hull said. "I sure am a lucky lad, aren't I?"

That was why Chicago fans were so horrified when Blackhawks management could not come to terms with Hull on a salary at a time when the WHA was knocking on the door. Hull was frustrated by his Blackhawks dealings. He was the biggest star in the league and one of a few who could put bodies in the seats. WHA officials reached out and Hull told them he would only play if they gave him a million dollars. To the shock of Hull the WHA did just that.

Hull was given a $1 million signing bonus from the league itself with all teams chipping in and about $2 million more spread over ten years.

At the time Hull was making about $60,000 a year from the Hawks. By then Hull was cynical about being underpaid and the hardness of the Blackhawks' negotiating stance bothered him. Hull, who already had one holdout on his résumé, called Tommy Ivan and coach Billy Reay "puppets" of William Wirtz.

There were often rumors that Hull and Stan Mikita, the two biggest stars on the team, were on the outs. But that was not true. It was true that at times Hull was such a big star there were gaps between his status and the rest of the players. Some may call it jealousy. Others said Hull took advantage to go his own way too often.

Nonetheless, Hull departed and it was always regretted in the city where he made his name. It was not for decades that there was a true rapprochement between the greatest star in team history and the team.

Nearly forty years later Hull was asked what he would tell the thirty-three-year-old who left the Blackhawks.

The team, he said, "backed me into a corner. They never offered me a contract while they were off floating around in their 110-foot ship in the Caribbean. They didn't seem like my fifteen years of blood, sweat, and tears for them made any difference."

Hull had a lot of hockey left in him. Hull began his career during the Original Six era, played during the NHL expansion era, and wrapped it up when there were two professional leagues going, all over a span of 23 seasons. He was forty-one when he retired after breaking in at eighteen.

"I've really never, ever had a job," Hull said. "I played hockey."

Dennis Hull

When your older brother is the most flamboyant star in the National Hockey League, it's not going to be easy to stand out on your own merits.

Dennis Hull was forever overshadowed by Bobby Hull, but was still a fine player who made major contributions to the Blackhawks in an NHL career that spanned 1964 to 1978, although his last season was with Detroit. Dennis and Bobby were teammates in Chicago for eight years.

Dennis scored 303 goals in 959 games and in one year scored as many as 40 while also topping 30 three other times. Little brother, who was actually the same size as big brother at 5-foot-11 and 198 pounds, made one All-Star team. Dennis, about five years younger, was durable, leading the league in games played three times.

Overall, Dennis Hull had a first-class career, but said he was never really appreciated by Chicago fans for who he was as an individual.

"When Bobby left Chicago and went to Winnipeg a lot of the fans here thought I should have gone and Bobby stay," Dennis said. "The fans never really accepted me in Chicago. In other cities like Toronto, Montreal, Boston, and Buffalo where they knew their hockey I wasn't given a rough time. They knew I wasn't Bobby Hull, that I was Dennis and we just happened to be brothers. But in Chicago it was different. Bobby was an established star when I got there and maybe they thought I'd be as good or better. I got used to the booing, though."

As a young player Dennis came into the NHL when the Original Six days still prevailed. It was an achievement just to earn a job.

He ended up playing 14 seasons in Chicago without receiving the love his sibling got.

"I had to decide early in my career that this was the way the people were going to be and there was nothing I could do about it," Dennis Hull said. He called the earliest years in Chicago the best, "especially when there were only six teams. The hockey was better and maybe I was better, too."

Dennis said he never harbored jealousy toward Bobby and Bobby was always upset if Dennis was mistreated by the fans.

"Sometimes when they booed me he probably felt it more than I did," Dennis said. "But he couldn't stop being a superstar just because I was his brother any more than I expected to be a carbon copy of him."

Dennis said he could have gone to the WHA, but preferred sticking with the Blackhawks. He was good enough to be selected for the Canadian team for the first Canada-Russia series of 1972 and scored a goal. Unlike Bobby, Dennis never got his name etched on the Stanley Cup. Three times the Blackhawks reached the Finals while he was playing, but lost to Montreal every time.

Despite his reputation, Bobby Hull said fans wrongly claimed he had the hardest shot in hockey. It was Dennis, he insisted.

"It is true that the guy who has the hardest shot is a member of this club [Chicago]," Bobby Hull said. "His name is Hull, but everybody picks the wrong one."

In a fascinating occurrence, a group of blind children, fans through the radio, attended a Blackhawks practice and then were asked for their impressions. Based on the sound of the two Hulls' shots, they chose Dennis's as harder.

"He gets his power from his timing and from the great strength in his legs," Bobby said. "Dennis has a great set of pins."

Dennis Hull said Stan Mikita's playmaking and ability to draw the defense to him helped make him a better goal-scorer. Earlier in his career he had a champion in coach Billy Reay, who spied his potential but realized there was going to be some on-the-job training. For a time Reay only put the younger Hull into games when the Blackhawks had large leads.

The first time Dennis got a true chance to shine, in a close game against the Red Wings, he ran up against Gordie Howe. Everyone always knew Howe was a fantastic hockey player, but the average fan did not always recognize just how strong he was. Dennis recalled rushing to the net and suddenly being lifted off the ice by Howe with a hand grabbing him by the back of his hockey pants.

Howe said, "Just where do you think you're going, son?" Dennis replied, "Anywhere you are."

The Hulls' dad, or as he was known in the family, the real Bobby Hull, fathered eleven children and was a sharp wit. Once, after returning to Ontario he was walking down the street when a citizen asked, "What's the latest dope in Chicago, Bob?" Hull said, "My youngest son."

Another time, much later, after Bobby and Dennis were retired, they returned home for the first large-scale family reunion with all eleven siblings in many years. Everyone greeted them on their parents' lawn except for dad. The hockey players searched him out in the kitchen and he said, "See, I told you guys you'd never make it."

Actually, Dennis Hull did squeeze the $100,000 out of the Blackhawks that his brother always wanted, a sign of him playing later when money was looser.

Dennis Hull eventually earned a degree from Brock University, the same college that bestowed an honorary doctorate on Stan Mikita. He also taught classes in history and geography at Ridley

College in St. Catherines and coached hockey there. As a full-time adult freshman accepted into the mature student program after passing examinations, Hull, who left full-time high school as a tenth grader to play juniors, just tried to blend in with other students. It took two weeks before a French teacher who was a hockey fan realized the Dennis Hull in the class was the hockey player.

"I was thunderstruck," the instructor said.

Dennis developed a knack for entertaining audiences at events with his humor, and no one was more amazed by that transformation than Blackhawk teammate Doug Jarrett.

"In Chicago they used to pay us $100 to go around and speak and tell jokes at schools and parties," Jarrett said. "Dennis never said a word. I did all the funny stuff. The only time he'd talk was on the way home when he complained how tough it was to earn $50 these days."

Back at school, Dennis had a very good experience.

"For a while I thought the teachers were treating me differently because I'd played pro hockey," he said. "Then I found out they helped everyone else just as much. This has to be the greatest university in the country."

Much later Dennis Hull wrote a book about his life called *The Third Best Hull*. He ranked himself behind Bobby and his nephew Brett, Bobby's son, who scored 741 goals in the NHL. Brett and Bobby are the first father-and-son players in the Hall of Fame. Brett won two Stanley Cups, as well.

Dennis also became the athletic director at Illinois Institute of Technology. Both of his children grew up in Chicago and that motivated him to seek this job. Still, after his schooling and finding a new career, Hull admitted he missed playing hockey, if only for the offbeat things that happened.

Former Kansas City Royals star George Brett, a future baseball Hall of Famer, had the mostly highly publicized hemorrhoids surgery of all time during spring training of 1981. Dennis Hull underwent the same type of operation, had just gotten out of the hospital, and returned to the team.

When he took the ice for the first time with linemates Pit Martin and Jim Pippen a heckler shouted, "Dennis, how was your brain surgery?"

Hull said the trio was laughing so hard Billy Reay had to send a substitute line onto the ice.

Glenn Hall

Since people called Glenn Hall "Mr. Goalie," he had to be pretty good. He played in the National Hockey League from 1952 to 1971, mostly with the Blackhawks, but also with Detroit at the start and the St. Louis Blues at the end.

Some years Hall played every single game in net. Some years he was sensational, three times winning the Vezina Trophy after also winning the Calder Trophy as rookie of the year. Another Hall contribution to the sport was developing the "butterfly" method of goaltending, dropping to the ice with spread pads in order to stop low shots. But despite all of his successes, by all accounts Hall did not exactly love his job. It was so stressful he threw up before almost every game he started.

Teammates knew Hall was ready to go when he was tense enough to flee to the toilet and vomit.

"I sometimes ask myself what the hell am I doing out here?" Hall said. "But it's the only way I can support my family. If I could do it some other way I wouldn't be playing goal."

He sometimes used the word hate to describe his feelings about being the target of thousands upon thousands of shots. For the most part Hall was known as "Mr. Goalie," but he was really "Mr. Nervous Wreck."

"There's nothing really wrong with my stomach," Hall said. "Usually, I can eat anything that can be jumped on or hit with an ax. But on the day of a game, or on a day when I face something I don't particularly want to do, nothing helps."

An unnamed one-time teammate suggested "Hall's bucket belongs in the Hall of Fame." Gross.

After the 1965–66 season the native of Humboldt, Saskatchewan, decided he should quit. He bought a farm and began looking for a new profession. When the Blackhawks' general manager Tommy Ivan called to see if Hall was going to show up at training camp Hall said he was too busy. But Ivan gave him a substantial raise, to all of $38,000, and Hall returned.

The irony was that sportswriters and headline writers routinely referred to Hall as "steel-nerved." He pretty much had to display that approach since at one time Hall had a consecutive games playing streak that reached 502 games. No wonder Hall was tense. The Blackhawks presented him with a new car in recognition of the playing streak, a gift he said in gratitude "was really ridiculous" for a mere hockey player.

"I've been lucky, I guess," Hall said. "A lot of goalies get broken bones when they're injured, things like fractured cheekbones, fingers, things like that. Most of my injuries have just been facial cuts, nothing that would keep me from playing."

Hall said he did not want to alternate with another goalie when he was with the Blackhawks.

"People who advocate substitutes for goalies are not speaking for goalies," he said. "At least, they're not speaking for me.

This job is tough enough without having somebody looking over your shoulder. When you know there's somebody waiting for your job your concentration suffers."

Hall looked at his situation as a meritocracy. He earned the right to be the starter. In 906 regular-season games Hall's lifetime goals against average was a sterling 2.49 and he recorded 84 shutouts. If it weren't for Glenn Hall fans probably would not have known there were 4,200 possible minutes a goalie could play in a 70-game season. One year he missed 10 minutes, the slacker.

There were only six regular starting goalies at the highest level of play and the best guys could not be dislodged. At one point the Detroit Red Wings had Hall and Terry Sawchuk, two Hall of Famers. Inexplicably, they traded Sawchuk to Boston and they traded Hall to Chicago after his first four seasons.

Opponents knew Hall was good, but until the Blackhawks saw him play every day they didn't completely comprehend his capabilities.

"I always knew Hall was a tough guy to beat, but I never realized how great a goalie he is until I played on the same team," said Chicago's Bronco Horvath.

At various times Hall tried to get over his puking habit by taking pills. The pills took away the nausea, but made him sleepy. That was the end of that. He once smoked two packs of cigarettes daily, but gave that up. He refused to read books in order to preserve his eyesight. He tried sipping hot tea, which didn't cure him, but did make his stomach hurt less.

"Goal-keeping is such a strain that you're so tired and fed up by the end of the season in April that it takes to July to get over it," he said.

It didn't do Hall any good to face Bobby Hull and his wicked shot in practice every day, either.

"There's nothing that Bobby liked to do more than shoot the puck," Hall said. "The day after a game when we would be practicing, the cleaning crew, mostly women, would be working in the stands. He would see a lady bent over, maybe thirty-five or forty rows up, sweeping. He'd bounce a puck off the seat next to her. He'd grin." Hall said Hull shot so hard that even if he blocked the puck with his chest he could be knocked over.

Hall was much more willing to get hit with a Ping-Pong ball. To work on keeping his reflexes sharp, that's something he did for recreation and a workout.

"I like to get up very close and have a big fellow slam at me harder and harder," he said. "I keep moving in against his slams. I know the Ping-Pong ball won't hurt me and I'm trying to make a habit of moving in."

For all the talk about high-speed shots, Hall seemed more disgusted when he was bested by a slow-moving puck. After allowing such a goal to the New York Rangers he annoyingly dissected the shot.

"A knuckleball," Hall said of baseball's fluttery pitch, which has the habit of twisting and turning in the air in unpredictable fashion. "He beat me with a flicking knuckleball. It dipped."

When the NHL expanded for the 1967–68 season Hall went to the St. Louis Blues. By then he was making $47,500. He was still an outstanding player, still an edgy one, but he started sharing the job, playing just 40-something games a year in his old age. Mostly, the others were true backups, but Jacques Plante, another Hall of Famer, came along to share at the end of his career, too. St. Louis, representing the new Western Division squads, went to two straight Stanley Cup Finals.

By then Hall wasn't even pretending he enjoyed doing what he did.

"Every game I have to play these days is an hour or so of hell," Hall said.

Given Hall's attitude one might think he would have taken to the Plante innovation of adding a mask to the forty pounds of equipment he was already wearing, but he refused.

"What worries you most is the eyes," Hall said, "and a mask may not help there. You wouldn't want to go stopping a puck with an eye, even if you were wearing a mask. A mask might throw me off. You don't want to look the fool out there, out in front of all these people."

The slap shot complicated matters because the puck came faster at the man in net.

"Well, you don't want to get hit with one," Hall said. "You watch the puck. You never let the puck out of your sight."

Hall joked that had seen too many pucks up close and personal.

"If you don't think I'm familiar with that puck," he said, "let me tell you exactly what's written on it. 'Art Ross, patent number 2226516.'"

When Hall genuinely began looking retirement in the face, he knew he would miss many aspects of hockey.

"Ooh, I know that," he said. "The fellowship. Where else can you find fellowship like in hockey?"

While he disdained wearing a mask when he played, from the viewpoint of old age and receiving more than 200 stitches, Hall said, "It was a little stupid. But there were two or three guys on each team that could shoot the puck, not like today where everyone can shoot."

Hall did don a mask for a while with St. Louis, but overall said of how he and his contemporary netminders played, "We were tough and we took our chances."

He still believed Bobby had the hardest shot of all and laughed when people said he was fortunate he didn't have to play against him.

"They seem to forget that I practiced with him every day," Hall said. "We didn't practice with marshmallows or tennis balls."

Hall was inducted into the Hall of Fame in 1975 and his hometown in Saskatchewan raised a statue in his honor.

Tony Esposito

The younger brother of Hall of Famer Phil Esposito by fourteen months, goalie Tony Esposito joined him in the Hall eventually. Tony broke into the pros in 1967 and first appeared in the National Hockey League with the Montreal Canadiens before becoming a star in Chicago.

A three-time college All-American at Michigan Tech, the younger Esposito led his school to an NCAA title during the mid-1960s just before the Original Six expanded.

Esposito only played 13 games for Montreal and then played 873 more for the Blackhawks, basically serving as the replacement for Glenn Hall when he moved on to the St. Louis Blues. Esposito even played the puck the same way, relying on the butterfly style.

A five-time All-Star, Esposito was the rookie of the year when he posted 15 shutouts and earned the nickname "Tony O" or "Tony Zero." He won three Vezina Trophies. His lifetime goals against average was 2.92 and his finest season was 1971–72 when his mark was 1.77.

You didn't have to be related to Tony Zero to realize how special he was. Eddie Johnston, who played the position, was briefly the Blackhawks coach, then took over in Pittsburgh.

"He's the best goalie in hockey," Johnston said. "Any time Chicago doesn't want him, they can ship him to me."

Goalies are supposed to have impeccable reflexes and eyesight, but whether many people knew it or not, Esposito needed glasses from the time he was a schoolboy. To counteract any psychological advantage opponents might get, Esposito resorted to contact lenses.

Tony did try wearing glasses, but they fogged up on outdoor rinks where the family lived in Sault Ste. Marie. Phil recalled his younger brother's struggles.

"He wore glasses, right?" Phil said. "Any goalie wearing glasses had to be suspect, right? They'd call him 'Homer' after the pigeon that wore glasses. They'd call him a lot of other names and they all hurt. Even off the ice I noticed a change in his personality. A lot of the sparkle had gone out of him. It was as if wearing glasses set him apart and inhibited him in some way. The big change in Tony came when we got him contact lenses."

Tony Esposito was about fifteen at the time. The Espositos' father Patrick felt Tony would never be able to make it as a goalie with poor eyesight.

"His eyes are too weak for goaltending," he said. "But he won't even let me bribe him to play up front."

By the time Tony Esposito joined the Blackhawks, Phil had regretfully (in the eyes of the players and Chicago fans) been traded to the Boston Bruins. That made them forever opponents.

"In the games, it's a different story," Tony said. "There's no way Phil's going to score if I can prevent it."

Away from the ice the two hockey men did advise one another.

"If I'm doing something wrong, Phil will tell me after a game," Tony said. "And if I think he's hesitating with his shot, I'll tell him.

Hell, it doesn't bother me. I won't be playing against him for a couple of weeks and he'll have forgotten what I told him by then."

At the time Toronto was carrying three goalies and Chicago coach Billy Reay harkened back to the recent past when goalies took pride in playing in every single game on the regular-season schedule.

"It never occurred to fellows like Gump Worsley or Glenn Hall that they needed even one backup, never alone two," Reay said. "Okay, today you often get four games in five days with long road trips in between and obviously one goalie isn't going to be enough. He's sure to need relief. But I think the thing's out of hand."

The longer Esposito minded the Blackhawks' net the more he sounded like Glenn Hall. He began to tell people he hated playing the position. Although his father said Tony always wanted to play goal, he said in his junior days he was pressured to play the position.

"They needed a goaltender and they kept harassing me," he said. "I didn't want to play. I don't like it. It's no fun playin' goal, y'know. There's the pressure and everything. I still don't like it."

By the time Esposito made the NHL the mask was the rage for goalies. He said he could not identify with the goalies of the past playing with naked faces.

"This guy's not an idiot," he said. "He's got something up here. Hell, I'd be scared to play without a mask. I'm scared with one. It isn't fun. It never was fun. But it's a living."

Billy Reay

During his long National Hockey League coaching career, including two seasons in Toronto and 14 years with the Blackhawks,

Billy Reay stood behind the bench for 1,102 games, won 542, lost 385, and tied 175.

Three times he led Chicago to the Stanley Cup Finals, in 1965, 1971, and 1973.

Reay turned to coaching after 10 seasons as a player with the Montreal Canadiens and Detroit Red Wings between 1943 and 1953.

Reay is the answer to a trivia question that few people in the modern world of hockey think about: Who was the first player to raise his hands in the air, stick included, after scoring a goal?

The occasion came about in 1947 and the gesture has become so ingrained in hockey that no one thinks of its origins, as if it had always been done since the sport was invented.

Reay is also famous in Blackhawks annals for a very different reason. He was fired as coach in midseason in the least classy of ways, a story that is still remembered in the Windy City.

After leading the team since the beginning of the 1963 season, the Blackhawks dismissed Reay in December 1976 without doing so face-to-face. A few days before Christmas the team canned him by slipping a note under his office door. At the time general manager Tommy Ivan had announced plans to retire and Reay was supposed to move from the bench to the front office. Instead, he was ousted from the franchise he had long served.

Ivan expressed "complete disbelief over the series of events." Owner William Wirtz, who made the call and apparently botched the manner in which the decision was carried out, issued a statement saying Reay was a good friend, but a change had to be made.

When Reay died in 2004 at age eighty-six, the *Chicago Tribune* story on his death referred to the incident as "unconscionable."

Keith Magnuson

The rugged defenseman did not begin play for the Blackhawks until 1969, but he had an Original Six hard-nosed demeanor.

Back in the days when every club had an enforcer who really enforced when someone threatened its high scorers, Keith Magnuson was pretty much a bodyguard for Bobby Hull and others. In parts of 11 seasons with Chicago, Magnuson scored just 14 goals, but accumulated 1,442 penalty minutes.

Yet he became a fan favorite for his role as a protector. Magnuson had way more fights than Mike Tyson. Twice he led the league in penalties.

"You've got to fight," he said, "or they'll run you out of the league. I don't feel that I can stand by and watch the bigger defensemen and forwards around the league pushing our smaller men around. It bothers me to see it and if the other teams succeed in intimidating our wings, the Hawks will suffer."

After his rookie year, Magnuson, who played college hockey at Denver University, signed up for boxing lessons. It was a precautionary move and represented thinking ahead. If he was going to have all of those fights he figured he'd better learn how to defend himself and how to win them.

"He really taught me a lot about footwork," Magnuson said of his trainer, a former bantamweight champ named Johnny Coulon, who won the title in 1910.

To the surprise of some, Magnuson, whose playing career was over by the time he was thirty-two, became the Hawks' head coach for two seasons in the early 1980s.

On December 13, 2003, Magnuson was a passenger in a car driven by former NHL player Rob Ramage. On their way back from a funeral, with Ramage driving, the rental car swerved and then crashed near Toronto, killing Magnuson. Ramage was hospitalized, but then was convicted of impaired driving after drinking. Although the Magnuson family requested leniency with no incarceration time, Ramage was sentenced to four years in prison.

The Magnuson family did sue the rental car company and won $9.5 million.

Magnuson was fifty-six when he died and he was buried in the Chicago suburb of Lake Forest where he lived with his family. At Magnuson's funeral, former teammate Cliff Koroll praised the former defenseman's work ethic and said, "The one thing that will always stick out in my mind about Maggie was the size of his heart on the ice and off the ice."

Doug Wilson

Drafted in the sixth round by the Blackhawks, Doug Wilson was a completely different type of defenseman than Keith Magnuson during his 16 years in the NHL, 14 of them with Chicago. He scored as many as 39 goals in a season for the Blackhawks.

In 1,024 regular-season games, Wilson, who is currently general manager of the San Jose Sharks, scored 237 goals with 590 assists. Wilson made three All-Star teams for Chicago and won a Norris Trophy as the best defenseman in the league for the 1981–82 season.

Wilson roomed with Stan Mikita, the revered Blackhawks star, when he was a rookie and said the pairing was worthwhile.

"He was like a second father to me," Wilson said. "He taught me a lot about hockey and a lot about life, namely to treat other people with respect."

Wilson had to learn some things on his own, however. He admitted that as a young player he enjoyed going out at night and having fun, but realized he had to change his ways to make the most of his career.

"It used to be that when I missed a night of going out on the town I thought I really missed something," he said. "Now I want to win first and then have a good time, not the other way around. I had some things to learn, on the ice and off. I had to learn to make contributing to the team my top priority."

Wilson, who did not retire until 1993, was one of the last players in the National Hockey League to compete without wearing a helmet. He was among the group of players grandfathered in when the league made headgear mandatory, one of the last throwbacks to Original Six days.

For one season Wilson tried wearing a helmet, but he never got comfortable and reverted to his old style of going bareheaded on the ice.

"I never shook the feeling that I was protecting an injury," he said. "So I took it off again because I knew if I ever played another season as bad as that one I probably wouldn't have a job today."

One of the other last seven players in the league to go without helmets was Randy Carlyle of the Winnipeg Jets.

"Everybody knows who everybody else in the group is," he said. "But I'm not sure that isn't just because we're some of the oldest guys around. I guess we're like dinosaurs that way. I think it's just a case where we all got into a habit and it's too late to change. I mean, it's not a macho thing. It's not like we're all trying to beat each other out and be known as the last guy around without a hat."

That turned out to be Craig MacTavish.

In 1983, Wilson first gave a helmet a try after breaking his nose. In order to play he wore a helmet with a visor for 15 games. In the first game he took it off, Wilson was hit right in the forehead by a slap shot and suffered a fractured skull.

That still didn't convince Wilson to don the hat for good after he recovered.

Chicago Blackhawks Since

Denis Savard

Denis Savard was the third overall pick in the 1980 National Hockey League career. He played 1,196 games, scored 473 goals, and recorded 865 assists. That was good enough to get him elected to the Hall of Fame.

Most, but not all of Savard's career was spent with the Blackhawks. He was gone for five years in the middle and returned to play his final two seasons with Chicago. He eventually coached the Blackhawks, too, and now serves as a team ambassador.

Savard perfected a trademark shot that is akin to a 360-degree dunk in the NBA. His complete turnaround shot was named the "Savardian Spin-o-rama." Five times Savard scored more than 100 points in a season for the Blackhawks with a high of 131 and he ranks third in team scoring history behind Bobby Hull and Stan Mikita. The Blackhawks retired his Number18.

In 1986, Savard scored a goal four seconds into a second period, tying a record for the fastest goal scored at the beginning of a period.

In 2008, during a coaching rant that became one of the most memorable in NHL history, Savard blew up at his players. He wanted them to work harder, play harder, and above all, look at the insignia they displayed on their jerseys and "Commit to the Indian!"

The phrase caught on and became a team slogan. There were even T-shirts made up with the mantra printed on it. Probably each of the thirty-five Blackhawks head coaches who preceded Savard wished they had said "Commit to the Indian."

Chris Chelios

Defenseman Chris Chelios was one of the most durable NHL players of all time. It seemed as if he played close to forever.

Chelios broke into the league in 1983 and did not retire until 2010. Chelios played in 1,651 NHL games and was chosen for the Hall of Fame.

Chelios left his mark wherever he played, but his Chicago tie was precious to him. He grew up there and his father owned Greek restaurants. A man of eclectic interests, Chelios hangs out with Hollywood actors in Malibu, California, owns restaurants in Dearborn, Michigan, and once tried to qualify for the Winter Olympics in the bobsled. Using his Greek heritage, Chelios sought to learn the sport well enough to make the Greek team for the 2006 Games in Turin, Italy, during the 2004 NHL lockout.

However, by the time the 2006 Games rolled around Chelios was busy as captain of the US hockey team in Turin. He had first played in the Games twenty-two years earlier and the gap between his appearances was a record.

There did not seem to be much call for legalized mayhem in bobsled. One thing the 5-foot-11, 190-pound Chelios could do was bodycheck. Chelios was forty-eight when he retired after being selected for seven All-Star teams and winning the Norris Trophy three times.

Outside of Gordie Howe, who accepted one retirement from the Detroit Red Wings only to resurface in the World Hockey Association and skated well into his fifties, Chelios is probably the oldest player ever to compete in the NHL.

Chelios retired at forty-eight, but some said Johnny Bower, a Hall of Fame goalie, was older than his announced forty-five at retirement.

Kane, Toews, and Quenneville = Cups

It may be that the true glory days of the Chicago Blackhawks, the best of times and of all time, are right now.

The arrival of Patrick Kane and Jonathan Toews for the 2007–2008 season formed the cornerstone of a new generation of Blackhawks The duo is mentioned together as if they are joined at the hip, or as widely known professional partners as the Lone Ranger and Tonto. Add in the work of coach Joel Quenneville and Chicago copped Stanley Cups at the end of the 2010, 2013, and 2015 seasons.

This marked the greatest stretch in team history and Kane and Toews became the dual stars, the toasts of the town. It was Kane who won the Calder Trophy as rookie of the year when he was a baby-faced nineteen and Toews who became captain of the team. Toews, from Winnipeg, played for Canada in the Olympics and Kane, from Buffalo, played for the United States.

Kane was a precocious player. By the time he was ten, he scored so many goals that other kids in his league were asking for his autograph.

Toews won the Conn Smythe Trophy as Most Valuable Player in the playoffs and then Kane won the same award. Kane was the number-one overall pick in the 2007 draft. Toews was the third pick in the same draft. As of the 2015–16 season both players were twenty-seven.

In 2007 Kane threw out the ceremonial first pitch at a Chicago Cubs game. As part of the Cubs and Wrigley Field tradition of having guests lead the fans in singing "Take Me Out to the Ballgame," Kane, along with then-coach Denis Savard, sung the tune.

Toews, who played some college hockey at the University of North Dakota, had a body of water named after him north of Flin Flon in Manitoba when he first won the Stanley Cup and brought it home. It is called Toews Lake. Kane was offered college scholarships, but went the junior route.

Toews could score and could check and was a leader in the locker room—it seemed as if he was born mature—but one thing no one counted on him doing was bringing them home for dinner.

"I can't cook," he said.

At the beginning of the 2015–16 season Kane set a record for an American player by scoring in 26 straight games. It was the longest such streak by any NHL player in 23 years. Ending in the third week in January 2016, the Blackhawks set a franchise record by winning 12 straight games.

Joel Quenneville, who took over the Blackhawks for the 2008–09 season and presided over all three recent Stanley Cup triumphs, played more than 800 games in the NHL.

On January 14, 2016, Quennevile won his 783rd game as coach, moving into second place all time behind Scotty Bowman.

"I feel fortunate and honored to be in some great company over the years," Quenneville said.

5

TORONTO MAPLE LEAFS

Founded: 1917
Home Arenas: Mutual Street Arena, 1917–31; Maple Leaf Gardens, 1931–99; Air Canada Centre, 1999–present
Stanley Cups: 1918, 1922, 1932, 1942, 1945, 1947, 1948, 1949, 1951, 1962, 1963, 1964, 1967

Beginnings

Twice the Toronto Maple Leafs won Stanley Cups three years in a row, but they are now stuck in the middle of an embarrassing and disappointing championship drought, not having won it all since 1967.

Professional hockey at the top level of the game predates the creation of the National Hockey League and the biggest city in Canada has been host to a flagship team for decades. There was always great pride in having a first-class club in Toronto.

There was a team named the Toronto Blueshirts representing the city before the start of the NHL, but when the new league formed the owners did not want the owner of that franchise to be a member. However, they did want a Toronto team in the circuit.

The team that entered the league in 1917 was called the Toronto Arenas, named for the ice rink where the team competed. It was not a terribly slick nickname and by 1919 the team name was the St. Patricks. In 1927, when Conn Smythe gained control of the club, he named the team the Maple Leafs.

Although the Leafs became an iconic name across Canada there has always been lack of clarity about how it was chosen. Depending on who was doing the talking the Maple Leafs represented a World War I military regiment, or more generically represents blue skies and white snow.

However, that overlooks the fact that from 1868 on, the maple leaf had already become a symbol of Canada and was included in the coat of arms of both Ontario and Quebec. This makes for the best explanation for why the maple leaf became the team nickname and why it has always been so warmly embraced. The Montreal Canadiens have been more successful over the years, but they were seen as being more a representative of French-speaking Quebec. The Leafs early on developed a national following that was ingrained long before the NHL expanded to such communities as Vancouver, Edmonton, Calgary, and Winnipeg.

A major reason why the Maple Leafs became widely popular early on was Foster Hewitt. Hewitt was born in Toronto in 1902 and his father, W. A. Hewitt, was a sportswriter, and then sports editor of the *Toronto Star*. Foster sought the same career path. However, Foster soon learned about a new medium coming into use—radio.

Foster Hewitt was fascinated by the new technology and through his dad's influence in 1921 the two listened in on a radio demonstration made possible by General Electric in Detroit.

They heard Detroit Tigers star baseball player Ty Cobb speaking from Navin Field. Young Hewitt was smitten.

When the *Toronto Star* company established a radio station, Foster Hewitt, who was already writing for the newspaper, was in on the ground floor of broadcasting. By 1923 Foster Hewitt was on the air broadcasting everything from rowing to horse racing, but not yet big-time hockey.

By the time that opportunity rolled around Hewitt had developed his own style. Although commonplace as a call on goals nowadays, Hewitt was the first to employ the enthusiastic phrase, "He shoots! He scores!" That was in the 1920s. In 1931, when Maple Leaf Gardens was being constructed, Conn Smythe gave Hewitt the rights to broadcast all events in the building, including the Maple Leafs games.

No one threw himself more energetically into the role of early sportscaster in Canada than Hewitt. He was involved in the first broadcast of a horse race, and in an era before there were sophisticated broadcast facilities to accommodate his efforts, Hewitt, who simultaneously broadcast big news events as well as his sports coverage, was sometimes stuck in odd places behind a microphone. Stadiums and arenas had no place for him, so he set up his own vantage points. Sometimes he wedged himself into cold and wet places to view the action. On one occasion at the Kingston Racetrack, Hewitt froze his clothing to the roof and could not stand up after his broadcast. Emergency assistance freed him, but the seat of his pants could not be salvaged.

So Hewitt had some experience with complex broadcast scenarios when he was granted the Maple Leafs broadcast rights in an unfinished building. Hewitt had input into his new location. Experimenting by visiting other tall buildings, Hewitt established what he felt was the perfect viewing height—56 feet. An overhanging broadcast booth (for lack of a better word) was built that extended outward and gave him an unobstructed view of the ice. Upon first seeing its elongated shape and the way it appeared suspended in air, a Hewitt friend said it resembled a gondola. The description stuck and for decades it was referred to as Hewitt's gondola.

Over time Maple Leafs broadcasts essentially morphed into *Hockey Night in Canada* on the radio years before there was such a thing on television. Enormously popular, Hewitt turned Maple Leafs players into household names thousands of miles from their own households. Once, Hewitt received 90,000 fan letters in a single year.

Hockey and Hewitt made the shift to television in Canada in 1952. Foster's son Bill followed him into broadcasting. For some years they teamed up on Maple Leafs broadcasts and then Bill handled them for twenty additional years.

From the start in the NHL, the Toronto team was a winner. The 1917–18 club went 13–9 and won the championship. Reg Noble scored 30 goals. Toronto bested the Vancouver Millionaires over five games to claim the franchise's first Stanley Cup.

In 1922, Toronto was faced with an interesting development. The team's regular goalie held out for more money and he walked away. The team signed a free-agent replacement and went all the way to the title. Toronto again reached the Finals with Babe Dye scoring 30 goals and once again tackled the Millionaires. The result was the same, a Toronto victory in five games.

Conn Smythe

Born in Toronto in 1895 as Constantine Falkland Cary Smythe, Conn Smythe went with the short version of his name most of his life, beginning at age twelve. Although he played hockey and rugby when he was young, Smythe's principal claim to fame in the sporting world was his ownership of the Toronto Maple Leafs and acknowledgement as one of the key builders of the National Hockey League in its formative years.

Secondarily, and lesser known to non-Canadians, Smythe was a major figure in the horse racing world. His thoroughbreds won 145 stakes races. In their early years Smythe helped establish the New York Rangers.

Coincidentally, Smythe grew up in a neighborhood not far from Maple Leaf Gardens—only before it existed. He played a large role in seeing it built. His future was down the block and Smythe did not yet know it. He served in World War I, but also returned to service in World War II. He walked with a minor limp because he was hit by shrapnel in the back during the second war. He told people it was no big deal; since Franklin D. Roosevelt ran the entire United States from a wheelchair, he could run a hockey team with a minor foot problem. Smythe relied on a cane to get around.

In between, in 1927, he became the boss of the Toronto professional hockey team and gave it the Maple Leafs name. Under Smythe's leadership, which lasted until 1961, the Maple Leafs won eight Stanley Cups.

After his first military stint Smythe started a sand and gravel company. When the Toronto pro team came up for sale it was nearly shipped to Philadelphia for the best offer. Smythe formed an ownership group and together it paid $160,000 for the club. In 2015, the Maple Leafs were valued at $1.3 billion in US dollars, the most valuable team in hockey.

Smythe named the team, built its home arena, and provided the team colors of blue and white. He also coached the Leafs and oversaw personnel as general manager. Maple Leaf Gardens, constructed during the Great Depression, became known as "The House That

Smythe Built." One way he got the work done was by asking builders to accept shares in the structure rather than cash.

People marveled that he got the task done during such a serious economic downturn.

"It was tough, but I had a theory," Smythe said. "'The government is still printing money,' I told everyone. 'Therefore, there must be more money today than there was yesterday. How can we be worse off?'"

For a time it seemed Smythe's partners were trying to ease him out of hockey. It took time and trouble, but Smythe eventually took complete control of the Leafs and the Gardens.

Smythe preferred to see his Maple Leafs play an aggressive, even combative style of hockey. That's how he was as a person and that's what he wanted to see on the ice. He was known for saying, "If you can't beat them in the alley, you can't beat them on the ice."

Between 1942 and 1951, the Maple Leafs won six Stanley Cup championships. They did not always dominate the regular season, but Smythe's team was usually ready come playoff time. He used to say, "Winning sells tickets." He meant winning championships, not winning a Tuesday night game in February.

Smythe periodically made strange personnel decisions. That was due to being autocratic by nature. He twice demoted players to the minors because they got married without his permission. Talk about revenge for being snubbed without a wedding invitation.

During his prime years running the club Smythe was virulently anti-union. He paid his players reasonably well, but he wasn't pals with them. He did want to control their everyday lives.

"The rules are simple," Smythe said. "Aside from what you wear, what you say, what you eat, what you drink, who you're with, where you're going, how much you weigh, and what you think, the club has little, if any interest in the hired help's outside working hours."

That was a little Big Brotherish, but Smythe looked upon himself as a benevolent dictator.

"There's one thing about it," he added. "The pay is good and it's always on time. There's more civil liberty in digging a ditch. But most of these guys are in a rut. They still seem to prefer hockey."

Smythe did install pride in being a Maple Leaf early on in his regime.

"It was something very, very special to be a Maple Leaf in those years," said Joe Primeau, a 1930s player, who was the center on a line called "The Kid Line."

As a community figure contributing to charity, Smythe was known to be more generous than to his players, especially where children's needs were concerned. His name adorned a wing of the Ontario Crippled Children's Centre in Toronto. He also raised money for the Ontario Community Centre for the Deaf.

In 1958, three years before he surrendered his stake in the Maple Leafs, Smythe was inducted into the Hockey Hall of Fame as a builder.

Smythe's parting from the Leafs as he was turning sixty-six was a bit messy. He meant to keep the team in the family for good. He sold most of his shares in the team and arena to a group headed by his son Stafford. Only Stafford's partners, John Bassett and Harold Ballard, had more clout. Although Smythe netted $2.3 million, annual payment of $15,000 for life, a car, and an office, he was furious with the deal when he realized his son wasn't going to be truly in charge, but be a one-third operator.

There was considerable friction for a time.

"When I sold the Gardens I thought it was to my son," Smythe said later. "It took three days and Stafford said to me, 'Nothing is going to be changed around here, dad. What are you worried about?' What he meant was that he wasn't going to fire anybody, which he didn't. Later, when I learned he was not going to keep control himself, I was angry."

Then Stafford got into trouble with the law, being charged with fraud in 1971. He also became ill. When Stafford was dying in a hospital he told his father, "See, Dad, I told you they wouldn't put me in jail."

Much later, after Ballard had become the team's kingpin, Smythe passed a message along.

"Tell him I may be an old son of a bitch, but I'm still not in his class," Smythe said.

For a time Conn Smythe wrote a hockey column in the *Toronto Star* and that forum allowed him leeway to say just about anything about hockey. In the 1970s he began wintering in Miami Beach, Florida, saying it helped his ailing leg. He said he would have preferred being in Toronto, but the warm weather was good for him.

"The cold plays hell with my leg," Smythe said. "Even here I can tell when we're in for rain. I may know nothing, but I could be a weatherman."

As he aged, Smythe sometimes turned reflective. When he was about to turn eighty he said, "They say the good die young. That's some kind of mark against me."

Smythe died in 1980 at eighty-five. The Conn Smythe Trophy is given to the Most Valuable Player in the Stanley Cup playoffs. Before the NHL went to geographical names for its divisions one was named the Conn Smythe Division.

Ace Bailey

As excellent a hockey player as he was and for however long Irvine "Ace" Bailey was affiliated with the Toronto Maple Leafs starting in 1926, a year before even Conn Smythe took command, he is unfortunately most famous for being badly injured.

On December 13, 1933, Bailey, then in his eighth season in the National Hockey League at age thirty-one, was hit from behind by the Boston Bruins' Eddie Shore. Bailey fell to the ice and fractured his skull on impact. Bailey was so severely injured it was feared he would die. While he survived that blow Bailey was forced to retire from hockey.

It was touch-and-go for Bailey's life after he was rushed to a Boston hospital where he remained on the critical list for weeks.

"It was something that could have happened to anyone," Bailey said. "I met him (Shore) many times in later years when he visited Toronto, but I never held a grudge."

Bailey said he was sure Shore was after Toronto teammate Red Horner for a revenge check and didn't realize he hit the wrong man until afterward. Horner had just checked Shore into the boards.

However, Bailey's father did hold a grudge. After Shore's brutal hit, the older Bailey traveled to Boston and checked into the Copley Plaza Hotel because he knew that's where the Leafs stayed. Carrying a .45 pistol he sought out Conn Smythe to ask where he could find Shore. Smythe, with the assistance of two hotel detectives, subdued Bailey senior, confiscated the gun, and knocked him out with a drug and put him on a train back to Toronto. The incident was hushed up. The gun was mailed to Toronto a few weeks later.

Bailey was unconscious for fifteen days after he went into convulsions on the ice and underwent brain surgery to ease a blood clot. Police said if Bailey died they were prepared to charge Shore with manslaughter. Immediately after the injury, Boston team officials donated the proceeds from another home game to Gladys Bailey.

At least one paper a week after the incident referred to Bailey in the caption under a photo of his wife and three-year-old daughter Joanne with Toronto owner Conn Smythe as the "dying Toronto Maple Leafs' right winger." In fact, the *Toronto Star* editors decreed that an obituary story be prepared for Bailey. As is said in the newspaper business, the story was spiked when Bailey survived.

The 5-foot-10, 160-pound right winger was a mainstay of Toronto's 1932 Stanley Cup champions. During his career Bailey scored 111 goals and added 82 assists. Three times in a 44-game season, Bailey scored either 23 or 22 goals. As the end of the 1928–29 season concluded, Bailey became the first Toronto player to lead the NHL in scoring.

"It was during that '28–29 season that the sportswriters gave me the name Ace," Bailey said. "I'm glad they did because my mother named me Irvine."

When Bailey was catapulted into retirement by his misfortune, players competed in a benefit game in Toronto, raising nearly $21,000. The game between the Maple Leafs and stars from the other NHL clubs took place on February 14, 1934, a few months after the hit by Shore. The two men shook hands at center ice on the occasion as more than 14,000 fans applauded. The All-Star game itself was unique. The regular NHL All-Star game did not begin until 1947.

That was Bailey's first time in attendance at a game since his injury and it was Shore's first time in Toronto since the infamous hit on Bailey.

On March 6, Bailey returned to Boston to drop the first puck in a game between the Maple Leafs and Bruins. The Boston fans gave Bailey an ovation.

Physically, Bailey looked fit, but he was not completely well, at least not hockey-playing well.

"I have not done anything in the line of work, but am carefully preserving my energy," Bailey said at that time. "I take a walk every morning, drive my own car, and, as far as I can determine, except for a feeling of weakness, am in perfectly good shape. I eat and sleep regularly, am on no special diet and do about as I please."

Bailey did thank Boston medical people for their care and the way they nursed him back to health.

After his recovery, Bailey learned details surrounding his case, including the difficulty people had in removing him from the ice. Smythe led the interference like a football lineman trying to clear a path through fans. One drunken fan refused to move and accused Bailey of taking a dive and faking his injury.

"Get out of the way or I'll put you out of the way," Smythe shouted.

The man didn't budge and Smythe punched him. A Bruins official got Smythe arrested and he remained in jail till 2 a.m. Eventually, the charges were dropped, but Smythe had to pay for the obnoxious fan's dental work.

Those were not the only fisticuffs that night. Horner, the perhaps-intended, skated over to Shore and ordered him to put his hands up because he was going to fight him. Shore did not protect himself, but Horner belted him anyway. Shore fell to the ice and hit his own head. He was also carried off on a stretcher and needed sixteen stitches to close his wound.

Shore was suspended for 16 games and Horner for six. Smythe sought to have the suspension for Shore extended by the board of governors. Instead the board approved that benefit All-Star game.

After Bailey retired from playing he attempted to become an official, but the league turned him down. Between 1938 and 1984, Bailey worked as a timekeeper at Maple Leaf Gardens at Leafs games. That year, when he was eighty-one, owner Harold Ballard fired him.

The Maple Leafs retired Bailey's Number 6 jersey, the first number to be retired in NHL history. In 1975, he was enshrined in the Hockey Hall of Fame. Bailey was eighty-eight when he died in 1992 after suffering a stroke, though some listed the cause of death as lung failure. Some noted it was only then that the second obituary was written for Bailey.

Frank Selke

Frank Selke was there with the Toronto Maple Leafs almost from the beginning of the franchise. He was Conn Smythe's right-hand man in management and helped build three Stanley Cup–winning champions in 1932, 1942, and 1945.

However, he and Smythe had a falling out after World War II and Selke left for the Montreal Canadiens where he was part of six more Stanley Cup titles.

Selke was born in Berlin, Ontario, in 1893 (which changed its name to Kitchener because of wars with Germany), and lived for ninety-two years. He made his mark in hockey on the management side because he stood only 5-foor-2, or maybe it was 5-foot-5, depending on who was asking and who was writing. He was a giant in administration, however, and was around the sport for a half century.

Despite being involved with so many great Canadiens teams and many great Canadiens players, Selke chose an early Maple

Leaf player as the best he ever saw. In a 12-year career, nine of them with Toronto, the 6-foot-1, 195-pound Charlie Conacher led the National Hockey League in goals five times. He scored as many as 36 goals in 47 games.

That's why Selke picked Conacher.

"I have no hesitation in saying Charlie Conacher," Selke said, "the flashing right winger of the Maple Leafs' famous Kid Line of the '30s. He ranks as the greatest all-around athlete I have managed in my fifty years with sport. I have never known any player who has reduced the scoring of goals to as exact a science as Charlie Conacher. Those who remember will tell you that Charlie always made the right moves going in on goal. If he failed to score it was only because other teams also had great defensive players and goalkeepers."

Selke played a role in the construction of Toronto's Maple Leaf Gardens, but also helped get other palaces of the game under way from Cincinnati to Rochester, New York. He also built teams, instituting a sophisticated feeder system for the Maple Leafs, and then brought the same farsighted idea to Montreal.

Smythe and Selke had a close relationship that became strained. Selke was the man in the hinterlands searching for talent and believed he had one of the steals of the century when he tripped across Milt Schmidt, later a Hall of Famer for the Boston Bruins. All it would have taken to sign Schmidt was $250, but Smythe vetoed the deal, Selke said because Schmidt was German.

"He was such a great young player at eighteen that I almost signed him without asking for Smythe's okay," Selke said. "But I thought I should tell the Major I was spending his money. His reaction was astonishing, to say the least."

Mostly, Selke refused to criticize Smythe even when they parted. He credited Smythe with the brilliant early hire of Clarence "Hap"

Day, also called Happy Day. Day was going to college and Smythe persuaded him to turn pro.

"One of the smartest moves Conn Smythe ever made . . ." Selke said. He lacked a "solid citizen" to lead his team and he needed Day to shoulder the responsibility of team captain. From the first, Happy Day proved to be one of those rare fellows prepared to sacrifice all personal ambitions for the good of the team."

Day was a leader on the ice and when he retired became coach of Maple Leafs clubs that won five Stanley Cups in the 1940s. Add in one Cup as a player and one as an assistant team manager and Day was part of seven championship teams.

"I have always contended that he never did get full credit for his ability as a player," Selke said. "He often lamented the fact himself that he lacked that mysterious quality called color. Day was a nonsmoker and nondrinker. He never drank tea or coffee or ate chocolates. And every day in the year he was fit to play 60 minutes of hockey."

Selke actually was a hockey figure long before joining the Leafs, working with minor-league clubs in Toronto. His first Leafs assignment was selling program ads, a job for which he made $50 a week.

The breaking point, the split, between two of the pioneers of the NHL, occurred when Smythe returned from his stint in World War II. Against his instructions, Selke had traded for Ted Kennedy, who became a Hall of Famer. Rather than be grateful, Smythe grew angry. There were some who felt Selke did a better job running the team and the Gardens than Smythe and some who felt he needed to be put in his place because of the way he ran things.

"I found myself without a job in the spring of 1946," Selke said. "And believe it or not, I was greatly relieved. Conn Smythe had been good to me in countless ways, but he was a severe taskmaster and I was his whipping boy more years than I like to remember. I knew I was in hot water after Conn returned from overseas in the Second World War. Some of the directors and some of the people around the Gardens apparently resented my activities. There was a lot of sniping at me from the background. By 1946, I was fed up. I knew the $5,000-a-year salary wasn't worth it."

Their divorce changed the course of the NHL. Selke was hired in Montreal and turned the Canadiens into a powerhouse over the next generation.

Selke played a founder's role in helping to create the Hockey Hall of Fame in 1943 and was elected to it in 1960.

"Up until the Hall came into being, the game was ignoring its history," Selke said.

In 1978, the NHL established the Frank J. Selke Trophy, given each season to the best defensive forward in the league. Late in life, Selke, who died in 1985, didn't like the way owners ran the game.

"There are too many owners who don't give a hoot about hockey," he said. "It's all business. There's no question those owners were the worst thing to happen to hockey. How can you help a game unless you love it?"

King Clancy

One of the most influential figures in National Hockey League history really did have another name besides King, but almost no one knows it. His given name was Francis Michael and the King nickname was borrowed from his father, but the younger version also deserved it.

Clancy played 16 seasons as a defenseman with the old Ottawa Senators and then the Maple Leafs. He also worked in team administration for decades, earning a second nickname of "Mr. Maple Leaf."

When he was just starting out at eighteen, Clancy was wooed by Ottawa. His contract was for $800, but Tommy Gorman, the general manager, played a psychological game on the teenager, arraying 500 one-dollar bills on his desk and informing Clancy he would promptly give them to him if he signed with the franchise. Clancy provided his autograph and immediately bought a Harley-Davidson motorcycle.

"The best you could buy," he recounted at sixty-nine, "and rode it home and parked it in front of my house. I bought it unbeknownst to my dad, Lord have mercy on his soul. When he came home he asked who owned it. I said, 'Why I own it.' 'Take it back,' he said. 'I'll have my supper first,' I said. 'We'll wait supper,' said my dad. So that was the end of my motorcycle."

The last seven of Clancy's playing years were with the Leafs, up through the 1936–37 season. A first- or second-team All-Star four times, Clancy was a hardy defenseman. In his diverse career Clancy also coached the Leafs for three seasons in the 1950s. He was assistant club manager in the 1960s when the Leafs won three more Cups.

Immediately after his playing days he became a referee. On the occasion of officiating his first playoff game Clancy was extraordinarily nervous. Another official tried to soothe him by saying, "King, this is just another hockey game. Remember that once you drop that puck you're the only sane man in the rink. The guys in the seats are nuts and the players and coaches are too fired up to think straight."

After the game while exiting the arena, Clancy came across a $10 bill lying on the ground. He scooped it up and kept it. His officiating partner laughed and said, "About 3,000 fans walked past that bill without seeing it and they had the nerve to call you blind."

Clancy was always blindly in love with hockey, virtually from when he was born in Ottawa in 1903 until he died in 1986 in Toronto. Conn Smythe recognized the King's value after his star performances with the Senators and in 1930 gave up two players and $35,000 for his rights in trade. That was a very serious price to pay at the time.

In another officiating adventure, Clancy was an extra ref on the premises at the Boston Garden when a fan went after an official. Clancy intervened, pushed him into the referees' dressing room, and saw fellow ref George Hayes knock the interloper down with a punch and break his glasses by stepping on them. The fan sued Clancy for assault.

Hayes was called as a witness for the defense and spun a pretty yarn, as did Clancy. The judge sided with Clancy, although it seemed somewhat reluctantly.

"Mr. Clancy, I find it hard to believe your version of this disgraceful affair and I know the complainant told anything but a true story," said the judge sifting through the evidence given. "But I want to congratulate Mr. Hayes for the straightforward way in which he presented his evidence."

Clancy was cleared, though he barely believed how he escaped.

"That Hayes came up with the prize piece of fiction of all time," Clancy said. "I stuck to the truth and got hell. And the poor fan didn't even get a pair of glasses out of it."

Referees always took grief. A partisan Bruins fan of the female persuasion once yelled at Clancy, "If you were my husband, I'd feed you poison." Clancy had an answer for that. "Madam, if I was unfortunate enough to be your husband, I'd take that poison."

So many offbeat conversations took place while Clancy was an official that he could have compiled his own joke book.

He once sent Maple Leaf Bob Davidson to the box for an infraction, but received a complaint about the whistle.

"What the hell, King, you used to do that yourself," Davidson said.

"I know," Clancy replied, "but I never used to get caught."

Clancy had a rule that enraged players. They could call him a name once in an argument, but if they didn't stop and skate away then they were in trouble.

"They can call me what they like," Clancy said. "Once."

It was no wonder Clancy gained a reputation as someone who always got the last word.

When Clancy was coaching the Leafs his teams were not high scorers, but were skilled defensively. They also fell short in the playoffs. In Boston a spectator yelled at him. "King," he said, "they named a town after you."

"What town?" King said.

"Marblehead," the fan said of the Boston North Shore suburb.

Once on the bench, Clancy called for a player named "Bashin' Bob" Bailey to go into a game and start a fight, only to be reminded that he had sent Bailey to the minors a week earlier.

In 1972, at age sixty-nine, Clancy took over as interim boss of the Leafs when coach Johnny McLellan became ill. Under Clancy Toronto went 9–4–3 and sneaked into the playoffs. Since Clancy was at least temporarily the oldest coach in playoff history he was asked a number of questions about his age.

"I never felt better," Clancy said, explaining that his routine of sleeping quite a lot kept him feeling young. "I think it's the secret of it all. I'm with young men and I consider myself just as young as they are."

When Clancy turned seventy-five, the Leafs threw a birthday bash for him at a game. The highlight was a 300-pound cake, 180 pounds of it edible and the rest decorations that included hockey pucks and miniature hockey sticks. He gave the cake to the Hospital for Sick Children. He kept the standing ovation Toronto fans delivered at the Gardens.

Clancy was friendly with just about everyone. He tried to play a rough game as a defenseman, but avoided fights that might cause him harm.

Once, Clancy dropped tough guy Eddie Shore with a hard check. Shore came up prepared to fight, but Clancy disarmed him.

"Why, hello Eddie," Clancy said. He grabbed Shore's fist and turned the grasp into a handshake while adding, "And how are you tonight?"

Dick Irvin

Born in Hamilton, Ontario, in 1892, from the time he was a little boy Dick Irvin was enamored with hockey. So were his five brothers. Their father drove them to games by horse and sleigh. Their Santa Claus approximation sometimes relied on the horse's nose for the trail to bring them home since fierce blizzards were never considered an excuse not to go.

Irvin was good enough to become a professional hockey player in 1916, the year before the National Hockey League was formed. His first club was the Portland, Oregon team out west that ended up melding into the NHL when the Pacific league folded. Most of Irvin's playing career was spent in Western Canada before a three-year stint with the Chicago Blackhawks. Irvin was thirty-four before he suited up for his first NHL game.

Irvin's coaching career began with Chicago, but he was at the helm when the Toronto Maple Leafs won the Stanley Cup in 1932. Six other times Irvin led the Leafs to the Finals, but could not emerge victorious on even one of those occasions. However, in his 1,448-game NHL coaching career Irvin won three more Cups with the Montreal Canadiens. In a 27-year coaching career his teams missed the playoffs only four times.

Many appreciated Irvin's talents, including NHL president Clarence Campbell, who said that he was "one of the greatest figures the game has ever known. Everything he did was dedicated to the welfare of hockey."

Irvin was known as an innovative coach, and during the playoffs of 1955 he alternated two goalies for seven or eight minutes at a time. It was a bold move that defied the thinking of sticking with a hot goaltender. This was not one of the years when Irvin presided over a Cup winner, though.

"The coach in the National Hockey League is different from a coach in any other sport," Irvin said. "Now, take your baseball manager. It is taken for granted that under certain conditions he will play the percentages. Whether his move works for him or fails him, it is accepted as a perfectly legitimate method of eliminating himself from personal blame. Look at your football coach. He has maybe 10 games a season. All right, but he has a week between games—a whole week to get his injured players back in shape, a whole week to think up new plays, devise new strategy, rebuild morale and confidence within his club. A whole week, mind you, seven days and seven nights. Then, what happens in the game? The football coach, when he sees things going against him, has a time-out to reorganize his team. Ah, wouldn't I just love to yell for a time-out once in a while when I see a Rocket Richard or Gordie Howe coming down on my nets!"

Irvin, who died in 1957 at age sixty-four, was inducted into the Hall of Fame the next year. His son, Dick Jr., spent decades broadcasting Montreal Canadiens games and also appeared on *Hockey Night in Canada*. The younger Irvin was astounded by how his national profile rose and how readily he was recognized on the streets after he became part of the *Hockey Night* crew.

Irvin Jr. won the Hockey Hall of Fame's Foster Hewitt Memorial Award given to broadcasters for excellence.

Dick the Elder called hockey "The roughest game in the world."

Beyond that Irvin had compliments for the sport. "It is my life," he said. "It is also, I think, the greatest of all games, for it is fast, there is continual action, bodily contact, cleverness and finesse."

Turk Broda

The magician in the nets for the great Toronto Maple Leafs teams of the 1940s was Turk Broda, who became a Hall of Famer after playing his entire career with the team and protecting goal for five Stanley Cup championship clubs.

He was a four-time All-Star and won the Vezina Trophy twice while compiling a lifetime goals against average of 2.53.

The end product was magnificent, but Broda had some flaws when he first broke in. Coach Happy Day thought he wasn't quick enough with the glove hand, so he relentlessly drilled Broda, taking away his stick and making him reach for everything.

"In practically no time at all he was catching pucks like a baseball shortstop," Day said.

In later years Broda was so accomplished spearing the puck out of the air that one sportswriter applied one of the greatest of all goalie descriptions. Broda, it was said, "could catch lint in a hurricane."

While Broda's mother referred to him as Walter, his teammates gave him an awkward nickname as a young player. "Turk" was the outcome after being shortened from "Turkey Face." That name was slapped on him because Broda had so many freckles.

Born in Brandon, Alberta, Broda was of Ukrainian heritage. He began playing hockey as a tyke and didn't have the size to battle with bigger boys up front.

"I was one of the smallest of the gang that used to play on a pond at Brandon," he said. "They put me in goal and I never got out again."

Broda was a top goalie until 1952, but he was one of the best ever when it came to crunch time. He shrugged off pressure and played his best in the postseason. Broda's lifetime goals against average in the playoffs was 2.08.

"For one thing, I always needed the money from the playoffs," Broda said.

The one constant aggravation Broda seemed to have during his playing days was pleasing Conn Smythe with his appearance. Broda must have been the object of someone's optimism when his measurements were listed as 5-foot-9 and 165 pounds. That could not be right. Otherwise, teammates wouldn't have called him "Fat Boy."

Smythe threatened Broda's job if he did not lose weight. Later, when Broda was at the top of his game, the nickname morphed into "The Fabulous Fat Man."

Smythe was merciless on this topic, saying Broda wouldn't play if he didn't slim down. Other times he insisted he would take money from his check.

"Get that weight down in three days or it will cost you one hundred bucks," Smythe roared. When his pocketbook was put in jeopardy Broda lost weight. The long series of poundage discussions played out in the Toronto newspapers and were called "The Battle of the Bulge."

Smythe was the boss.

"An overweight netminder can't stop goals," he said once. "I'm taking Broda out of the nets and he's not coming back till he loses seven pounds."

Broda went to a health club and took a steam bath and went home and drank orange juice instead of eating ice cream. When Broda's shrinkage convinced Smythe to put him back on the ice, he was greeted at Maple Leaf Gardens by a band playing "The Too-Fat Polka." However, when he recorded a shutout victory, the same band played, "Happy Days Are Here Again."

While many believe superb reflexes make a goalie, one thing Broda had going for him was serenity. He almost never blew his cool and never seemed to change demeanor, even after rough nights in the nets. Broda's excellence in goal did earn him a more respectable nickname, too. Day began calling him "Old Eagle Eyes" because Broda always seemed to have his eye on the puck even if it was flying at him at high speed.

He was a genial man who never succumbed to braggadocio and spent time giving back. When Broda was thirty-seven and famous around Canada he visited hundreds of patients at a tuberculosis sanitarium, his presence not advertised in advance. He was greeted as a hero.

"Makes you feel humble, see," Broda said. "Gives you a funny feeling, see."

Broda signed autographs until his hand just about cramped, but ironically, his audience repeatedly asked, "How much do you weigh?" The once-slender Broda admitted he weighed 195 pounds and had to lose five more to satisfy Smythe.

When nearing the end of his NHL career, Broda was asked what he planned to do and said he might switch to officiating.

"At the kind of money they get paid, I wouldn't care who hated me," Broda said.

In an era long before there was such a thing as a sports memorabilia market and many professional players did not even save their own stuff, a unique Broda goalkeeper stick was preserved from 1942.

Toronto won the Stanley Cup with Broda in goal. After the playoffs ended, with the Maple Leafs stunning the hockey world by bouncing back from a 3–0 deficit in the Finals over the Detroit Red Wings, Toronto players all signed the stick. It was given to referee George Hayes, who later lost it in a poker game.

The claimant in the card game gave the stick to his son, who at first did not take good care of it and used it to play hockey on the streets. Later he realized his error and changed his ways. After thirty-seven years in one family the stick was sold as memorabilia and given to a new owner as a birthday present.

By then, Broda, who died at fifty-eight from a heart attack, had long before passed away.

Syl Apps

When it came to athletic genes Syl Apps had more than his share and passed on more than his share to future generations. Apps, from Paris, Ontario, was a sturdy six feet and 185 pounds and before he became a star for the Toronto Maple Leafs between 1936 and 1948, he represented Canada in the 1936 Summer Olympics in Berlin as a pole vaulter.

Apps made the shift from track and field to hockey in one year and won the Calder Trophy as National Hockey League rookie of the year in 1937 when he scored 16 goals and 29 assists. Apps was the first Calder winner. He became a many-time All-Star and Hall of Famer and played for three Toronto Stanley Cup winners in the 1940s.

When the hockey player was born in 1915, he was named Charles Joseph Sylvanus Apps. Everyone knew him as Syl. Although most people considered his name unusual, Apps said he came by it in a logical fashion.

"My mother's people came from England—their name was Wrigley, like the chewing gum—and there was a Sylvanus Wrigley," Apps said. "I was named after him."

He learned to skate as a youngster when his father flooded the front lawn. When he got a bit older Apps improvised, flooding a slightly larger area that led to a garage on the property. He nailed a garbage can lid to the door and used it for shooting target practice.

"I sure made a lot of noise back there trying to bang the lid on that garage door," he said.

Although he placed sixth in the Olympic pole vault Apps said his biggest moment in sport, perhaps bigger than winning Stanley Cups, was winning the British Empire Games pole vault in 1934.

"Just being in London as a nineteen-year-old was quite a thrill," he said.

Conn Smythe actually first noticed Apps when he was playing in a college football game for McMaster University. He was so impressed by his skills he added him to the Leafs' negotiating list. Because of amateur rules, he could not approach Apps, though, until after he competed in the Olympics.

Ranking right behind was winning the 1942 Stanley Cup, his first. Watching his team play inconsistently, coach Hap Day shook up a key line, inserting Apps into a trio with Don and Nick Metz.

The Leafs won that night and won the next three to top the Red Wings. Apps scored five goals and added nine assists.

That solidified Apps's stature in Toronto. So did making community public appearances.

"We always did a lot of speaking to boys' groups and whatnot," Apps said. "I guess players do that today, too, although we did it for nothing."

Apps was a clean, stylish player known for his stick-handling and smooth skating. He did not swear and when he got angry he issued such exclamations as "Jiminy Christmas!" As a rookie his teeth were rearranged by a stick to the face, and while enraged enough to engage in fisticuffs, the nastiest words emanating from Apps's mouth were, "By, hum!"

"I didn't swear, so I substituted other words that didn't sound so bad," Apps said. "To say 'By, hum,' I guess you have to be as mad as somebody who's just had two teeth knocked out."

Fighting was not a usual part of Apps's repertoire. He was a Lady Byng Trophy winner.

"It's funny how you learn to play the game," he said. "When you are a rookie you chase after the puck in the corner and the defenseman shoves you into the boards. A couple of years later you go into the corner together with the defenseman. And toward the end of your career you let the defenseman go in first and then you shove him into the boards."

Apps completed his career with 432 points in 423 games. He had stated a desire to reach 200 goals in his playing days, but when he announced his retirement he was just shy of the milestone. To hit 200 he scored a hat trick in his final game. That put him at 201.

Apps was only thirty-three when he retired. A year later Apps wrote an article entitled, "My Advice to All Young Hockey Players."

He offered a six-part program discussing the desire to play, staying in shape, working hard to improve skating, practicing hard, being known as a team player, and making sure to believe in one's self.

"Once you have made a place on a hockey team," he wrote, "don't become an individualist. Cooperate in every way. Be a real team man. Don't blame anyone. Take a share of the blame yourself."

Apps won a seat in parliament after hockey and was awarded an honorary degree from York University.

Family members most assuredly kept the Apps name alive in the athletic world. His son Syl Jr. played for the New York Rangers, primarily for the Pittsburgh Penguins, and finally the Los Angeles Kings. This Apps scored as many as 99 points in a season on 32 goals and 67 assists. Lifetime, Syl Jr. scored 183 goals, just short of his father's total.

Syl Apps III was a star for Princeton University and spent four years in the minors. A granddaughter, Gillian Apps, won three Winter Olympic gold medals, in 2006, 2010, and 2014 while playing for Canada's women's hockey team. Another grandson, Darren Barber, Gillian's cousin, won an Olympic gold medal in rowing.

Syl Apps died of a heart attack at eighty-three in 1998. He was later pictured on a Canadian postage stamp.

Teeder Kennedy

A Hall of Famer who was brilliant at winning face-offs, Teeder Kennedy was the Toronto Maple Leafs' captain for so long he should have been promoted to general. Kennedy held the honor for eight years while playing his entire 16-season NHL career with the

Leafs. During that period, between 1942 and 1957, they won five Stanley Cups.

Born in Port Colborne, Ontario, Theodore Kennedy was introduced to hockey in an unusual manner. His father died eleven days before he was born and so his mother, raising four children, entered the workforce at a local ice rink. Kennedy spent much post-school free time on the premises. Young friends could not pronounce Theodore, so he became Teeder.

Only eighteen when he broke in with the Leafs, Kennedy was not actually known as a superior skater. Other elements of his game, from defense to forechecking to controlling those face-offs, were more significant. Howie Meeker, a Kennedy line mate, said Kennedy made up for lack of skating speed by skating through opponents. His true trademark was a supreme work ethic. He gave that 110 percent 110 percent of the time.

Conn Smythe called Kennedy "the greatest competitor in hockey. Ted Kennedy was not a superbly gifted athlete. But he accomplished more than most by never playing a shift where he did not give everything he had."

Kennedy understood if he did not skate as fast as other stars he had to bring other things to the table.

"I never had much speed," Kennedy said, "certainly not the way Syl Apps or Max Bentley or Milt Schmidt, the great centers did, so I compensated by using my wingers. To be able to pass reasonably well made up for my lack of speed."

By the 1944–45 season Kennedy led the Maple Leafs in scoring with 29 goals and 25 assists. He finished with 231 goals and 329 assists. The Leafs of that era were considered the first dynasty in NHL history. After the 1954–55 season Kennedy won the Hart Trophy as the league's Most Valuable Player.

Some called the 1947–48 Maple Leafs the best team ever. The roster featured Kennedy, Syl Apps, Max Bentley, Turk Broda, Howie Meeker, and Fleming MacKell.

When it became apparent that Kennedy won more than his share of face-offs, fans in Maple Leaf Gardens began chanting for him when the puck dropped. They yelled, "Come on Tee-der, come on, Tee-der."

Kennedy put his all into each face-off.

"I always went all-out at face-offs, especially those in our own end," Kennedy said. "A face-off is the only time when play is at a standstill and you can set up a system, predetermining what happens next. Everything was decided by signals. I would gesture with my hand or nod my head. I wouldn't always go for the draw. In the other team's end I would send the puck into the corner and Meeker, [Vic] Lynn, or [Sid] Smith would usually go there."

Kennedy turned face-offs into a science. Once, later in life, he drew diagrams using paper and pencil for a reporter explaining how he won so many.

"Strength and reflexes are important," Kennedy said long after retirement. "I still have good reflexes, something I was blessed with. Never watch the referee's hand. Watch the ice. And keep your eye out for the other fellow's weakness."

Kennedy said it was an honor to be a longtime captain of the Leafs and he was conscious of Conn Smythe's high standards.

"He ran the team like an army," Kennedy said. "Discipline counted, officers must show leadership on the battlefield, that sort of thing. He demanded his respect for his captains. And look at the captains he chose. Hap Day was a disciplinarian. Syl Apps led an exemplary life. There was a tradition of top guys and you had to adhere to standards when you were captain."

Kennedy was involved in a play that nearly cost young Gordie Howe his career. On one play he was slicker than Howe. Howe was attempting to take him out with a check, but Kennedy sidestepped it.

Howe crashed into the boards headfirst at high speed with teammate Jack Stewart falling on him. Howe incurred a concussion, facial fractures, and cut one of his eyes. For a time it was felt Howe's life might be in danger.

Kennedy was accused by Detroit officials of somehow causing the mishap, but all he did was escape the hit.

"Everybody saw that Howe ran himself into the boards," Kennedy said. "When Howe hit the boards he almost landed in Clarence Campbell's lap. He was sitting right there and saw everything, the president of the league."

Kennedy knew when the time was right to retire.

"I retired because I'd had enough," he said of his 1957 choice. "When you're young, hockey's a lark. After a few seasons it changes. It's a pick-and-shovel job. And you're under pressure all the time. That gets tiring. I could never sleep on trains. I'd have to wait till we reached whatever city we were going to and sleep all day in the hotel."

When Kennedy retired he was given an unusual gift—a grandfather clock. Near the end of Kennedy's life at eighty-three in 2009 his family donated the clock to the hometown Port Colborne history museum. By then the local hockey rink had long been named the Teeder Kennedy Youth Center.

Some of the Boys

Wherever Red Kelly went the Stanley Cup seemed sure to follow. Over twenty years in the National Hockey League between 1947 and

1967, Kelly split his career between the Detroit Red Wings and the Toronto Maple Leafs and he played for eight championship clubs.

A Hall of Fame defenseman for thirteen years before shifting to center and who coached ten years in the NHL, as well, Kelly served as a Liberal member of Parliament in the 1960s—while still active with the Leafs. Although everyone called him Red, Kelly's given name was Leonard.

After thirty years at the highest level of the game Kelly's hair was not as bright in color as it used to be, but his attitude about success in the NHL had not changed.

"If I've succeeded in anything it's because I try to outwork the next guy," Kelly said. "Work is simply a synonym for effort and as I tell my players, 'If there is one thing that will cost you your job in a hurry, it is lack of effort, lack of try.'"

The 5-foot-11, 185-pound Kelly was a prolific scorer for a blueliner. He tallied 281 goals with 542 assists in 1,316 games. Kelly won the Lady Byng Trophy four times and a Norris Trophy as the best defenseman in the league in 1954. He was selected for eight All-Star teams.

"To me, if you've given your best and lost, you need never hang your head," Kelly said.

In some quarters Kelly was not even viewed as a solid prospect. But he showed enough to become a regular by age twenty. A scout told him he wouldn't last 20 games in the NHL, a dramatic miscalculation.

"Certain people were saying I wasn't good enough," Kelly said. "I've always been fortunate to realize the value of hard work and extra effort. The world belongs to those who aim a little bit higher each time out."

By 1950, Kelly's third year in the NHL, Tommy Ivan, then Detroit's coach, was in love with his skills.

"Kelly is the greatest all-around player in hockey and also the most underrated," Ivan said. "We've used Kelly at every job except as goalie and he's been outstanding wherever we put him."

Demonstrating toughness, Kelly played at the end of the 1958–59 season with a broken foot taped tightly. The foot, as well as the injury, was kept under wraps.

Kelly coached the Los Angeles Kings—that team's first coach—the Pittsburgh Penguins, and the Maple Leafs.

"I've occasionally been disillusioned with management, but never with hockey," he said. "I loved hockey. I loved playing. Can you imagine playing for twenty years in the NHL? There's the rink and there's a little black puck and every day you chase that thing up and down. Can you imagine that?"

Kelly grew up on a farm and the center of home activity was the piano. He said the family held barn dances. Most of the adults besides the farmer father were lawyers or priests, Kelly said, noting "the idea of me playing pro hockey was frowned upon." But as a youth he rode a pony three miles to a pond to practice. Hockey was in his blood.

"That little puck spins this way and it spins that way and you have to learn what is the best way to approach it, how if you're traveling 30 miles an hour you can pass it to a player going just as fast," he said, "or to one who is standing still, how to lift the puck over an obstacle. You learn all those things and you don't do it overnight."

Many observers thought the most unusual thing he managed to pull off in his career was serving in parliament between 1962 and 1965 while playing.

"I just did it," was Kelly's explanation for how he found the time. "There were some jokes about the Member for Center Ice.

We won an election, the Stanley Cup, and I had a son. We went through two elections, three Stanley Cups, and two children."

Once, Kelly nearly missed a game because of duties in parliament. He was driven to the airport, jumped on a flight to Montreal, and got to the Forum just in time.

"As I tore into the dressing room the other players were heading out on the ice for the warm-up," Kelly said. "I practiced by myself every day. I rented the ice over in Hull."

That was not even close to Kelly's most bizarre incident in pro hockey. His baby son Conn was put into the Cup for a picture and he went to the bathroom through his diaper.

"He did a full load in the Cup, so we all chuckle when they drink out of it now," Kelly said years later.

Howie Meeker

There was actually precedent for an NHL player to serve in parliament. Howie Meeker, who played ten seasons for the Leafs between 1946 and 1955, was a Conservative member of the legislative body.

Meeker scored 27 goals with 18 assists and won the Calder Trophy as rookie of the year in his first season. He spent his entire NHL career with the Leafs, playing in three All-Star games and as part of four Stanley Cup championship teams. Meeker had a five-goal game in his career.

After his playing career, Meeker coached the Maple Leafs for one year and served as general manager. He spent years teaching hockey to youths in camps and then he assumed a major role on *Hockey Night in Canada*. That earned him a spot in the Hall of Fame.

Meeker said deciding to run for parliament was tough and even after deliberating very carefully with his wife he never expected to win.

"If I'd thought I would have won the whole thing I wouldn't have run," he said. "Everybody figured the Liberals would win."

Prime Minister Louis St. Laurent was a Montreal Canadiens fan and the first time Meeker returned to chambers after a losing game against Montreal, sporting a black eye, as well, St. Laurent exercised privilege to make Meeker tell about the loss. Meeker said St. Laurent repeated this act until Toronto won a game.

When that happened, Meeker crossed to a seat next to St. Laurent and said, "Mr. Prime Minister, we kicked ass in Montreal last night. Tell me about it!" Members of parliament roared with laughter.

Jimmy Thomson

Born in Manitoba, Jimmy Thomson broke in with Toronto in 1945. A defenseman who played in seven All-Star games, Thomson never scored more than four goals in a season and scored just 19 in his career, but he hit hard and often.

Thomson became the Leafs' captain for the 1956–57 season, but got on the wrong side of owner Conn Smythe by working as an organizer of the league's players' union. Smythe exiled Thomson to Chicago for the last year of his career in 1957–58.

"The only difference between Thomson and me," Smythe said, "is that he thinks he's a great hockey player and I think he was a great hockey player."

Thomson said Smythe's opinion changed because of his union activities.

"He specifically took issue with me a couple of months ago when he charged I was a poor influence on the young Toronto players by representing them on the Players' Association Committee," Thomson said.

Thomson was ready for a trade.

"I want to play hockey in the NHL again next season," he said at the time, "but certainly not with the Leafs because I feel my loyalty has been questioned."

After one season in Chicago, Thomson's rights were turned back to Toronto. No other team wanted him. There was a belief Smythe blackballed Thomson and he left the game at thirty-one.

It was shabby treatment for a four-time Cup winner and a perennial All-Star. When Thomson left hockey he became a successful businessman before dying of a heart attack at sixty-four.

More Good Guys

Allan Stanley

Although Allan Stanley began his National Hockey League career with the New York Rangers in 1948 and finished it with the Philadelphia Flyers in 1969, a major part of his career (ten years) was spent with the Toronto Maple Leafs. His Toronto time made his best case for acceptance in the Hall of Fame, where he was inducted in 1981.

A four-time Stanley Cup winner, Stanley only twice scored as many as 10 goals in a season. He scored 100 goals exactly in regular-season games. Not the swiftest of skaters, Stanley's nickname was "Snowshoes."

Stanley was a hotshot minor leaguer and New York paid $70,000 for his rights, hence a label of "The $70,000 Beauty." However, he didn't seem to be a hard-nosed enough guy for demanding Broadway fans.

"Fans would boo me in the warm-ups," Stanley said of his stay in New York.

It all worked out for Stanley as he got his name repeatedly engraved on the Stanley Cup because of his association with the Maple Leafs.

"I'd hate to think of our defense without Sam," said Leafs coach Punch Imlach, using part of another of Stanley's nicknames, Silent Sam. "I use him on the power play, to kill penalties, and to take a regular shift."

Stanley was also one of those old-time guys whose fortitude sometimes overruled common sense. Once, his calf was nicked by the skate blade of an opposing player. He limped home, but prepared to play right after.

"It hurts in practice," he said, "but it doesn't hurt in games."

Stanley was forty-two when he went to the Flyers on a sort of elder statesman valedictory tour.

"We listen to him and we learn," said Philadelphia defenseman Joe Watson.

Stanley laughed at himself that year when he made a return trip to Maple Leaf Gardens in Toronto and pretty much forgot what team he belonged to after 10 years with the other side.

"It was amazing how many things I did wrong," Stanley said. "I was getting in the wrong lineup. I went to the wrong bench. I constantly had the urge to skate with the blue sweatered team."

As a card-carrying member of the Original Six for the last two decades before expansion, Stanley said doubling the size of the league was hard to get used to.

"I'd look up, see a stranger, or a comparative stranger," he said, "and say to myself, 'Who the heck is this guy and what can he do?' That made me play a hesitant game until I learned their individual styles."

After he retired, Stanley operated a golf resort. When he was sixty, a reporter asked if he was going to play senior hockey. He said he wasn't old enough. Stanley lived to be eighty-seven.

Ron Stewart

A winger from Calgary, Ron Stewart played thirteen of his twenty-four years in the National Hockey League with the Maple Leafs, scoring 276 goals in 1,353 games. A member of three Stanley Cup–winning teams, Stewart was good for about 15 goals per season. His career high was 21 goals.

Scoring may not have been his forte, but Stewart was deployed in a variety of roles, often assigned to do the dirty work killing penalties and checking.

As a kid, Stewart, one of two children, was taught to skate by his older sister May. They were close growing up and sis thought of herself as a pretty good skater. Stewart was not even five years old yet and surprised members of the family with the way he took to the ice. As soon as he stood up on skates he glided away on his own, showing he did not need lessons at all.

"I just stood there amazed," May said.

Talk about a natural-born skater.

Eddie Shack

Although he played for the New York Rangers, Boston Bruins, Buffalo Sabres, Pittsburgh Penguins, and Los Angeles Kings—just about anyone who would have him in his 1,047-game career—Eddie Shack was best known for his years with the Toronto Maple Leafs.

Actually, he was probably best known for being the unique Eddie Shack. Shack was from Ontario and seemed destined for a career as a butcher when he tried hockey and found out he was pretty good at it. The 6-foot-1, 200-pound wing was part of four Stanley Cup championship teams in Toronto. He was given credit for the winning goal in the 1963 Finals, but later said the puck hit him in the butt as he was trying to get out of the way of it.

Shack's nickname was "The Entertainer" and his personality was more outsized than his game, although he did score 239 regular-season goals. He was also good enough to play in three All-Star games between breaking into the NHL in the late 1950s and his retirement in the late 1970s.

A hard-nosed player who pleased fans with his checking, Shack was also known for having a big nose. He was so popular in Toronto that a song was written about him called "Clear the Track, Here Comes Eddie Shack."

To some degree Shack was musical. He once played the maracas with a singing group and made a guest appearance with the Toronto Symphony. Featuring an extra-large mustache, in some photographs from the 1960s Shack resembled Ringo Starr of the Beatles. Some called Shack "The Clown Prince of Hockey."

He also became popular on the banquet circuit. Shack could talk a good game. He had little formal schooling and was illiterate. He once said, "I tried learning reading and writing a few times and finally gave up. When you're a dummy you have smart guys around you. Also saved me money because I didn't buy scrapbooks. What's the use of keeping clippings if you don't know what they say?"

It didn't seem as if Shack tried to master those school subjects.

"Hockey was just a way to get out of Sudbury," he said of his hometown. "I hated school. I didn't like my teachers. They used to give me a lickin' and I'd run home, then they'd bring me back for another lickin'."

Shack said he was working as a butcher's assistant by the time he was eight and dropped out of school in the third grade. Another time he said he was kicked out of second grade for not shaving. He also said he was promoted from grade three because he lent the teacher his car.

"I was a little bastard, always getting into fights," he said. "I was a big kid and I looked older so I was able to get my driver's license when I was thirteen. Then I lost my license at fourteen."

Many years after retiring from hockey, Shack became involved in efforts to promote literacy.

"I always tell kids to make an effort in school," Shack said. "It's no fun going through life not being able to read street signs or maps. I've had to lean on a lot of people for help in my life, especially my wife."

Growing up, one neighbor was future Leafs great and teammate Tim Horton. Shack called Horton his hero, but said he didn't get to know him until they were on the Toronto roster together.

Shack was fairly business-savvy and said his strength was promotion, of events and of himself. People liked Shack and they liked to hear him sing or talk. He did not think of himself as an elite player and sometimes issued self-deprecating comments. Of those 239 goals, Shack said, "That's pretty fair in eighteen seasons, especially when you figure how much time I spent on the bench."

Far from being haughty, Shack made jokes about himself. Of his 1937 birth, he said, "I was an 11.6-pound little boy and that included a two-pound nose." Shack, who perhaps fancied himself as the second coming of Jimmy Durante, once insured his nose for $1 million, admitting he did so for publicity.

Shack obtained endorsement contracts for various products, and when surveys were conducted he had tremendously high name recognition across the country and name brand identification with his companies.

One reason was how beloved Shack was by hockey fans. He could not readily pinpoint that appeal, either.

"I just love to play hockey and maybe the crowd knows how much fun I have doing it," Shack said. "Ya know, when I watch myself on videotape I laugh like hell because I look pretty funny when I skate, funnier when I shoot, and really hilarious when I try to make a fancy move on some guy. Maybe the crowd thinks it's funny, too."

There was a running joke during Shack's early days with the Leafs that he played all three forward positions—at the same time. He seemed to be skating all over the ice rather than undertaking one assignment. When he hit athletic old age, however, he covered less territory.

"I don't run all over the ice the way I used to," Shack said. "That stuff's for the eager youngsters. My style is more suitable to a veteran of my age. Now I just skate from Point A to Point B. That will surprise a lot of people who figured I didn't know the second letter in the alphabet."

Shack made it seem as if he had withdrawn from excess verbiage as a habit, too.

"I'm not pontificatin' much any more, either," Shack said. "I don't know quite what that means. I learned the word from Carl Brewer when we were with the Leafs. Carl used to say he was doing that a lot and I figured if Brewer, who'd been to college, was doing it all the time, then it had to help me. But it didn't, so I've stopped doing it."

Shack did okay. He pretty much owned a palace of a home that included his own sauna, pool table, large yard that he drove around in with a dune buggy and was located next to a golf course. Oh yes, he owned the Toronto-area course. The *Toronto Sun* featured the house in its Homes section after Shack's retirement, crediting wife Norma as the decorator of record.

As only familiarity in the Original Six era could bring, Detroit general manager Jack Adams routinely talked trash to Shack. He yelled that he could not spell goal, never mind score one. When Shack did score on the Red Wings, he skated over to the boards, leaned in to Adams and said, "S-C-O-R-E."

Bob Baun

Except for a four-year hiatus with other teams in the middle of his 17-year National Hockey League career, defenseman Bob Baun spent all of his ice time with the Toronto Maple Leafs between 1956 and 1973.

Known for his hard checks, Baun issued far more body checks during his career than he scored points. His contributions did not show up in the box score, but were in the eye of the beholder.

In 964 NHL games, Baun scored just 37 goals, never more than eight in a single year. He added 187 assists. He did accumulate 1,491 penalty minutes. He earned his keep that way and some called him "The Gorilla" for his hard-hitting ways. Baun was good enough to play on four Leafs Cup champions, however.

Besides hitting hard, Baun, who sometimes was called "Boomer," also rubbed it in, or teased opponents into making illegal hits on him with verbal assaults.

"I'm an aggravating son-of-a-gun," Baun said. "I'm so aggravating even my wife wonders why more guys don't TKO me."

The 5-foot-9, 182-pound Baun was known for his toughness. He fractured an ankle in a 1964 playoff game against Detroit and returned to the game to score the winning goal with the leg heavily taped.

"I knew it was broken, but I wanted to get out there in overtime," he said. "The trainer gave me a shot of painkiller and we laced the skate up tight."

Even then Baun did not submit to an X-ray. The victory was in a sixth game of the series. He played in the seventh game, won by the Leafs, and then got the X-ray showing the break.

"I never saw it as anything especially brave," Baun said. "I never even thought of not going back in the game. That's the way it was then. It was all emotion. It was still sore as blazes eight weeks later."

Baun once suffered a cut in his neck from a skate blade and was hemorrhaging blood before teammate Tim Horton got him to a hospital. Medical personnel placed Baun in a bed next to his wife, who was giving birth. That's one version of the story. Another is that wife Sallie heard on the radio that Baun might die from his wound, only to wake up and find him by her bedside to tell her the seriousness of the matter was exaggerated.

Baun played with a broken neck for five years and only retired at thirty-six because of the need for a spinal fusion.

The Leafs made him available in the big expansion draft when the NHL doubled in size from the Original Six and Baun was selected by the Oakland team. He said it was difficult at times to psyche himself up for games in Northern California.

"It's murder trying to concentrate on hockey when the temperature hovers about the 75-degree mark and the sun is shining," Baun said. "I had two winter scenes, good paintings, in my living room. I'd pull the drapes on game days, light the lights over the paintings and light the fireplace in an effort to get in the mood for hockey.

It may sound ridiculous having a fireplace going with the weather a balmy 70, but I think it helped a little."

His first job outside the game was operating a cattle ranch, but he coached the Toronto Toros of the World Hockey Association for one season before being fired for losing.

Baun may not have been much of a goal scorer, but he was pretty much a Renaissance man. Baun came to that role gradually after first being viewed as a country bumpkin from Lanigan, Saskatchewan, as an eighteen-year-old rookie.

"I didn't dress very well then and when we were out anywhere the other fellows on the team made me walk a hundred feet behind them," Baun said. "I didn't like that much. I've always gone first-class ever since then in everything."

Baun helped form the NHL Alumni Association, was awarded an honorary doctorate, and drove a hard bargain over his contract with Imlach. Sometimes he disappeared from team transportation as a protest statement against being underpaid.

"I'll never get ulcers," Baun said. "When I put my head on that pillow I go to sleep. I'm not a worrier."

Baun invested in his future. Among other things he operated an automobile dealership, became a representative of an Italian restaurant, and ran a contracting company. He started a gourmet club because he was a fine cook. Baun had a wine cellar going, too. He might be the only NHL player to compare his sport to cooking.

"Cooking is very much like hockey," Baun said, no doubt speaking over the head of young players who live at McDonald's. "You've got to have a bit of an edge going in. And you've got to be excited about what you're doing. You've got to have those taste buds going for you, salivating a bit."

Once, after Baun had committed to a duck hunt on a day off, Imlach called for a morning practice. Baun tried to notify the coach of his alternate plan, but couldn't reach him and he went hunting anyway. But then he told Imlach he had been a no-show because his grandmother died. Unfortunately for Baun, a Saskatoon sports section got wind of his hunting trip and reported on it.

Imlach blew a gasket, but Baun yelled right back when Imlach threatened to send him home.

"You send me home and I'll go moose hunting and really visit my grandmother," Baun said.

In retirement, Baun retained his Maple Leafs seasons tickets. In 1983 he said they cost more than he made as a rookie in 1956–57.

George Armstrong

No one expected young George Armstrong to become a National Hockey League player because he was not a good skater as a kid. His father blamed spinal meningitis, incurred at age six, but Armstrong overcame early limitations to put together a Hall of Fame career for the Maple Leafs.

Armstrong played for Toronto between 1949 (just two games that season) and 1971, appearing in 1,187 games. He scored 296 goals, later he was an assistant general manager for the club, and coached the team one year. He was Leafs captain for 13 seasons.

Armstrong, who was from Ontario, was nicknamed "Chief" because part of his heritage was native. In retirement Armstrong was famous for working for charitable causes and also for bringing attention to Native needs and helping groups providing good role models for Native children.

When he was a boy, Armstrong experienced some discrimination. While never ashamed of his heritage, Armstrong told his mother one reason he worked so hard at the game was to prove any doubters wrong.

The most famous goal Armstrong didn't score came in the 1958–59 playoffs against the Montreal Canadiens. At a crucial point, Armstrong fired at netminder Jacques Plante. No goal was signaled and Armstrong was livid. He was correct, he had scored, but no one in authority saw it. The puck went through the webbing of the net behind Plante. A minority of people saw it. That included Montreal coach Toe Blake, and he wasn't about to tell the officials they blew the call helping his team.

Armstrong protested. Officials shook their heads no.

"I tell you, I just scored!" Armstrong said when he skated to the bench.

There was no such thing as instant replay at the time, but the next day a film version of the play was examined—in those days it took until overnight for them to be readied for viewing—and Armstrong was proved right, if too late. The "score" became known as Armstrong's "invisible goal" or "phantom goal."

Despite his longevity, Armstrong's 6-foot-1, 185-pound body may not have been cut out for big-league hockey. That's because he began suffering from ulcers at nineteen.

"And I was plagued by them during my entire playing career," Armstrong said. "Just ask my former roommates, Johnny Bower or Dickie Duff. They'll be able to tell you the many tablets I used to take to make the pain bearable."

Right after retirement, Armstrong was filmed playing a role in the 1971 movie *Face-Off* about a fictional hockey player. He even had a love scene, but it ended up on the cutting room floor.

"I didn't care one way or the other, but it would have been a big laugh, right?" he said.

Apparently Armstrong's wife cared. She told Armstrong she was going to inform the director the object of her hubby's love in the movie had to be her, his mother, or his daughter.

"Honest, though, I never ever dreamed of being in a movie," Armstrong said. "I never thought of it until they phoned me last week. Then I said why not. But I told them it had to be on the condition that if I wasn't any good, they'd fire me."

In the film Armstrong played a hockey player named George Armstrong, but not himself, actually.

Armstrong said he made $7,000 for his first contract with the Maple Leafs and his mother witnessed the deal.

"You were happy to sign," Armstrong said. "You felt it was a privilege to sign. Nine out of ten rookies got the minimum $7,000 and that's all there was to it."

Rookie Armstrong was thrilled to be a teammate of legends Max Bentley, Turk Broda, and Teeder Kennedy.

"I absolutely went ape when they told me I'd be rooming with Bentley," Armstrong said.

Armstrong's newcomer responsibilities were buying Bentley a newspaper and a sandwich on command.

"I'd be thankful for the privilege," Armstrong said. "It was like running errands for the prime minister."

Punch Imlach

As coach of the Maple Leafs George "Punch" Imlach demanded strict discipline, a strict dress code, had no sentiment about keeping players instead of trading them if he felt he was trading up, and often insulted them to their faces.

Defenseman Tim Horton once said of Imlach's tough approach, "Well, George preaches a strange gospel, but it seems to work."

For all of that Imlach's tenure produced 402 victories and four Stanley Cup championships. The record sent him into the Hall of Fame.

Imlach was impugned because of his lack of communication skills, but he wasn't trying to become friends with his players. Imlach later got the expansion Buffalo Sabres in business, but returned to the Leafs as assistant GM, reporting directly to owner Harold Ballard.

In 1981, Imlach's connection with the team ended when he came to work and saw his private parking place had been eliminated.

"I wish I could be behind the bench," he said. "That's where the fun is. It's the best thing in the world. That's the thrill, the real thrill."

Imlach died at age sixty-nine in 1987, after his fifth heart attack.

Tim Horton

There are some people who don't even realize that Tim Horton's donut shop chain has anything to do with a Hall of Fame hockey player. They don't even realize there was a Tim Horton hockey player. Probably not so in Toronto, but that's definitely true in the United States.

The hockey player earned enough fame and respect based on his accomplishments over a 24-season career between 1949 and 1974. Most of them, 19 seasons, were representing the Maple Leafs.

Horton, a 5-foot-10, 190-pound native of Ontario, was a defensive specialist who scored 115 goals in his career and never more than 12 in a season. Horton five times was chosen either a first- or second-team league All-Star.

Although he was sturdily built, Horton was no giant. But even Gordie Howe, who was often depicted as the strongest man in the

National Hockey League disagreed. Nope, he said, "Horton is the strongest."

Horton's personality did not come on strong. He did not curse, drink, or make off-the-ice waves. Horton did not have it in him to be an enforcer. Coach Punch Imlach was simply a hard-hitting clean player and that was scary enough.

"You can't call Tim a really tough player because he's not really mean," Imlach said. "But he's the toughest player in the National Hockey League when he's riled up."

Horton was both muscular enough and strong enough to apply a signature bear hug move on rushing forwards, as if it was a wrestling match.

Derek Sanderson, the former Boston Bruin, said, "I heard a cracking noise and figured it was my ribs going one by one."

Horton was still drawing compliments from opposing players as he approached his fortieth birthday.

"Horton's the hardest bodychecker I've ever come up against," said Montreal's John Ferguson. "He's as strong as an ox and hits with terrific force."

To some extent Horton's reputation improved with age.

"My style hasn't changed," Horton said. "But I don't rush up ice as much as I used to. I've learned that the most important thing is to check well in our end. I'll only carry the puck more if we're behind."

To some extent Horton changed his game.

"I was young and reckless in my early years in the league," he said. "I had a very bad temper. I guess I still have one, but I've managed to contain it as much as possible. Otherwise, I would have spent much more time in the penalty box."

Unlike professional athletes of today who make staggering amounts of money from their teams, Horton got rich from his entrepreneurship off the ice. Tim Horton Donuts became an international sensation after he lent his name to the sweet shop and co-founded it in 1964. The first store opened in Hamilton, Ontario, and these days it features a statue of Horton the hockey player out front.

"I love eating donuts," Horton once said, "and that was one of the big reasons that I opened my first shop. Buying donuts was costing me too much money."

Horton had a partner named Ron Joyce who ran things while the defenseman was playing hockey. Horton was the one who scouted new sites and secured financing. Once, a sportswriter asked Horton if he ever actually made any donuts.

"I have fooled around with it," he said. "But I never did go through the whole process. One day I will have to do it just to see whether I can do it. Mind you, they don't need my help in that respect. We're successful because we offer a good product. They're buying it because of that and not because of my name."

By 1974 there were forty Tim Hortons in the chain. In February of that year, Tim Horton the person was killed in an automobile accident. His car was traveling 100 mph when it crashed in St. Catherines, Ontario, taking his life at age forty-four. There were suggestions he may have been drunk, but no official statement was made on that topic. More than thirty years later it was revealed Horton was driving drunk.

"No finer person, teammate, or hockey player has ever lived," said Horton's former Leafs teammate George Armstrong.

When Horton died he left behind a wife and four daughters. Joyce bought out their interest in the chain for $1 million. Then he embarked on a super expansion program that put Tim Hortons on seemingly every occupied corner in Canada and spilled into the United States, as well.

As of the end of 2014 there were approximately 4,500 Tim Horton's donut shops. Surprisingly, there are more than fifty of the stores in the Persian Gulf. In the late 1980s a franchise operator put Tim Hortons and Wendy's, the hamburger chain, in nine locations. In 1995, Tim Hortons partnered with Wendy's for more than $540 million when there were 1,000 outlets. At the end of 2014, Wendy's bought out the operation for $11.4 billion.

Horton never lived long enough to see the spectacular success of the donut chain, but he lived long enough for it to make him wealthy and know his idea had blossomed.

The hockey player's legacy lives on at the Parry Sound, Ontario, Tim Horton Memorial Camp for kids who otherwise could not afford a summer camp experience. Thousands have attended the camp in the last forty years.

Johnny Bower

Perhaps the most beloved athlete in Toronto sports history, Maple Leafs goaltender Johnny Bower, still going strong in his nineties in early 2016, was an unlikely star in the sport that at first seemed to spurn him.

If it seemed it took forever for Bower to break into the National Hockey League it probably seemed even longer to him. By the time he found his way to the NHL with the New York Rangers Bower was twenty-nine. He didn't make his first start for the Leafs until he was thirty-four.

Bower was from a Saskatchewan family that was not well-fixed. The price of equipment during the Great Depression, especially in a family of eight kids, was prohibitive. Bower found his goalie trade because he couldn't afford skates and sticking to the net allowed him to play with the other kids. He cut up an old mattress for pads and used a tree branch for a stick.

Horse pucky was turned into hockey pucks. The kids followed a horse, sometimes for a half mile, until it relieved itself. The residue froze and was shaped.

"They'd be like rocks in no time," Bower said. "Made great pucks."

Bower lasted in the big-time until he was forty-five, squeezing in 15 seasons good enough to earn him a place in the Hall of Fame. Along the way, Bower, whose lifetime goals against average was a splendid 2.51, won the Vezina Trophy twice and four Stanley Cups. Bower played in five All-Star games.

The funny part of the whole age business was that despite Bower's date of birth being announced as November 8, 1924, he often lied about his age, confusing everyone. People wondered if he was really two or three years older, although ultimately it appeared the regularly used date of birth was accurate.

He was so tough to score on that Bower earned the nickname "The China Wall." He actually acquired the nickname as a star in the American Hockey League with Cleveland.

A man of Ukrainian descent, Bower was originally known as John Kiszkan. He said he changed his last name to make life easier on sportswriters. That may be the only time in sports history such a reason was given for such a drastic change.

Bower, who was honored with a star on Canada's Walk of Fame, also appeared on a postage stamp and was featured in a four-coin commemorative set of Maple Leafs legends. He is the oldest goalie to appear in an NHL game, at forty-five years, one month, two days old.

Toronto coach Punch Imlach, with a nod to Bower's seeming imperviousness to age, called him "The most amazing athlete in the world. Bower just hated to lose."

Somewhat later, when Bower was forty-five, the Leafs were in a pinch and suited him up as a back-up netminder for a night.

"I don't want anyone to think I'd try to make every goalie play my style," Bower said. "But there are certain things all goaltenders must do to be successful. Another goalie can look and see if he's doing the right things. And there are a few little tricks."

Bower, who even despised giving up goals to teammates in practice, was known as an expert at reaching out with his stick and swiping the puck away from charging forwards.

As talented and accomplished as Bower was, as the years went by it was impossible to overlook his age. "In those later years all kinds of people would come up to me and say, 'John, how do you do it? What's your secret?' I always told them that it was just hard work and that was the truth."

It wasn't as if the Leafs were unaware that Bower was aging on the calendar. Year after year they brought challengers to training camp and let them loose trying to win the job. Bower kept repelling them.

"When competition got stiffer I worked three times as hard," he said. "Competition drove me."

If the oldest player on the team kept putting out, letting the sweat pour down his face, then it was difficult to be a younger guy and not give it your all.

"He was an inspiration to us," said longtime teammate George Armstrong. "He shamed others into hard work. John gave everything he could in workouts and we weren't going to let that old guy show us up."

Since the Maple Leafs have not won a Stanley Cup since 1967, Bower remains the last Toronto goalie to win the biggest prize in the sport. When the clock ran out and the Leafs clinched the title, Bower threw his stick in the air in celebration. He did not remember to catch it and when the lumber fell from the sky it conked him on the head. The wound required six stitches.

After he finally stepped away from the ice, Bower stuck with the Leafs as an assistant coach-goalie instructor specialist under Red Kelly. He had to climb high above the ice to watch and then go down to the dressing room between periods and climb back to his seat again. He counted 99 steps up. He could call a time-out for a reward. "Sometimes I can get back in time to grab a sandwich at the buffet in the press room," he said.

On somewhat of a lark in retirement one of Bower's projects was singing a children's song named "Honky, The Christmas Goose."

"I only sing in the shower," Bower said. "And when I told my wife about it later, she just said, 'Oh, my God.'"

The song sold 40,000 records and endured in the public mind for years.

"I got hundreds of calls about that record," Bower said. "People want to know where they can still get a copy. But I used to get calls from angry parents, too. It seems their kids would get up and put the record on at 6 a.m. when the parents were trying to sleep."

Bower remained in demand in retirement. He signed autographs at sports memorabilia events, gave speeches for corporations, in both cases earning money. Other times he helped minor-league hockey teams and charities for free.

"He has absolutely no pretension," said one-time teammate Brian Conacher. "When you get an autograph from Johnny Bower you actually feel like you know Johnny Bower as you walk away. I think he has actually grown in stature since he left the game and the adulation boggles his mind."

In 2007, Bower lost his 1967 Stanley Cup ring in of all places the parking lot of a Tim Hortons donut store. A passerby found it and returned it, but it had been run over by a car and crushed. The manufacturer made a duplicate and presented it to Bower.

"Eddie Shack offered to sell me one of his," Bower joked. "This one sure looks nicer than the other one did. I was so worried I would never get it back. It had a happy ending."

Frank Mahovlich

"The Big M," Frank Mahovlich, could blow just about any other hockey player away with sheer numbers. In 20 seasons in the National Hockey League Mahovlich scored 533 goals in 1,181 games. He played in 15 All-Star games and competed for six Stanley Cup–winning teams. He won the Calder Trophy as rookie of the year, as well.

At the tail end of his career, the 6-foot, 200-pound Mahovlich, from Ontario, played four more seasons in the World Hockey Association, adding another 89 goals to his regular-season totals.

Mahovlich spent the first twelve years of his superb career with the Toronto Maple Leafs and when he scored 48 goals during the 1960–61 season it was a team record that lasted for twenty-one years. Later, with the Detroit Red Wings, Mahovlich scored 49 times in one season. Mahovlich did lament coming so close to bagging 50 and not making it.

During his 1956 to 1978 career Mahovlich was one of the biggest names in hockey. Mahovlich was chosen for the Hall of Fame in 1981 and found out in the most peculiar of ways. He was eating lunch at a club and when he came out to his car he saw a piece of paper flapping in the breeze under his windshield wiper.

For a moment Mahovlich thought he had somehow received a ticket. Instead, it was a note from his wife Marie informing him of his selection to the Hall. It turned out she was in a hurry to make another appointment and thought this was the best way to communicate. Obviously, it was long before cell phones became common.

Mahovlich suited up for four Maple Leaf Stanley Cup winners. The first one, in 1962, was the most special.

"That was probably the most important one," said Mahovlich, who also was on two Cup champs in Montreal. "It's quite a relief being on your first championship team. A lot of good players go through an entire career and never get on one."

By the time Mahovlich notched his 500th career regular-season goal—the fifth player in NHL history to reach that milestone—he was playing for the Montreal Canadiens.

"I couldn't believe it," Mahovlich of the magic number goal. He partially felt that way because he had been stopped earlier in the game on a breakaway that was much more likely to nestle in the net.

Mahovlich scored his 600th goal while playing for the Toronto Toros of the WHA. Only Gordie Howe and Bobby Hull were ahead of him on the goal scoring list at the time and both of them had totals combining their NHL and WHA appearances.

Teammate Steve Shutt said Mahovlich's 600th goal was no thing of beauty. It almost seemed to go in the net by accident. That prize-winner was something else altogether.

"It was a blooper," Shutt said. "It bounced and wobbled and ended up in the net. Frank picked up the puck with a grin on his face. The rest of us broke up."

Mahovlich, whose brother Pete also played in the NHL, came along at a time when salaries were beginning to increase. When he was nineteen he told his father, Pete Sr., to quit his job working in the mines.

"He said he would look after me and my wife because I had worked hard enough in my life," Frank's dad said. "It was hard work all right and I thought I would give retirement a try. It didn't last very long."

The elder Mahovlich went back to work, but not in a mine.

Although never as big a star as his brother, Pete Mahovlich scored 288 goals in 884 NHL games. During the 1974–75 season, Pete Mahovlich scored 117 points and another year he hit 105. Frank never topped 100 points in one year.

Later in life Frank Mahovlich represented Toronto as a senator in parliament. He served from 1998 to 2013 for the Liberal Party. He was already on a postage stamp, but Mahovlich's fame kept expanding. One newspaper headline referred to him as "Senator Slapshot."

"To tell you the truth, 75 percent of the senators, I never heard of them when I came here," Mahovlich said five years into his legislative career. "It's a pretty low profile place to be, to be honest. That's the way I am. Even when I played hockey, I kept a low profile. I was never a rah-rah guy."

Even in his new job, Mahovlich was mobbed for his autograph and it wasn't because he was leading debates on wheat in Alberta. Another senator once said there might be twenty people around Mahovlich at any given moment seeking his signature.

"There may be two people tripping over me," the senator said, "and that's to get to Frank to get his autograph."

Another senator said whenever she appeared at a public forum the first question asked was, "Do you know Frank Mahovlich?"

Dave Keon

Twice Dave Keon won the Lady Byng Trophy, somehow managing to be whistled for just one penalty in each year. Besides that unusual accomplishment a few years apart in the 1960s Keon was a member of four Stanley Cup winners and played in eight All-Star games.

He also won the Calder Trophy as rookie of the year and played in the National Hockey League and World Hockey Association for parts of 24 seasons. He spent the first 15 years of his career with the Maple Leafs. Overall, between his tenure in Toronto, where he gained his greatest fame—enough to be chosen for the Hall of Fame—and his WHA years, Keon appeared in 1,597 games and scored 498 goals.

Keon, who stood 5-foot-9 and weighed just 165 pounds, was an indispensable player. He not only could score, but he also made things happen on the ice. Once, when Keon was injured with the Leafs and had to miss some playing time, coach John McLellan said, "Frankly, I much would have preferred to get along without an arm and a leg. You become so accustomed to using Keon in difficult situations that when he's not there, it's a very insecure feeling."

The center was a master of penalty killing and for a time held the record for most short-handed goals. He was a speedy center and although he was not a hard hitter, he led the Leafs in other ways as captain.

Bob Baun, who played with Keon on the Leafs and then moved on, called Keon, "a hockey player's player. By that I mean he's consistent. He does everything that has to be done. When I played against him he remembered my moves."

Keon's name and the word "class" were often used in the same sentence, even in the same sentence as Joe DiMaggio's name. Keon stuck around from 1960 through 1982.

"Obviously, I can't skate the way I once could, not for any length of time, anyway," Keon said after he turned forty. "But basically I'm making the same assessments I used to make. The things I learned as a junior and in my early pro seasons, the work ethic, I guess, have become so important at this stage of my career."

Keon knew his strengths and weaknesses and didn't want to stick around too long.

"You can't afford to be embarrassed when younger guys begin out-skating you in drills," Keon said. "You can't accept it, either, and say, 'Well, after all, I'm forty.' You've just got to dig in and reduce the differential. If you find yourself taking shortcuts, or looking for excuses, it's time to pack up."

Toronto Maple Leafs Since

The Toronto Maple Leafs have won 13 Stanley Cups, but none since 1967. That represents one of the longest title droughts in North American professional sports. The Leafs remain remarkably popular, with sellouts at every game at the Air Canada Centre and a long season-ticket waiting list.

The fan base is both frustrated and impatient, but much like the Chicago Cubs in Major League Baseball, who haven't won the World Series since 1908, they remain eternally optimistic. The long ownership tenure of Harold Ballard has been blamed for failings. Ballard became part owner in 1961 and became principal owner and remained in a position of leadership until 1990.

In some quarters he was regarded as an eccentric uncle. In other ways he offended sensibilities. Ballard insulted women. He was charged with fraud and tax evasion and served time in prison. He was despised by fans for running off favorite Dave Keon and for not seeming to care enough about the Maple Leafs' fortunes to build a winner.

Ballard hired coaches, but second-guessed them in public and was accused of micromanaging the entire organization. Ballard refused to consider signing European players, but while he was in jail the team signed future Hall of Famer Borje Salming. Ballard did not want to pay the going rate for players as contracts soared in value. Ballard made obscene comments and feuded with members of the Toronto media.

In 1979, Ballard tore out the famed gondola used by Foster Hewitt from the earliest days of broadcasting. Despite a request from the Hockey Hall of Fame to acquire it, Ballard tossed it into an incinerator.

"Hell, we're not in the historical business," Ballard said of the forty-eight-year-old landmark, "and that gondola wasn't so old anyway."

On the positive side, Ballard was well-known for making generous contributions to charities. Cynical fans joked the Maple Leafs had become a charity case and that charity should begin at home.

In 1990, not long before his death at eighty-six, a judge ruled Ballard was mentally incompetent after reviewing documents submitted by three doctors.

Although more than a quarter century has passed since Ballard's death, the franchise has not completely righted itself. Not only have the Leafs not won a Stanley Cup since 1967, they have not reached the Finals. Between 2005 and 2016, the Leafs qualified for the playoffs only once.

Since the Original Six era ended in 1967, the Toronto Maple Leafs have featured some great, respected and well-appreciated players such as Doug Gilmour, Mats Sundin, Darryl Sittler, Wendel Clark, and Paul Henderson. But the Leafs have never put together a great season that carried them to the Stanley Cup.

Sundin was captain of the Leafs for 11 years, was selected for nine All-Star games, and was chosen for the Hall of Fame.

Sittler, another Hall of Famer, set an NHL record in a game against the Boston Bruins on February 7, 1976, by scoring 10 points in a single contest. Sittler scored six goals that day.

Gilmour spent six of his 20 NHL seasons with the Leafs and was nicknamed "Killer." Also a Hall of Famer, Gilmour scored 35 points during the 1993 playoffs when Toronto reached the conference finals.

Clark, a number-one draft pick who scored as many as 46 goals in a season for the Leafs, played for Toronto three different times in his career.

Henderson played seven seasons for Toronto, but his greatest fame occurred while representing his country. In the Summit Series of 1974, when Canadian ice hockey supremacy was challenged by the Soviet Union, Henderson scored the winning goal in the seventh and eight games to lead Canada to a come-from-behind victory. Henderson's final goal was voted the sports moment of the century in Canada when the 2000s began.

6

DETROIT RED WINGS

Founded: 1926
Home Arenas: Border Cities Arena, 1926–27 (Windsor, Ontario);
Detroit Olympia, 1927–79; Joe Louis Arena, 1979–present
Stanley Cups: 1936, 1937, 1943, 1950, 1952, 1953, 1955, 1997,
1998, 2002, 2008

Beginnings

The Detroit franchise was created for play starting during the 1926–27 season, with most of the players from the Victoria Cougars of the defunct Western Hockey League. For that reason the team's first nickname was not Red Wings, but Cougars.

During that first season the Detroit franchise did not even have a rink and played its first games in a building called the Border Cities Arena, across the national boundary in Canada in Windsor.

The name changed in 1932 after James Norris bought the club. He chose Red Wings based on a past group known as the Winged Wheelers, a bicycle club that had as its emblem the wings that became commonly associated with Detroit.

Even before Norris took over Jack Adams was in place as the coach and general manager. He started in the team's second year of existence and remained affiliated with the National Hockey League club for 36 years. Adams suffered through the early years as boss of the Detroit bunch when it was trying to catch up with the rest of the league by finding better players.

Norris agreed to keep Adams, sort of in a probationary manner. Their contract was a handshake. Norris liked Adams's work enough to keep him. And keep him. On and on he stayed.

The Detroit team did not qualify for the playoffs in four of its first five seasons. It took seven years for the team to go as far as the semifinals in the playoffs. In 1934, the Red Wings reached the Stanley Cup Finals, but lost to the Chicago Blackhawks. Two years later, in 1936, the Wings captured their first-ever Cup by beating the Toronto Maple Leafs.

This was not a team where the names of players stood out in the memories of Red Wings fans, although they were pioneers in a sense and some even made the Hall of Fame much later. The best players on that squad were center Marty Barry, who scored 40 points with a team-high 21 goals, Larry Aurie, who scored 16 goals, and Herbie Lewis, who scored 14 goals.

The real star of the bunch was Syd Howe, who was from Ottawa. His first team was the Ottawa Senators. No relation to Gordie, Howe played 17 seasons in the NHL, scored 237 goals, and had his best years with Detroit. Some of his other teams disappeared right under his skates such as the Philadelphia Quakers and the St. Louis Eagles. Howe stayed with Detroit well into the 1940s and played on three winning Cup teams during his 12 years in the Motor City.

Later teammate Sid Abel said of Syd Howe he "never received the recognition he deserved. He could play every position, including goal, and probably did. His basic position was center and he was a truly great player."

When Gordie Howe showed up with the Red Wings, he was asked, "Are you related to Syd Howe?" For 37-straight seasons Detroit had a star forward named Howe on the team. Soon enough Gordie would become the better one.

In 1944, Syd Howe scored six goals in one game. The record was seven, set in 1920.

"I had a good chance to break the all-time record," he said, "but I couldn't do it."

Near the end of his career, the Detroit club held a special night for Syd Howe to thank him for his service.

"I got a lot of gifts," he said, "including a piano."

Apparently nobody asked how he got it home.

Barry, who was chosen for the Hall of Fame, played 12 seasons in the NHL, made one All-Star team, and won a Lady Byng Trophy for sportsmanship. He had six 20-goal seasons without ever playing more than 48 games in a schedule. Aurie, who played at only 148 pounds and died at forty-seven, had one All-Star campaign when he scored 23 goals in the 1937–38 season. Lewis, who scored 148 goals in his 11-year career, was also chosen for the Hall of Fame.

The goalie was Normie Smith, who had a 2.04 goals against average. The next year Smith, who only played eight seasons, made his only All-Star team and his 2.05 goals against record won him the Vezina Trophy.

Although Smith did not wear a mask during his playing days he did wear a cap that pretty much resembled a modern baseball cap as he tended goal. He said it kept glare out of his eyes, making it easier to see the puck.

Smith was the backstop for Detroit on the franchise's first two Stanley Cup champs in 1936 and 1937. During the 1935–36 season Smith was in net for a Detroit showdown with the Montreal Maroons that lasted for more than 116 minutes of overtime after the 60 minutes of regulation, the longest game in league history. It took six overtimes to settle things. The game was played March 24 and March 25, at the Montreal Forum, not ending until 2:25 a.m.

Teammate Modere "Mud" Bruneteau scored the winning goal in the middle of the night. In that game Smith made a remarkable 92 saves, the single-game NHL record to this day. Not only is that total in the league record book, it also earned mention in the *Guinness Book of World Records*.

"You know, we figured it was going to go on all night," said Phil Caddell more than 60 years after the fact. Caddell, a long-living fan, was in attendance. "And our pact was we weren't leaving until it was over. Whether we were awake or not."

In 2012, ESPN rated the Game 1 Stanley Cup Finals epic with Smith's shutout as the eighth-greatest playoff performance of all time.

Sid Abel made his first appearance in a Red Wings uniform for the 1938–39 season and remained in the National Hockey League until 1954. His last two seasons were played for the Chicago Blackhawks, but otherwise he was a Detroit guy.

As a player Abel, from Melville, Saskatchewan, was part of three Detroit Stanley Cup victories. In 12 years as Red Wings' coach his teams lost in the Cup Finals four times. He also coached parts of four other seasons with other teams in a lifetime in hockey. In addition, Abel was a general manager and was eventually selected for the Hall of Fame.

Born in 1918, Abel was the most recognizable player on the Detroit roster for a time, and a member of the organization for three decades. A center who scored as many as 34 goals in a season, Abel contributed 189 goals during his career, along with 283 assists. In 1948–49 he scored 28 goals and led the league. Abel also missed several years of his prime serving Canada in World War II.

An oddity of Abel's first training camp with the Red Wings was that he was practicing well with the team and getting himself noticed when one day general manager Jack Adams called him over and informed the player that the team was missing his contract. Abel had given it to the team's western scout to turn into the club, but he never mailed it.

"I didn't know about the missing contract and I was having a good camp," Abel said. "By this time I was hoping they wouldn't find the original because I figured I could sign for more money."

Alas for Abel, the original document turned up.

Abel played, coached, and managed, though he admitted they were not equally enjoyable.

"Playing was the best," he said. "It was the fun part of the career. Coaching was headaches, while being a general manager was not as bad. Being a player was the best."

One highlight of playing for Detroit for Abel was being assigned to what came to be known as "The Production Line" with Ted Lindsay and Gordie Howe. All three became Hall of Famers. Abel was chosen for four All-Star teams and won the Hart Trophy as Most Valuable Player after the 1949–50 season.

When Abel died at eighty-one in 2000, Gordie Howe effusively praised him.

"I learned a lot from him from just listening," Howe said. "He was our captain and leader. He won in every aspect of the game. He had a full life as far as hockey goes."

Ted Lindsay

An icon of the Detroit franchise, Ted Lindsay, who was also known as "Terrible" Ted for the way he played the game with vigor and aggressiveness, joined the Red Wings in 1944.

Lindsay was from Renfrew, Ontario, and became a nine-time All-Star as a left-winger and a Hall of Famer whose career lasted for 17 seasons, although a few of them were with the archenemy Chicago Blackhawks, and there was a lengthy interruption near the end. In 1,068 games, Lindsay scored 379 goals and 472 assists.

He did have his moments on the ice.

"Some nights I was so good I could have become an egotist," Lindsay said much later.

Born in 1925, Lindsay turned ninety in 2015. His father, Bert, played locally for a team called the Millionaires, although the Lindsay family was not in that income bracket.

In one of the stranger episodes in old National Hockey League days—but representative of player-management relations—Lindsay was a vocal supporter of the new NHL players' union. General manager Jack Adams traded him to Chicago in 1957 as punishment even though Lindsay was at the top of his game.

A fascinating later development for Lindsay was that eventually he became general manager of the Red Wings and was very much at odds with NHL Players' Association executive director Alan Eagleson. In 1977, Lindsay referred to Eagleson as "the worst thing that ever happened to hockey. One of the biggest detriments in sports." Lindsay had become the Red Wings' general manager in 1977 after the team fell on hard times and dropped to the worst in the league.

Ultimately, in the late 1990s, Eagleson was disbarred as an attorney and convicted in the United States and Canada of fraud and embezzlement for his union activities. He served time in prison, and resigned from the Hall of Fame.

In 2010, taking note of his early accomplishments in the development of the union and the price he paid, the Players' Association changed the name of one of its awards to the Ted Lindsay Award. It cited his skill, tenacity, leadership, and role in establishing the union.

Between 1957 and 1960, Lindsay toiled three years for the Blackhawks. His heart was never really in it and his family stayed behind in Detroit. Lindsay announced his retirement, but in 1964, after he replaced Adams as GM, Sid Abel contacted Lindsay and asked him if he wanted to play again.

On the face of it, this was preposterous. Lindsay was thirty-nine and had been out of the NHL for four years. But he accepted. League president Clarence Campbell did not think the move passed the taste test and badmouthed it. "This is the blackest day in hockey history when a thirty-nine-year-old man thinks he can make a comeback in the world's fastest sport."

Campbell ate his words when Lindsay appeared in 69 games, scored 14 goals, and added 14 assists.

"This is one of the most amazing feats in professional sports," Campbell said. "I didn't think it could be done. He has to be rated a truly amazing athlete."

Perhaps Lindsay paved the way in Campbell's mind when Gordie Howe pulled off the same type of magic for much longer.

Lindsay was just 5-foot-8 and 160 pounds, but played bigger. Size did not inhibit him in taking on bigger guys in the corners or in fights. He gave his all to the team measured by any yardstick. He also collected more than his share of stitches from those in-the-trenches battles while accruing 1,808 penalty minutes.

"If you got me dirty, I got you twice dirty," Lindsay said. "There was never anyone who liked to win more than I did."

Lindsay did relish contact and one item of evidence supporting that became clear when he became a broadcaster. When battles broke out he admiringly spoke of players who used their sticks for things other than swatting at the puck. "That's laying the lumber on 'em," he said.

Lindsay really did earn the nickname "Terrible."

"I had the idea I should beat up every player I ever tangled with and nothing ever convinced me it wasn't a good idea," he said.

While Lindsay is credited with being the first player to lift the Stanley Cup above his head and skate around the rink with it in celebration, he later said he had no intention of starting a tradition. The motivation behind his heavy lifting, he said, was to give fans a better view of the trophy. But the practice caught on and became a staple of post-championship-deciding games' on-ice ceremonies.

Later in life Lindsay was very active in the Detroit area raising money for charity, especially for organizations researching autism.

In 2008, a statue of Lindsay was placed on view at Joe Louis Arena.

Lindsay, who said he loved the Red Wings' organization, expressed his devotion in a colorful manner. The team emblem features wings, but they are linked to a wheel. "I had that flying wheel tattooed on my forehead and on my butt," Lindsay said.

Craggy-faced Lindsay was still working out regularly at age eighty-nine in 2014, lifting weights three days a week and stretching seven days a week. With most of his contemporaries deceased, Lindsay was nearly the poster player for the Original Six era. There was some joking given his longevity that Lindsay should no longer be called Terrible Ted, but Durable Ted.

"I believe the body is a machine, a muscle from the bottom of your feet to the top of your head, and if you take care of it, it'll serve you very well," Lindsay said. "So far, my philosophy's been working out pretty good. Keep the legs strong. Even though you're getting weaker, keep the legs strong."

Even at ninety, Lindsay was still getting around. He made a public appearance speaking to Detroit-area steelworkers and donned a hard hat for the occasion. The event was connected to Lindsay's nonstop efforts to raise money for the autism cause and the group of about a hundred people came up with $4,000.

The red hard hat was a gift from United Steelworkers Local 1299. Once again this was recognition of Lindsay for being a union man way back.

"The owners and managers were too stupid to realize we had brains," Lindsay said.

Lindsay, the rabble-rousing labor organizer, did not seem so terrible to the steelworkers.

Bill Gadsby

The defenseman from Calgary, Alberta, who spent 21 years in the National Hockey League and was selected for the Hall of Fame only played his final five years with the Detroit Red Wings, but Bill Gadsby most closely identified with that team.

Gadsby had some excellent years with the Blackhawks and New York Rangers and was a seven-time All-Star in all, but after his playing days ended he coached the Red Wings and remained aligned with the team as an "Honored Member" of the Detroit Red Wings Alumni Association and actively raised funds for local charities.

Gadsby spent long enough guarding the Red Wings' blue line to compete in 323 regular-season Detroit games. Gadsby didn't shoot much and scored goals less often. He was quite dependable, however. Four times Gadsby led the NHL in games played, making it into all 70 contests. Also, during the 1958–59 season when Gadsby amassed 46 assists it was a record for a defenseman.

Still, Gadsby concluded his career with 130 goals in 1,248 games and contributed 438 assists.

Before he was a teammate with the Wings, the 6-foot, 185-pound Gadsby was an antagonist of Gordie Howe's. When Howe came up ice seeking to score, Gadsby backpedaled in his way. Known for his aggressiveness, Gadsby developed an annoying habit to bug onrushing skaters without breaking the rules.

"Gadsby would put that stick right up in your nose, but would never make contact," said Howe, who broke into the NHL the same season as Gadsby, 1946–47. "But it's distracting as hell." Howe was eighteen, Gadsby nineteen.

Another way Gadsby tried to get under the skin of charging forwards as they rolled down the ice was to yell at them. He shouted, "Shoot! Shoot!" hoping they would fire the puck off-target and sooner than they were ready to get off a good one. Once, when with the New York Rangers, he did that to Howe, Howe fired, and the puck went into the net to tie the game.

"So when I circled behind the net, Bill was there, and I said, 'Thank you,'" Howe said. "He turned bilingual, English and profanity."

Gadsby's coaching career in Detroit ended suddenly, fired in midseason of his second year. Ironically, the Wings had just played Chicago and the fans were putting pressure on the team to fire coach Billy Reay. He outlasted Gadsby.

"I felt so sorry for Billy Reay in Chicago Stadium the other night," Gadsby said after he got the ax. "I looked down at him and those 16,000 people were singing, 'Good-bye, Billy.' I felt really bad for him. Now I realize they were singing to me."

Howe, Gadsby's longtime on-ice and off-ice business partner, was aggrieved when Gadsby was canned.

"Bill Gadsby is one helluva fine man to play for in the players' eyes," Howe said. "I don't think it was his fault we didn't make the playoffs last season. I hate to see such a fine gentleman go out in that particular manner. I was just sick about it."

The coach was caught off-guard. He didn't sense any warning signs. At the time team president Bruce Norris fired him the Red Wings were on a two-game winning streak. Only a night earlier, Gadsby said, Norris had put his arm around him after a victory and told him what a good job the team was doing.

"The next afternoon he fired me," Gadsby said. "At first I thought he was joking. But then I realized he wasn't. It was the biggest shock of my life."

Gadsby's long career could have been terminated at an early stage. At twenty-five, when he was a member of the Blackhawks, it appeared Gadsby had polio.

"It was when my neck became sore that clinched it," Gadsby said of symptoms that alarmed him and doctors. "I was sent immediately to a hospital in Ottawa where I was put in isolation for ten days. Fortunately, the symptoms went away. I really lucked out. But the whole thing was pretty scary for a while."

Gadsby worked his legs and arms hard all day long and took a lot of medication. He was sent on his way to resume playing hockey after a week and a half.

That was not Gadsby's only close call. His first serious brush with death occurred when he was twelve. He and his mother had been visiting her family in England for three months when World War II began in Europe in 1939. They sailed on the last Canada-bound steamship in September, one named the SS *Athenia*, an unarmed passenger ship that sailed out of Glasgow, Scotland, en route to Montreal.

A Nazi submarine torpedo sank the ship off the coast of Ireland and the Gadsbys took to the sea for rescue. It was the first United Kingdom boat sunk by Germany in the war, although Germany did not admit responsibility until 1946, after the war was over, at the Nuremburg trials. The U-30 sub tracked the *Athenia* for more than three hours before attacking.

The commander realized his mistake and reported it to German navy officials, but they covered up the incident, even altering the ship's official logbook at the time. Later, the commander said he thought the boat might have been a troop ship or an armed merchant vessel and said it was following a zigzag course away from normal shipping lanes. The German hierarchy engaged in the cover-up and actually accused British Prime Minister Winston Churchill of staging the destruction of the ship to turn British neutrality leanings to war footing. It did indeed have such an effect on public opinion in Canada. The Germans were accused of committing a war crime.

It was night when the assault began and the Gadsbys were asleep.

"We were knocked right out of out berths," he said. "I was too young to realize our real predicament. My mother rushed me up to our lifeboat station. She was as calm as she could be, though terribly frightened. I'll never forget the sights I saw. Men and women going crazy with panic. I saw horrible sights I'll never forget."

Unaware that 128 civilians and crew members among the more than 1,400 people on board had been killed, the Gadsbys spent a few hours in the lifeboat before being plucked from the water. It took fourteen hours for the *Athenia* to go down.

"Our boat was jammed," Gadsby said. "Must have been close to fifty people. It was pitch dark in the water, rough and cold. I don't remember if we had anything to eat, but there was tea. The British always had tea no matter what happened.

"What the heck are a few bumps and bruises in hockey after that?"

Gordie Howe

The man nicknamed "Mr. Hockey" came the closest to playing forever as any National Hockey League player.

The amazing Gordie Howe may not only be the best hockey player of all time—Wayne Gretzky said so—but the longest playing. Howe, who was from Saskatchewan, broke into the NHL with the Detroit Red Wings in 1946. He played with the club through the 1969–70 season, when he retired. Then, after the Houston Aeros signed Mark and Marty Howe, Gordie's sons, he came out of retirement to suit up for the World Hockey Association franchise for the 1973–74 season.

In between, Howe, who had a wrist problem when he departed the Red Wings, underwent surgery to fix his nagging injury. He also found life in the Red Wings' office unfulfilling. So he returned to the ice. He played seven additional years with Houston and then the Hartford Whalers. That included a final stint with Hartford when it joined the NHL. Howe retired for a second time when he was fifty-one.

That made for a 32-season hockey career. Howe played in 2,186 regular-season games between the two leagues, scored 975 goals, and assisted on 1,083 goals. With Detroit he played on four Stanley Cup winners. He was chosen for 23 All-Star teams, won the Art Ross Trophy six times and the Hart Trophy six times. Howe, who stood six feet tall and weighed 205 pounds, was as tough as he was talented. It was joked that a special Gordie Howe hat trick was a goal, an assist, and a fight in one game.

Howe was stronger than most players who came after him. But he also had a saying, claiming he played "religious hockey." That is, it was better to give than to receive, a notable outlook in a fight. Howe picked up that outlook from his father, Ab, who planted the idea that it was important to watch out for himself and make sure he didn't take any sass or worse from anyone.

Ab put Gordon (what he called him) to work young, in construction, and said he could pick up 90-pound cement bags with one hand. He had equal strength in the left as the right. His father said he was ambidextrous and in the pros Howe did shoot with either hand.

Gordie did not stay in school past eighth grade, but he was an intelligent guy. He knew where he wanted to go and believed if he could become as good a hockey player as his body would let him he could become a star. That's why in his youth he practiced writing his autograph and asked his sister how she liked his penmanship.

The *Detroit News* issued a review of rookie Howe's opening day.

"Gordon Howe is the squad's baby, eighteen years old," the paper reported. "But he was one of Detroit's most valuable men last night. In his first major league game he scored a goal, skated tirelessly and had perfect poise."

Gretzky broke most of Howe's scoring records, but as a nineteen-year-old played with the over-fifty Howe in his last

All-Star game. Whoever is taking the poll generally lists Howe, Gretzky, and Bobby Orr as the top three greatest of hockey players.

Tommy Ivan, the Hall of Fame administrator with the Chicago Blackhawks and Red Wings, was coaching Detroit's Omaha minor-league affiliate when Howe was seventeen and was sent to Nebraska to play for him.

"Look, I'd like to be able to say I knew early at Omaha that we had a superstar," Ivan said, "but that wouldn't be true. I knew he had a chance to be a pretty good player. But how good?"

At the end of the season Ivan told upper management that Howe, who had not even played junior hockey, was good enough to be in the NHL right away. Sure enough, Howe, just eighteen, made his debut the next season.

Howe made the big jump readily, but wasn't sure he could make the team out of training camp. Eventually, Howe, Ted Lindsay, and Sid Abel formed the Production Line. That was a double-meaning description. First, the players were very productive. Second, it played off the Motor City image as the headquarters of auto manufacturing.

Lindsay and Howe were close friends and Lindsay said one reason Howe was a terror in camp was his insecurity about having a job.

"He was always worried he couldn't make the team," Lindsay said. "Every year he was tough on left wingers in training camp because of it. He lived to play the game and nobody was going to get the job away from him."

The most goals Howe scored in a season was forty-nine in 1953–54. In four other seasons he topped 40.

While Howe led the world in longevity, Gretzky was such a dominant scorer that debate sprung up over which of the two was the best hockey player ever. It was clear people loved watching them both and each had their adherents.

"Howe is the greatest hockey player I have ever seen or expect to see," said Emile Francis, one-time New York Rangers coach and Whalers general manager. "He tops Gretzky because he has ability and durability. Gordie is to hockey what Babe Ruth is to baseball."

Sid Abel, Howe's longtime teammate and coach, said Howe never sweated it as time for the opening face-off approached.

"You had to prod Gordie to remind him there was a game," Abel said. "He'd be dreaming of a rummy hand or something."

When he reached his late thirties and had been in the NHL for about twenty years, Howe couldn't escape repetitive questioning about how long he planned to play. Howe tired of the line of discussion.

"Everybody keeps asking, 'How long more, Gordie?'" he said. "For the luva Pete, WHY?" Howe didn't seem to realize not everybody played pro hockey into their forties, never mind their fifties.

Howe scored 29 goals and added 47 assists while playing in all 70 games for Detroit in the 1964–65 season, so he didn't see why the next year everyone was asking about his future plans.

"Knowing how good I felt at the end of last season, I honestly can't see any end in sight," Howe said.

People should have listened.

By the time Howe played in the WHA with his sons, something even he thought was inconceivable, a fan referred to him as a fossil. Howe might have become irritated, but he was playing like a much younger man, so he shrugged off the insult. The Howe siblings got ticked off on his behalf.

"The boys were mad, but I thought it was kind of funny," Howe said.

As strongly identified with Detroit as Howe was for a quarter of a century, he had a bit of a rift with management when he stopped being so accommodating about salary. He took it on good faith that the higher-ups were treating him right. Then Howe discovered he was only the third-highest-paid member of the club. Howe's wife Colleen took over managing her husband's financial affairs. First, she made sure he got a raise to $100,000 a year. Then she worked to market him as marketing took a convenient turn, more avidly courting professional athletes.

"I never had an ambition to be a millionaire," Howe said. "Just comfortable, with some extras."

Howe came to resent being misled by Jack Adams in the Detroit front office. Still, when Adams died, Howe was a pallbearer at his funeral. The group of them rode in a limousine to the cemetery and guys were telling nice stories about Adams. One other pallbearer interjected his thoughts, surprising many.

"I played for him and he was a miserable sonofabitch," the guy said. "Now he's a dead sonofabitch."

"You could hate that bastard," Howe said, "but he was a good man."

When Howe returned to hockey in the WHA with his kids, he underwent a thorough physical. Looking over Howe at forty-five the doctor was astounded by his training and strength.

"What I really found incredible was his pulse rate, which was around forty-eight," the medical man said. "That's almost the heart of a dolphin." After another physical preceding a different WHA season, another doctor said, "This man could run up Mount Everest."

It was as if Howe had never been away. He resumed his stature as a first-rate star. Coming back from a retirement he also knew he needed to prove himself again.

"If I'd failed badly," Howe said, "people would have remembered me more for trying to make a stupid comeback at forty-five than for all the other things I did in hockey."

Howe predicted that his sons were good enough to make it in pro hockey and he was right. They came up through the WHA since the Aeros were kind enough to unite the whole family. The joke after Marty later made his inaugural NHL goal was that he needed just 800 more to tie his famous father.

"Counting his goals in the World Hockey Association he must have over 1,000, so I think his records are safe," Marty Howe said.

While in the WHA, Howe, always a freight-train presence on the ice, did not back off because of old age, especially if one of his boys was in trouble. Once, a player jumped Mark and Gordie skated up. He quietly asked him to stop and the player ignored him and did not stop flinging punches.

"When he didn't," Marty said, "Gordie reached down, stuck his fingers into his nostrils and pulled him up off the ice. The guy's nose must have stretched half a foot."

For a while, the other son, Mark, made it seem possible he would break his dad's mark for longevity. Mark played six seasons in the WHA and 16 in the NHL and was also chosen for the Hall of Fame. This Howe played in five NHL All-Star games and one WHA All-Star game.

The Whalers team doctor thought the older Howe, playing with younger guys, was in no worse physical condition than many of them.

"The stamina is there," that doctor said. "It's the speed that goes."

Not many could tell. Howe made up for a decline in swiftness with his experience and savvy.

Howe never gave up being "Mr. Hockey." He made public appearances and signed many autographs. Much later, in his eighties, Howe had serious health problems, battling cancer and other woes. His family announced he was suffering from dementia.

In May 2015, when Howe was eighty-six, it was announced that when the long-term construction project was complete on a bridge connecting Detroit and Windsor, Ontario, it would be called the Gordie Howe International Bridge.

As a young player Gordie Howe was happy to be in the league. He didn't explain his aspirations.

"One of my goals was longevity," Howe said. "I guess I've pretty much got the lock on that."

Marcel Pronovost

One of the strangest traditions in all of sport, never mind just hockey, is throwing an octopus on the ice at Detroit Red Wings games.

Strangest and perhaps grossest of traditions, unless you are a Red Wings fan and in on the gag. This all began on April 15, 1952, when the Red Wings were in the playoffs. In those Original Six days it took just eight victories to capture the Stanley Cup. An octopus has eight arms. Brothers and fans Pete and Jerry Cusimano, who owned a store in a Detroit market, threw the first octopus. Indeed, that year the Wings swept eight playoff games to capture the Cup.

Defenseman Marcel Pronovost was nearby and skated over to take a look.

"Right away I knew what it was," Pronovost said, "and I knew that it was dead. It was an octopus. I scooped it up and skated over to the penalty box with it, but nobody there wanted to touch it, either. I didn't think about it, I just picked it up. Oh yeah, you better believe I wondered why they were throwing the octopus on the ice."

The octopus became a symbol of Red Wings good luck and periodically another is smuggled into the arena for key

Detroit games. In 1955, two co-workers at a seafood company threw a thirty-eight-pound octopus on the ice during the play-offs. A year later someone threw a fifty-pounder on the ice. It was displayed on the Zamboni machine as it cleared the ice over the remainder of the game.

Pronovost was a comparative innocent bystander to the octopus tradition, but he was there at the creation.

Originally from Quebec, Pronovost played junior hockey in Windsor, across the Canadian border from Detroit, and made that his home. He played 20 years in the National Hockey League beginning in the 1949–50 season, 15 of them with the Red Wings before competing for the Toronto Maple Leafs.

Two Pronovost brothers followed Marcel into the big-time. Claude, a goalie, played 11 seasons of professional hockey, but only a small number of games in the NHL with the Boston Bruins and Montreal Canadiens. Jean, who spent his prime years with the Pittsburgh Penguins, scored 391 goals in 998 games.

Marcel was born in 1930. Claude was born in 1935. Jean was born in 1945. Claude's career in the NHL was short, so Marcel never faced him. It took until his 19th season in the league before he got on the ice against one of his siblings. It was Jean's rookie year of 1968–69.

"I remember my kids got mad at me that night because I hit Jean pretty hard when he came over the blue line," Marcel said. "After the game they came up and said, 'You're not supposed to treat Uncle Jean that way.' It was kind of amusing."

For all of his physical play, Pronovost kept his penalty minutes low. Almost always his season total for time spent in the box was under 50 minutes. A reason for that was Pronovost's comparatively clean, if hard-nosed play. He realized that his best sport was hockey, not boxing, so he could not afford to get into many fights.

"I couldn't lick my lips," he said, never mind lick another player in combat. "But I made myself respected by using the body check effectively and I think I wrecked a few shoulders and knees along the way. I enjoyed the physical game."

One statistic next to Pronovost's name that he was proud of was 1,206 regular-season NHL games. When he hit 1,000, Pronovost knew he was nearing the end.

"I'd like to go for another thousand," he said. "But I'm afraid that's not possible."

Pronovost, who died in 2015 at age eighty-four, also had a long coaching career as a Detroit assistant, in the minors, as head coach of the Buffalo Sabres, and for one year in charge of Chicago in the World Hockey Association. Then he became a scout, helping the New Jersey Devils recruit talent in the 1990s. Pronovost spent virtually his entire life in hockey and was inducted into the Hall of Fame in 1978.

During Pronovost's year and a half coaching the Sabres, a local radio disc jockey named Stanley created coffee cups named after himself. They were his own personal Stanley cups and Pronovost got more than his share of the souvenirs. He said he had about 15 of them.

"I've got to admit they're nice for coffee, but not quite as nice as drinking from the real Stanley Cup," said Pronovost, who once drank champagne from the genuine article.

Pronovost played in 11 All-Star games and was part of five Stanley Cup–winning teams, four of them with Detroit.

"The most underrated defenseman ever to play in the league," said Detroit teammate Ted Lindsay of Pronovost.

At six feet tall and 190 pounds, Pronovost could deliver hard checks. Sometimes he sacrificed his body to do so, as well. Once, by accident, Pronovost missed a check on a Maple Leafs player, hit teammate Gordie Howe instead, and broke Howe's collarbone. That time Pronovost wasn't very popular in Detroit.

Only once in his two decades in the NHL did Pronovost score as many as 10 goals in a season. But he was plenty fast on skates. "I was as quick as Bobby Hull," Pronovost said. "I could skate like the wind."

Terry Sawchuk

Some call Terry Sawchuk the greatest of all goalies. He may also have been the most nerve-racked goalie of all time, too, playing a position where the pressure is highest and those who occupy it frequently are tested and strained.

As great as he was, there is little doubt that Sawchuk often fought a losing battle against his demons. He suffered from depression and died after an off-ice altercation at forty after playing 21 mostly superb seasons in the National Hockey League.

A four-time winner of the Vezina Trophy, Sawchuk played in 11 All-Star games. He spent 14 of his seasons with the Detroit Red Wings and compiled a lifetime 2.52 goals against average. More remarkable than anything, Sawchuk recorded 103 shutouts, three times notching as many as 12 in a single season. It was a performance that made him a Hall of Famer.

Sawchuk was a perfectionist at heart and collecting shutouts the way some collect baseball cards is what pleased him. But the journey from the first minute of a game to the last stressed him.

Born in Winnipeg, Sawchuk's NHL career was phenomenal. Off the ice he faced difficulties, even from the time he was a youth when two brothers died, one from scarlet fever, one from a heart attack at seventeen. At various times Sawchuk suffered a seriously injured right arm that went untreated, mononucleosis, ruptured back discs, torn hand tendons, and innumerable stitches in his face. Beyond that his personality had him on edge. He became an alcoholic and had a tumultuous home life eventually leading to a divorce. It was miraculous Sawchuk played as long as he did with as much success as he had.

Many years after the goalie incurred the break in his arm that resulted in its healing crooked he had three operations when with the Wings.

"They took 66 bone chips out of my arm," Sawchuk said. "Even now I can't bend it more than a 90-degree angle at the elbow, although it doesn't handicap me when I'm goal-tending."

In the minors, Sawchuk was hit in the eye with a stick and forever after was haunted by that shot and feared losing sight because of a puck traveling at high speed.

"They stitched it up," Sawchuk said, "but they were afraid I might lose the sight in that eye. In fact, they said there was even danger of an infection spreading to my other eye. I was in the hospital three weeks and luckily came out of it with no damage."

Overall, Sawchuk needed 400 stitches in his face from stopping pucks. While Jacques Plante, then in Montreal, invented the goalie mask, Sawchuk saw the wisdom of using such protection and became an early supporter of the equipment revolution.

"It was Terry Sawchuk who really made the mask popular for goalies," Plante said. "That was three or four years after I came out with one. Sawchuk went something like 10 consecutive wins while wearing the mask. That removed a lot of the doubts. Up to that time people had been suspicious of them."

None of this debilitating injury siege includes an appendicitis attack. Another time he was in an automobile accident and suffered chest injuries. Sawchuk was a grumpy young man.

Sawchuk created his own style in the net. He developed a peculiar crouch that kept him low to the ground, but which as a by-product gave him back problems.

"When I'm crouching low, I can keep better track of the puck through the players' legs on screen shots," Sawchuk said. "Also, the crouch seems to give me better balance and spring action when I have to move fast. I've noticed that if I have several bad games in a row and seem to be in a slump it's because I've unconsciously straightened up. When I go back to the crouch, I improve."

Some observers termed Sawchuk's bent-over style gorillalike.

Sawchuk's era from 1949 to 1970 was almost all part of the Original Six period and for much of his career teams carried one goalie. The best goalies played in every game unless so severely injured they couldn't skate, or crouch. Sawchuk seemed ambivalent about backups.

"I wouldn't go that far," he said. "But I do think it would be well to have a spare goalie good enough to perform while the regular is given occasional days of rest during the season. There isn't any doubt that there's a lot of pressure in goal-keeping."

Sawchuk was so good as a young goalie that in each of his first five full seasons in the early 1950s his goals against average was in the 1.90s. His presence, along with front-line players like Gordie Howe, made it possible for the Red Wings to record the best regular-season record in the league for seven straight years, a mark that still stands.

If there was one time that Sawchuk let physical ills divert him from his main assignment it was when he was with the Boston

Bruins after his initial splash with the Red Wings. He walked away from the team in 1956–57, fully intending to quit the game for good. He had hit a meltdown point.

The Red Wings regained his rights and Sawchuk did return to the sport for the 1957–58 season. He played all 70 games that year.

One thing no one could take away from Sawchuk was his extraordinary shutout count of 103 in the regular season and another 12 in the playoffs. Compared to the hockey world of today that is like Cy Young winning 511 games in baseball—untouchable.

"Certainly, I'm proud of it," Sawchuk said of that record, "and feel it means something. After all, for shutouts you're not allowed one mistake. The big scorers can make a dozen mistakes and still get a goal towards a record. A goaler makes a single goof and he has to wait until the next game to start all over."

Those who watched Sawchuk at his best viewed his career in awe.

"Sawchuk was the greatest goalie to ever play hockey," said Sid Abel, the longtime Red Wings player, coach, and front office official. "He was simply the greatest."

In 1970, Sawchuk and then–New York Rangers teammate Ron Stewart shared rent on a house on Long Island. One night in late April the two got into an argument and then a fight at a bar. Their disagreement, apparently over Sawchuk's nonpayment of rent, resumed soon after on the home's lawn.

In his version of events, Stewart said he fell over a barbecue grill and thought Sawchuk fell on top of him and "hit himself on one of the protusions on the cooker, or possibly against my knee." He said Sawchuk cried out in pain.

Doctors came to the scene and said Sawchuk told them he had gotten fed up with Stewart and "I punched him and knocked him down. They kicked us out of the bar and I hit him again. I just kept knocking him down. At the house I tagged him again and knocked him down again. I jumped on him and I fell on his knee."

Sawchuk was taken to the hospital and underwent more than one operation, the last one gall bladder surgery. Stewart actually visited him in the hospital. Then Sawchuk suffered a blood clot in the hospital and died a month after the fight. After Sawchuk passed away Stewart said the incident was "like a bad dream."

For Sawchuk, whose life was so often pockmarked by complications, this was the ultimate tragedy.

Alex Delvecchio

In 1970, the city of Thunder Bay, Ontario threw a testimonial dinner to honor Red Wings star Alex Delvecchio.

The menu included tossed salad, pickles, dinner rolls, olives, roast beef or fried chicken, mashed potatoes with gravy, mixed vegetables, beets, coffee or tea, and "assorted squares." Those were apparently for dessert, but sarcastic wags might have chimed in that they kind of described the guest of honor, too. That all stemmed from Delvecchio's so-called "clean" play on the ice after his then-19th Red Wings season.

Speakers included Red Wings luminaries Gordie Howe and Sid Abel and other guests from the hockey world included Vic Stasiuk, Parker McDonald, Doug Barclay, and Bruce Gamble. For once, the focus was on wing man Delveccio instead of Howe.

The man who thrived best in the gigantic shadow cast by Gordie Howe was Alex Delvecchio. While it is no disgrace to play second-string to greatness, it also makes it difficult for your own greatness to be recognized.

That was pretty much the story of Alex Delvecchio's career with the Detroit Red Wings. Howe was "Mr. Hockey" and the brightness thrown by his glow often overpowered contributions of others. Delvecchio was Scottie Pippen to the Chicago Bulls' Michael Jordan.

At one point Delvecchio played on an all–Hall of Fame line with Howe and Frank Mahovlich. For a while, too, out of team necessity, Delvecchio shifted to defense. Delvecchio, whose nickname was "Fats," not for the size of his belly, but because of the roundness of his face, got quite used to having Howe around.

"He usually plays his slot on attack, but not when the other team is pressing us," Delveccio said. "He is easy to play with because I read his moves so well. I know instinctively when he is going to break and when he is going to shoot." Mahovlich said it was easy to play alongside God.

"Well, I say the same, although I sometimes have to switch places when God wanders a bit because he always wants to be in the middle of things."

Delvecchio was born in 1931 in Ontario and made his first appearance in a Red Wings uniform as an eighteen-year-old—for one game—during the 1950–51 season. He did not retire until 1974, 1,568 regular-season games later. He only played 11 games that year, but in between he played in the maximum of 70 seven times. His appearances crossed 24 seasons.

For almost all of that time Delvecchio was a Howe teammate. For years he was also the Detroit captain. Delvecchio played in 13 National Hockey League All-Star games. His career totals were 456 goals and 825 assists. He also won the Lady Byng Trophy three times for gentlemanly conduct, and ironically the achievement got him booed on home ice. The fans thought Delvecchio didn't hit enough guys often enough.

"Yes, I do have my 'cheering' section," Delvecchio said. "I was looking forward to road games a couple of years ago when they really let loose on me. It seems that a couple of people start it and it spreads throughout the rink. I think they are angry at me for winning the Byng Trophy. They think I won't hit because if I get a penalty I will lose the Byng, but that just isn't so. You know, nobody ever booed [Red] Kelly, [Stan] Mikita, or [Bobby] for winning the Byng, but they get on me."

Sid Abel, the player, coach and general manager of the Red Wings during Delvecchio's long tenure, said even if Delvecchio didn't hit as hard as Howe he mixed it up in other ways, notably going after the puck and being elusive when others tried to hit him.

"Alex gets in there and digs along the boards and behind the net," Abel said. "He knows how to roll with a check so that no one ever really gets a good piece of him. He is fluid, not flashy."

Delvecchio was known more for being reliable than colorful and as a center he said he looked at his job responsibility as being more about setting up goals.

"The goals are nice, of course," Delvecchio said. "But I've always taken a lot of pride in assists. It's the centerman's job to get assists."

Famously, over one stretch in his career Delvecchio endured a long goal-scoring drought—31 games. It got to the point he was willing to try any superstition to break out of the slump. Delvecchio obtained what he called English holly and put it in a skate. The trick didn't work, perhaps because it was a sprig of white heather from Scotland and was mislabeled.

"It did tickle when I put on my skate boot, though," Delvecchio said.

People sent him lucky pins and he smeared his stick with tobacco juice (kind of yucky), but none of those alleged remedies solved the goal-scoring problem.

When Delvecchio snapped the streak it came on a controversial play. Ed Johnston was in net for Boston and when the red light went on he went ballistic, complaining to the refs that Delvecchio kicked the puck in.

"No, I don't care if he goes 62 games without a goal, that one shouldn't count," Johnston said.

The goal counted.

Delvecchio said he thought about kicking the puck in illegally, but didn't have to resort to that desperate move.

"It turned out I didn't need to because it bounced in itself," he said.

Delvecchio's personality was low-key. And even when Abel appointed him captain of the Red Wings he took that into account. Delvecchio's role would not necessarily be the captain who kicked butt. He was more of a pep talk kind of guy.

"Sometimes a player needs a little boost more often than a knock," Abel said. "I think Alex is that kind. He takes the captaincy seriously and he has the respect of the other players, especially the younger fellows."

A newspaper once described Delvecchio's career as "Second Banana, But He Seldom Slipped Up." The story referred to Delvecchio's marvelous bunch of lifetime on-ice accomplishments being eclipsed by Howe.

"Gordie Howe was the greatest, there's no doubt about it," Delvecchio said. "When you got to play with him you gave him the puck and you knew things were going to happen for your hockey team."

As he passed forty, with his hair turning gray, Delvecchio knew he would soon retire, but he still received praise for the almost magical way he skated. Longtime Bruins player, coach, and administrator Milt Schmidt loved Delvecchio's style.

"Alex is forty-one and he still moves like he's twenty-one," Schmidt said. "This man is a real craftsman—no unnecessary moves, no silly penalties, no wild shots."

Still, Delvecchio became reflective discussing how tough it was to be married with five children and be a full-time professional athlete.

"A professional athlete definitely cheats his family," he said. "He is not always there when his wife and children need him. His wife [Teresa] has to bear a lot of the burdens alone. The athlete so often is gone on the holidays—Christmas, New Year's, Thanksgiving, birthdays. He is home a little while, then gone again. The family gets used to the routine. At first maybe the little ones cry when you pack up to go away again. They want to pack up and go with you. Then they get used to it. For a father, that's sad, his family getting used to him being away."

However, even as Delvecchio hung up his skates, his other family still beckoned. Delvecchio spent four more years in the NHL as a bench leader.

Norm Ullman

Most of Norm Ullman's best years were with the Detroit Red Wings, but he also played for the Toronto Maple Leafs and for Edmonton in the World Hockey Association over the course of 23 seasons.

The first 13 of those seasons that led to the Hall of Fame came with the Red Wings for Ullman, who was from small-town Alberta before moving to Edmonton.

"I think I was eight years old when I first started skating," said Ullman in a typical report from Canadian boyhood. The location was not a typical backyard or pond. "There was an American Air

Force base right across the street from where we lived. They had a skating rink there and my dad arranged with the people there that we could go and skate. It wasn't hockey, just free skating."

Ullman turned to hockey at age ten and was good at it. By then the family was living in Edmonton and Ullman, who finished his career with an Edmonton team, began it with one. His junior club, starting at sixteen, was the Edmonton Oil Kings and it was owned by the Red Wings.

Up until then, Ullman, who listened to National Hockey League games on the radio, said he did not have a favorite team. But Detroit took over his affections.

"Detroit became my favorite because I belonged to them and I knew that some day, hopefully, I might end up playing there," he said.

Detroit began showing more than casual interest in Ullman's future when he scored 101 points in 36 junior games his second year with the Oil Kings. He was in awe when the Red Wings brought him to the bigs and he shared a dressing room with Gordie Howe, Ted Lindsay, Marcel Pronovost, Terry Sawchuk, Alex Delvecchio, and Red Kelly.

When the Wings shifted him to a line with Howe and Lindsay he could not believe his good fortune.

"It was amazing for a young guy coming in to get that chance," Ullman said.

Wherever he played, though, Ullman could score. Sixteen times in the NHL he scored at least 20 goals in a season with a high of 42 in 1964–65. Ullman was also durable, seven times leading his league in games played.

Ullman was twenty when he broke in with the Red Wings in the 1955–56 season. Overall, in 1,410 NHL games he scored 1,229 points. Counting Ullman's two years in the WHA, as well, he scored 537 goals and assisted on 822 goals. Ullman said he would have liked to win a Stanley Cup, the one big gap on his résumé, and finish in the NHL with 500 goals instead of 490, plus those WHA goals.

"Had I played on a Stanley Cup champion, just one, I would have felt more fulfilled," Ullman said. "We came close a couple of times, but never seemed to be able to go all the way. And I would have liked to get another 10 goals before I left the NHL. Four hundred and ninety doesn't have the same ring to it."

It was Howe who pinpointed reasons for Ullman's success.

"Ullman has unusual strength in his arms," Howe said. "He also has uncanny hockey sense."

In December 1955, Ullman had a six-point night, three goals and three assists, in a 10–2 victory over the Boston Bruins. In 1965, in a playoff game against the Chicago Blackhawks, Ullman distinguished himself in another way. Glenn Hall was in goal for Chicago and was never easy to beat. Yet Ullman blitzed him with two goals within five seconds.

"It was an uncanny situation," Ullman said. "The first goal I scored came from about 40 feet out. It went low along the ice and hit off the goalpost and past Hall into the net."

As always, a face-off followed a goal, and Chicago seemed to control the puck.

"After the face-off, I picked off a pass from Eric Nesterenko," Ullman recalled. "I took one or two strides and decided to shoot. When I shot the puck Matt Ravlich [of Chicago] stepped in front of me, putting a screen between me and Hall. Hall must never have seen the puck because it went right in. And all of this happened in just five seconds."

On other occasions Hall made acrobatic shots to rob Ullman, so he wasn't going to give the goals back.

"But you never argue how you score goals, just as long as you score them," Ullman said.

Ullman had a way of sneaking up on other teams.

"That man is a mystery to me," said Montreal coach Toe Blake. "He is not all that fast and sometimes I don't even know he is there. And then the loudspeaker announces, 'Goal by Ullman,' or 'Assist by Ullman,' and I know he was there all the time. I don't know how he does it. If I knew, I'd stop him. All I do know is he has been poison for us."

In Howe's mind Ullman was a quiet guy, too, off the ice.

"That Ullman was with Detroit for two years before I heard him utter one sentence," Howe said.

The words "yes" and "no" were major elements in Ullman's vocabulary when he was young.

"I really don't like the limelight," he said. "I'm kind of quiet."

Others noticed.

"Normie never opened his mouth when I managed the Red Wings," Jack Adams said. "So I called him 'The Noisy One.'" When the Red Wings brought Ullman to Detroit for that rookie campaign, Adams gave him a pep talk about working hard. Ullman never forgot it and always displayed a solid work ethic with his teams.

Once, a sportswriter asked the Detroit publicity man for stories about Ullman and he replied, "Ullman anecdotes? Are you kidding? He never talks." Of course that was an anecdote.

Ullman was known for his stick-handling and his forechecking. He shared a line with Howe and Lindsay. Later, Ullman, who played in 11 All-Star games, formed a line with Floyd Smith and Paul Henderson.

"Norm is a terrific player," said Smith in a testament to Ullman's playmaking skills. "All he needs is ice time. He doesn't have to depend on me or any other player."

After 21 years in the NHL, Ullman was approaching the end of his career when he got a chance to suit up for Edmonton in the WHA. The symmetry of that opportunity appealed to him.

"The reason I went there was because I was from Edmonton," Ullman said of his last move. "They wanted me so I thought, 'It might be nice to go back and finish my career where it started.'"

Detroit Red Wings Since

After the early Stanley Cup championships and four more in the 1950s, the Red Wings suffered their own Great Depression. This was one of the National Hockey League's all-time droughts. Detroit next won a Stanley Cup in 1997 after a gap of forty-two years. Between 1971 and 1983 the Red Wings missed the playoffs twelve out of thirteen years.

At last, in the 1990s, the franchise was revived and the Wings won additional Cups in 1998, 2002, and 2008. Some new great players came along and no player meant more to the club in the post–Gordie Howe years than Steve Yzerman.

Yzerman was born in 1965, just two years before the end of the Original Six era. He is from British Columbia and broke into the league for the 1983–84 season. Yzerman spent his entire 22-year career with Detroit, appearing in 1,514 games, scoring 692 goals, and assisting on 1,063 others.

The 5-foot-11, 185-pound Yzerman was selected for 10 All-Star games. In 1984, he was the first eighteen-year-old chosen. At various times Yzerman won the Lester Pearson Award, the Selke Award, the Conn Smythe Trophy, and the Bill Masterson Award.

As the Red Wings rebuilt into a championship team Yzerman was the heart and soul of the club and was rewarded with his name being etched on the Cup three times as a player. Later, when Detroit won again in 2008, he was a team executive. In different seasons Yzerman scored 65, 62, 58, 51, and 50 goals.

Nick Polano, who was a Red Wings coach and general manager, said the first time he saw Yzerman play was in 1983 at the team's training camp.

"Within five minutes of the first scrimmage he was the best player on the ice," Polano said. "I had no doubt he was headed for stardom."

Later in his career Yzerman played more of an all-around game and was recognized for his defensive ability.

"I've always considered myself a decent two-way player," Yzerman said. "It's just that I never got noticed about playing defense until I stopped scoring."

Yzerman served as Wings captain for years.

Yzerman was very earnest talking to sportswriters. He was once asked where fans' passion for the game came from and he replied with a serious answer.

"Not just in Canada, but in colder winter weather areas people play the game throughout the winter a lot," he said. "And a lot of people that follow the game are fans of the game. They played it or their brother played it, or nowadays, even their sisters are playing the game. So I think the passion mostly comes from people playing it and it really originates from the cities that are more cold-weathered where hockey was played."

When Yzerman retired the Red Wings retired his Number 19 jersey in a special ceremony. He received a two-and-a-half-minute standing ovation at Joe Louis Arena.

Although many other hockey-mad communities do refer themselves as "Hockeytown," in recent years it seems to be more often applied to Detroit and its connection to the Red Wings.

This was the Detroit era under Scotty Bowman, universally regarded as the greatest coach in NHL history. Bowman started with the St. Louis Blues, made his reputation with the Montreal Canadiens and then led the Red Wings from the 1993–94 season to his retirement after the 2001–02 season. Bowman presided over five Stanley Cup champion teams in Montreal, one in Pittsburgh, and three more in Detroit.

"I had the career I never thought I would," Bowman said after winning his ninth Cup. "Now it's time to enjoy what other people enjoy."

Bowman coached in 2,141 regular-season NHL games, won 1,244, lost 573, and tied 314. Although now in his eighties, Bowman works as a senior advisor to the Chicago Blackhawks organization, the place that employs his son Stan as general manager. The Blackhawks have won three Stanley Cups since 2010.

Another characteristic of the Red Wings during this period was the amount of reliance on Russian talent. In 1980, when a team of United States collegians upset the number-one ranked team in world hockey to capture the Olympic gold medal at the Winter Games in Lake Placid, New York, it was inconceivable that top Russian players would become regulars in the NHL.

Sergei Fedorov, Viacheslav Fetisov, Slava Kozlov, Igor Larionov, Vladimir Konstantinov, and Nicklas Lidstrom made for a colorful group from overseas who boosted the Red Wings. All but Swedish star Lidstrom were from Russia, free to play after the breakup of the old Soviet Union. Lidstrom won the Norris Trophy as best defenseman seven times, played in 12 All-Star games, and was chosen for the Hall of Fame in 2015. He retired after 20 years with Detroit in 2012.

Lidstrom admitted knowing very little about NHL history when he came to the United States from Sweden. He asked the Red Wings if he could wear Number 9. That was Gordie Howe's retired number, so it was not available.

"I got my first lesson in Red Wings history," he said.

Festisov did not reach the NHL until he was thirty-four and played his last four years in Detroit. Kozlov was just nineteen when he joined the NHL and played 18 years, the first 10 with Detroit. He scored as many as 36 goals for the Red Wings in one season.

Larionov spent eight years as a Detroit defenseman and was elected to the Hall of Fame in 2008. The journey from Russia was not an easy one for him. He was held back from joining the NHL for years.

"Everything was opened up except for sports," Larioniov said after Mikhail Gorbachev changed Russian society. "Nobody knew players got no respect and were treated like dirt."

Larionov, who was called "The Professor," once challenged world champion Anatoly Karpov to a game of chess. He won two Olympic gold medals and three Stanley Cups. He married a Russian figure skater and after his retirement Larionov went into the wine business. He produces wines with such names as "Hattrick" and "Triple Overtime." Late in his career he talked about his wine imbibing.

"I like to drink wine every night, about two glasses," he said. "When I turned forty, I started to drink two-and-a-half."

A documentary film was made of Larionov's last game and he said he really enjoyed being involved with it.

"It was great to watch the editing," he said. "We had fifty-five hours of footage with the boys in Moscow and we had to cut it down. We wanted it to be flawless."

Some said Larionov was a flawless player. He grew up in the Soviet Union system developed by Anatoly Tarasov and his international powerhouses. He taught a fast-moving, weaving style, but stressed awareness of what was going on.

"His famous expression to players was that even when you were playing the game and controlling the puck and going five-on-five you still have to see the nice-looking blonde girl in the second row," Larionov said. "You have to see the other things around you."

Konstantinov was a rugged bodychecker who earned the nickname "Vlad The Impaler." He came to the league in 1984 and was still going strong in 1997 when the Wings won the Cup. Just six days after the victory, following a celebration party a limousine carrying Federov, Konstantinov, and team masseur Sergei Mnatsakanov crashed at the hands of a driver who was filling the job despite having a license suspended for drunken driving.

Mnatsakanov and Konstantinov were seriously injured. Both were in comas for a period of time. Kontsantinov's career ended and he needed a wheelchair to get around. Inspired by Konstantinov's improvement, the next season the Wings adopted the motto "Believe" as a slogan and won the Cup again. The team received special permission from the league office to include Konstantinov's name on the Cup as a member of the winning team, and when Detroit clinched the victory, Konstantinov took to the ice in his wheelchair with the Stanley Cup in his lap.

Fedorov wore Number 91, spent 20 years in the league, 13 of them with Detroit, won a Most Valuable Player award, and was chosen for the Hall of Fame in 2015. He was more outspoken than his countrymen and made sure he had fun off the ice. He was also viewed as somewhat of a swinging bachelor. Once, he was pictured in the *Toronto Star* with his arm around an attractive blonde bursting out of her dress under the header "Hey, Fedorov, that's two minutes for holding."

Fedorov and tennis player Anna Kournikova, who was known as much for being a babe making somewhat provocative poses for cameras as her on-court results, knew each other from the time she was sixteen. They were seen together often and rumors about the extent of their relationship followed both.

Ultimately, Fedorov confirmed he and Kournikova had actually married—but had split. She was twenty-one at that time, in early 2003. The marriage took place in 2001.

"They are true," Fedorov said of the stories. "We were married, albeit briefly, and we are now divorced."

Fedorov scored 483 goals in 20 NHL seasons, 400 of them for Detroit. When the Red Wings won the Stanley Cup in 2002 and players got a chance to display it at a place of their choosing for a day, Ferorov brought the Cup to Moscow. (Larionov was along, too).

That was a remarkable day Fedorov could not have foreseen when he defected from the Soviet Union in 1990, a year after the Red Wings drafted him. He had to sneak away from his team in Portland, Oregon. Fedorov spoke no English when he came to the United States. He wanted to play in the NHL and get paid well for it.

"Trying to make one step at a time with one big thought behind it," he said.

What he and the team achieved in Detroit is something he relives whenever he can.

"Those days are unbelievable," Fedorov said. "As I grow older, as I gain more experience, I'm ecstatic sometimes. Sometimes I get chills."

EXPANSION:
THE SECOND SIX

FROM 1942 TO 1967, the National Hockey League consisted of six teams, four in the United States and two in Canada.

Compared to other professional sports leagues hockey was grossly underrepresented on the sports landscape. The other sports had expanded gradually. Hockey stood pat for a quarter of a century.

But the world was changing. Previously remote outposts were now growing major cities. The only care hockey had to take in its growth plan was to cautiously approach the American South. There were vast regions of the United States where it hardly ever snowed and where the only ice around was clinked in glasses.

Those southern markets were too risky for the moment, but Sunbelt hockey did eventually catch on. In the meantime, NHL administrators thought big, expanding in one swoop into new communities.

They chose Minneapolis, Pittsburgh, Philadelphia, St. Louis, Los Angeles, and the San Francisco Bay Area for their experiment. Only the California Golden Seals failed, although the Minnesota franchise eventually moved to Dallas and was replaced by different ownership.

Much of the initial argument driving expansion focused on obtaining a nationwide American TV contract. There was also the threat of the Western Hockey League turning into a major league and owning the West.

The incoming teams were charged a $2 million fee, which also massaged the pocketbooks of existing owners.

One major element overlooked—and resented in some quarters—when the expansion franchises were announced was that none were located in Canada. Hockey is Canada's national sport. No populace bleeds for the game the way Canadians do, so that maneuver seemed shortsighted. There were hard feelings, especially since it was generally believed Vancouver was ripe for a team.

The NHL did not rush into the decision, either. The plan was discussed for several years. A two-game set of Boston-Toronto exhibitions was played in Los Angeles and each drew about 10,000 fans. Maple Leaf legend Conn Smythe proclaimed the region, "a hockey gold mine." New York Rangers official Bill Jennings was the driving force in making sure expansion became reality. He was totally devoted to seeing big-time hockey grow beyond the northeastern section of the US and Canada.

From a player's standpoint the doings were of great interest. The NHL offered the narrowest opportunity of any North American sports league. In one stroke, 120 jobs were added. This would provide borderline players with opportunities and would extend careers of older players.

It can also be said that although NHL owners did not see it coming, their decision to expand into six new cities protected their flank from serious siege when the World Hockey Association started in 1972. The financially less stable WHA took risks in choosing cities and hockey did not catch on in several of them. For the most part, the NHL staked claims in more reliable places with its new clubs and Original Six teams had little trouble fending off challenges in their longtime homes.

During that first season the expansion teams' record against the Original Six teams was 40–86–12. Nobody was surprised. But that was the genius of the expansion plan. By placing the six new teams in their own division they competed for playoff spots against one another with one team from that side of the bracket guaranteed a slot in the Stanley Cup Finals. That maintained maximum fan interest for the entire season.

It took until 1974 for a new club to capture the Cup. That was the Philadelphia Flyers, the Broad Street Bullies, who won two in a row.

VICTOR LYNN

NOT NEARLY AS famous as many of his contemporaries in the National Hockey League, Vic Lynn is unique in league history. He is the only player to skate for all of the Original Six franchises.

Lynn was born in 1925 in Saskatoon and broke into the NHL in 1943 by playing one game with the New York Rangers. In subsequent years, spread out through the 1953–54 season, Lynn traveled around the league as if living in a moving van.

Before he ever played a game at age six, Lynn said he aspired to become an NHL player. Most of those earliest games were played on outdoor rinks.

"We played in Saskatoon at Victoria rink at seventeen below zero one time," Lynn said. "It was an open-air rink. It had boards around it and everything but it was still open air. No roof. You wore a toque over your ears and you had heavy sweaters on, you got sweaty, but you've got to work at it. . . . Out here it gets to forty below."

Known by the nickname "The Saskatoon Streak," that was Lynn's only appearance with the Rangers. During the 1943–44 season he played three games for the Detroit Red Wings. In 1945 he played two games for the Montreal Canadiens. He kept being returned to teams in the high minors only to fight back into the league on another team's roster, until finding a home with the Toronto Maple Leafs.

Between 1946 and 1950 Lynn played the majority of his NHL games with Toronto, appearing in 213 regular-season contests while scoring as many as 12 goals in one season for the Leafs.

Lynn teamed on a line with famed Leafs players Ted Kennedy and Howie Meeker. Together they formed The K-L-M Line. That trio was part of Maple Leaf Stanley Cup crowns in 1947, 1948, and 1949.

"We felt like heroes, you know, everybody cheering you, everybody giving you a pat on the back, until you went back to training camp the next year, then you had to start all over again," Lynn said. "We had a pretty good hockey team. It was pretty well equalized, everybody was the same, everybody got their turn to play, and everybody played good. We had a good coach and we had good management, and that's what made it.

"Those were my best years in the NHL. I had some good years with Boston, too. Played there, we didn't win the Stanley Cup, but we were in the playoffs every year I was there. That makes a difference, especially in the pocketbook."

Lynn joined the Boston Bruins for the 1950–51 season and scored a career-high 14 goals that year. He played just a couple more games for Boston the next year, and then completed his NHL career with the Chicago Blackhawks spread over two different years.

During his NHL career Lynn scored 49 goals, gathered 76 assists, and appeared in 327 games. Lynn died at age eighty-five in 2010.

DON CHERRY

A **MAN WHO HASN'T** played the game in decades and hasn't coached it in nearly as long, Don Cherry may be the most famous man in hockey.

That is not only because of his forum on *Hockey Night in Canada*, the coast-to-coast Saturday night television show delivering the National Hockey League across that nation, but because Cherry will seemingly say anything controversial and because he owns a wardrobe consisting of sport coats that even deaf people can hear.

They are so loud in color some of the jackets seem to be made of Scottish kilts and others must borrow their brightness from a Crayola box. He is a peacock in clothing. His sidekick was a dog named Blue, although the original Blue predeceased Cherry and has been succeeded by a series of bull terrier Blues.

Now past eighty years old, Cherry began playing minor-league hockey in 1954. His only NHL skating time in nearly 20 years on the ice was a single playoff game for the Boston Bruins in 1955.

More accomplished as a coach, Cherry twice led the Bruins to the Stanley Cup Finals in 1977 and 1978, but could not claim the championship. He also coached the Colorado Rockies.

Cherry's broadcast debut for the Canadian Broadcast Corporation began in 1980 and it was over the airwaves that he found his true niche.

Hockey Night in Canada is a Canadian institution predating television with radio broadcasts going back to the 1920s. Cherry's role in the proceedings is essentially to be himself and spout opinions in a game segment called "Coach's Corner." It is now an iconic feature of Canadian television. He gained fame five minutes at a time during those segments.

Harry Neale, a longtime *Hockey Night* color commentator and another former coach, once said to Cherry, "When you were playing you were a cement-head and now you're the cement that holds us together."

At one time years ago while arguing over airtime with other members of the crew, Cherry blurted, "F . . . guys wouldn't know a hockey player if you slept with Bobby Orr."

Consistent themes of Cherry's outspokenness are Canadian nationalism, hockey toughness, including favoring fighting, player work ethic, and criticizing dirty play. Cherry dislikes fancy celebrations following goals. While regarded as a breath of fresh air in many quarters, he also infuriates others by being politically incorrect and periodically issuing political pronouncements that have nothing to do with hockey.

Cherry owns a string of restaurants and has written popular books, one with the title of *Grapes*, his nickname.

As a career minor-leaguer Cherry had some strong opinions on the Original Six world, if only from the standpoint of there being so few jobs. He singled out other players who were deserving of NHL slots, but could not break in. One long-ago player named Frank Mathers for the Pittsburgh Hornets impressed Cherry as a rookie. "If he can't make the NHL, who can?" Cherry remembered thinking.

Mathers played in 23 NHL games during his 1948 to 1962 career, but was enshrined in the Hall of Fame in the builder category. There were only 30 defensemen in the entire NHL at that time.

In an expansion-friendly era, Cherry is sure that he, Mathers, and many others, would have moved up.

"All of us playing in the minors in those days would be playing in the NHL," he said, "and we could have had another six teams to fill."

Cherry said the real reason he did not make it with the Bruins was his defiance of a team edict not to play baseball in the summer. Cherry loved that sport, but broke his shoulder, and while the Bruins did not cut him loose, in his mind they perpetually kept him in limbo.

"They showed me their displeasure and sent me to the dregs of society and the Siberia of hockey, the Springfield Indians of the AHL and Eddie Shore," Cherry said. "That was at the age of twenty-two and I was doomed to the next twenty years in the minors and a million miles on the buses."

Cherry said he got his "Grapes" nickname while playing for Shore. The owner agreed to pay the fines of another player, but not Cherry's. Cherry said most people think the nickname came from the coupling of it with Cherry, another fruit, but it is short for "sour grapes" for all of the complaining he did while in Springfield about Shore.

Cherry said the greatest player he ever saw who is not remembered today was Rene Chevrefils. Chevrefils might have been mentioned with the all-timers, but saw his career ruined by alcohol. As a young player in juniors Chevrefils was ranked just behind Hall of Famer Jean Beliveau.

He rose to the Bruins and had seasons of scoring 18, 19, and 31 goals, but "the Bruins sent him to the minors to teach him a lesson and to dry out." Chevrefils became a teammate of Cherry's in Springfield. "We did everything we could to help him. We gave up beer so he had no temptations. He was such a warm, funny guy. We were rooting for him all the way."

It didn't work. Chevrefils was only forty-eight when he died in 1981.

Cherry once described his favorite stay-at-home night after dinner as involving lifting some weights, taking a sauna while listening to the Toronto Maple Leafs on the radio, then settling in to watch other NHL games through satellite TV as he munched on cheese and crackers and drank beer.

As a broadcaster, Cherry speaks hockey and knows his audience.

"There's a lot of mothers and women who don't like it," Cherry said. "There's a lot of college professors that don't like it. But I'm talkin' to the guy that goes in the beverage hall. Every time I drive by those guys that are workin' on the highway with a jackhammer, I have a guilty feeling that I should be there, too."

Hockey Night in Canada was Cherry's breakthrough in the broadcast world, but he had his own radio show airing on 90 stations and developed a syndicated television show. Everyone knew Canadians could never get enough hockey, but no one anticipated they wouldn't be able to get enough Don Cherry.

Don Cherry may not have been able to crack a roster on an Original Six team, but he is an original.